MW01291833

Explorations in the Learning Sciences, Instructional Systems and Performance Technologies

Series Editors

J. Michael Spector, University of Georgia, Athens, GA, USA
Susanne P. Lajoie, McGill University, Montreal, Quebec, Canada

For further volumes:
http://www.springer.com/series/8640

John Sweller · Paul Ayres · Slava Kalyuga

Cognitive Load Theory

 Springer

John Sweller
School of Education
University of New South Wales
Sydney, NSW, Australia, 2052
j.sweller@unsw.edu.au

Slava Kalyuga
School of Education
University of New South Wales
Sydney, NSW, Australia, 2052
s.kalyuga@unsw.edu.au

Paul Ayres
School of Education
University of New South Wales
Sydney, NSW, Australia, 2052
p.ayres@unsw.edu.au

ISBN 978-1-4419-8125-7   e-ISBN 978-1-4419-8126-4
DOI 10.1007/978-1-4419-8126-4
Springer New York Dordrecht Heidelberg London

Library of Congress Control Number: 2011922376

Printed on acid-free paper

Springer is part of Springer Science+Business Media (www.springer.com)

Preface

Without knowledge of human cognitive processes, instructional design is blind. In the absence of an appropriate framework to suggest instructional techniques, we are likely to have difficulty explaining why instructional procedures do or do not work. Lacking knowledge of human cognition, we would be left with no overarching structure linking disparate instructional processes and guiding procedures. Unless we can appeal to the manner in which human cognitive structures are organised, known as human cognitive architecture, a rational justification for recommending one instructional procedure over another is unlikely to be available. At best, we would be restricted to using narrow, empirical grounds indicating that particular procedures seem to work. We could say instructional procedure *A* seems better than procedure *B* but why it works, the conditions under which it works or how we can make it work even better would be rendered unanswerable and mysterious.

In contrast, knowledge of how we learn, think and solve problems – human cognitive architecture – can provide us with a coherent, unifying base that can be used to generate instructional hypotheses and data. That base can explain why some instructional procedures work while others fail. Seemingly disparate, even contradictory data can be explained and reconciled. Most importantly, human cognitive architecture can be used to generate instructional procedures that we otherwise would have considerable difficulty conceiving. The structures that constitute the framework of human cognitive architecture provide an essential prerequisite to instructional design for both researchers and professional educators. Those structures allow us to make sense of instructional design issues. Further, we can use our knowledge of human cognitive architecture to devise instructional theories.

One such theory is cognitive load theory that was explicitly developed as a theory of instructional design based on our knowledge of human cognitive architecture. Cognitive load theory consists of aspects of human cognitive architecture that are relevant to instruction along with the instructional consequences that flow from the architecture. This book begins by considering categories of knowledge in Part I, human cognitive architecture in Part II, categories of cognitive load in Part III, followed by the instructional effects that flow from these theoretical considerations in Part IV and the conclusions in Part V.

In recent years, the cognitive architecture used by cognitive load theory has been expanded and anchored within a biological evolutionary framework. Evolution by natural selection has a dual role in cognitive load theory. First, as indicated in Chapter 1 of Part I, we can classify information into two categories. The first category, known as biologically primary knowledge, consists of information that we have specifically evolved to acquire while the second category, known as biologically secondary knowledge, is information that we need for cultural reasons but have not specifically evolved to acquire. Educational institutions were devised to facilitate the acquisition of biologically secondary information and cognitive load theory deals almost exclusively with that category of information. Chapter 1, by analysing these distinct categories of knowledge, provides an introduction to the evolutionary base used by cognitive load theory.

Evolution by natural selection has a second, equally important role in cognitive load theory. Evolutionary theory is usually considered as a biological theory explaining how biological structures, including entire species, arose. That function is, of course, the primary purpose of evolutionary theory. Nevertheless, evolutionary theory can be considered from an entirely different perspective, as a natural information processing system. By thinking of evolutionary theory in terms of the manner in which information is processed, we can extend evolutionary concepts to other information processing systems such as human cognition.

Biological evolution is not normally considered in information processing terms but there are advantages to thinking of it in this way. When considered as an information processing system, biological evolution is able to tell us about a particular class of theories, natural information processing theories. These theories tell us how information is processed in nature and evolution by natural selection provides us with the best known and most detailed natural information processing theory. By treating biological evolution as a natural information processing theory, we can throw substantial light on the characteristics of this class of information processing systems because of the large amount of knowledge that we have available to us about biological evolution.

Knowing how natural information processing systems such as biological evolution function is particularly important because human cognition provides another example of a natural information processing system. If we know how biological evolution functions as a natural information processing system, that knowledge can be used to tell us how human cognition functions because human cognition also is a natural information processing system, analogous to evolution by natural selection. Knowing the characteristics of natural information processing systems in general can tell us about some of the central characteristics of human cognition.

Thus, if we know how biological evolution works, it may tell us much about how human cognition works, assuming both are natural information processing systems. If we assume the way we learn, think and solve problems is part of nature because we are part of nature, we need to know how nature learns and solves problems. That aim can be achieved by treating both evolution by natural selection and human cognition as a natural information processing system. Chapters 2–4 of Part II establish and discuss the suggested analogy between evolution by natural selection and human cognition. In the process, those chapters provide the cognitive architecture that lies at the heart of cognitive load theory.

Cognitive load theory's emphasis on human cognitive architecture and its evolution is not an end in itself. The ultimate aim of the theory is to use our knowledge of human cognition to provide instructional design principles. The cognitive architecture discussed in Part II tells us that when processing biologically secondary information, human cognition includes a working memory that is limited in capacity and duration if dealing with novel information but unlimited in capacity and duration if dealing with familiar information previously stored in a very large long-term memory. Instruction needs to consider the limitations of working memory so that information can be stored effectively in long-term memory. Once appropriate information is stored in long-term memory, the capacity and duration limits of working memory are transformed and indeed, humans are transformed. Tasks that previously were impossible or even inconceivable can become trivially simple. Accordingly, the aim of instructional design is to facilitate the acquisition of knowledge in long-term memory via a working memory that is limited in capacity and duration until it is transformed by knowledge held in long-term memory. The characteristics of that memory can provide guidelines relevant to designing instruction. The initial process of specifying instructional design principles begins in Part III of this book.

The cognitive load imposed on working memory by various instructional procedures originates from either the intrinsic nature of the instructional material, resulting in an intrinsic cognitive load, or from the manner in which the material is presented and the activities required of learners, resulting in an extraneous cognitive load. Chapter 5 in Part III introduces the instructional applications of cognitive load theory by outlining the categories of cognitive load, their interactions and their instructional consequences. Chapter 6 discusses techniques that have been used to measure cognitive load.

The chapters of Part IV discuss the range of instructional effects generated by the theory. Over 25 years, researchers from around the globe have used cognitive load theory to generate a variety of instructional procedures. Those procedures characteristically are tested for effectiveness by comparing them to more traditional methods using randomised, controlled experiments. When the results of such comparisons indicate the superiority of a new procedure over a commonly used procedure, a cognitive load effect is demonstrated. Cognitive load effects provide us with novel instructional guidelines that constitute the ultimate aim of cognitive load theory. These guidelines constitute the major justification for devising cognitive load theory and are discussed in Chapters 7–17. Each chapter describes one or more of the cognitive load effects generated by the theory with each effect indicating an instructional procedure, tested for effectiveness, and recommended for use. The conclusions of Chapter 18 tie together the various strands of the preceding sections.

Over the two to three decades that cognitive load theory has been used as an instructional theory, it has undergone considerable development and change. In an example of a feedback loop, the changes to cognitive load theory have been driven largely by the instructional effects generated by the theory. Most commonly, the theory has generated a new instructional procedure at a point in time and that procedure has been demonstrated in a particular curriculum area using a specific set of materials. On occasions, the effect has failed to generalise to a different area and different conditions. Such failures require an explanation and that explanation usually results in both theory development and new instructional effects and procedures. In this manner, the edifice that constitutes cognitive load theory has been constructed.

Ultimately, the theory stands or falls according to its ability to generate novel, useful, instructional procedures, a justification common to all instructional theories. We hope cognitive load theory passes this test. The most recent version of the theory, along with the instructional procedures generated by the theory over many years is presented in this book. We begin, in the next chapter, by using evolutionary theory to categorise knowledge.

John Sweller
Paul Ayres
Slava Kalyuga

Acknowledgements

There are far too many people who have contributed to cognitive load theory over the years to be able to thank in anything other than general terms. The first group to thank is the army of research students who ultimately did most of the work associated with the theory. Many of those students from around the world have since become highly respected international scholars in their own right. Without them, this book would not have been written. We owe them a debt of gratitude that can never be repaid. One of those ex-students, Elizabeth Owen, carefully read the manuscript and eliminated many of our more clumsy efforts. We thank her for her work, emphasising that any remaining confusions are entirely our responsibility. Another research student, Chee Lee, funded by the Faculty of Arts and Social Sciences at UNSW, did a magnificent job of organising our reference list and assisting with the figures. Her patience knows no bounds!

The empirical work described in this book and largely carried out by research students required the testing of countless students (using those randomised, controlled experiments!) in many of the population centres around the world. They deserve a special thank you. We hope that as small compensation, our procedures have assisted them in their studies.

Our many collaborators from around the world have contributed far more to cognitive load theory than we could ever achieve. The theory is theirs, not ours.

Lastly, and most importantly, we would like to thank Susan, Robyn and Marika. They have put up with us and for them, cognitive load theory has been a near lifetime sentence!

Contents

Part I
Preliminaries to Cognitive Load Theory

Chapter 1
Categories of Knowledge: An Evolutionary Approach

The first step that we need to make in considering the manner in which human cognition is organised is to categorise knowledge. Different categories of knowledge may be acquired, organised and stored in different ways and require different instructional procedures. Understanding how we deal with different categories of knowledge is a requirement in determining which aspects of human cognition are important from an instructional design perspective.

There are a very large number of ways of categorising knowledge but fortunately, most knowledge category distinctions that can be made are irrelevant from an instructional point of view because they have no demonstrated differences in their instructional implications. One category that is relevant concerns the distinction between knowledge we have specifically evolved to acquire, known as biologically primary knowledge, and knowledge that has more recently become important for cultural reasons, known as biologically secondary knowledge. In Chapter 1, we discuss the distinction between biologically primary and secondary knowledge and the instructional implications that flow from that distinction.

We deal quite differently with biologically primary and biologically secondary information. Recognising faces, recognising speech, using general problem-solving strategies, and engaging in basic social relations provide examples of biologically primary knowledge that we have evolved to acquire. Such knowledge is modular. We evolved to deal with the various types of primary knowledge at different times and in different ways. For example, we might expect that the cognitive processes required to allow us to learn to recognise faces is likely to be very different from the processes that allow us to recognise spoken words. While we have an ability to easily learn to recognise a large range of human faces or to recognise the immense number of sounds required by our native language without tuition, the manner in which we acquire those skills is likely to be quite different with divergent cognitive processes. Furthermore, not only do the skills required to recognise faces and sounds differ from each other due to their modularity, such biologically evolved primary abilities require a different form of cognition from the general information processing required to acquire biologically secondary knowledge.

Biologically secondary knowledge is knowledge more recently required by societies for cultural reasons. Examples are reading, writing or any of the many other

J. Sweller et al., *Cognitive Load Theory*, Explorations in the Learning Sciences, Instructional Systems and Performance Technologies 1, DOI 10.1007/978-1-4419-8126-4_1, © Springer Science+Business Media, LLC 2011

topics for which instruction is provided. Instructional design is largely concerned with biologically secondary, not primary knowledge. When dealing with secondary knowledge, human cognition provides an example of a general, information processing engine. It is general because, in contrast to the structures that process primary information, the secondary processing engine is capable of processing a wide range of information categories. Furthermore, since instructional design is concerned largely with secondary, not primary knowledge, a description of the cognitive machinery driving the acquisition of secondary knowledge can lead directly to instructional design procedures.

Why Instructional Design Needs to Distinguish Between Biologically Primary and Secondary Knowledge

Human structures and functions are the product of evolution by natural selection. Everything, from structures such as our opposable thumb to functions such as oxygen/carbon dioxide transfers in our lungs, exists due to a long history of evolution over countless generations. While the evolution of our physical structures and functions tend to dominate our awareness when we consider our evolutionary history, the evolution of the human mind tends to take a back seat. We less frequently think of the human mind as an entity that evolved and even more rarely consider the consequences of an evolutionary view of human cognition. There are some important educational consequences that flow from considering brain structures and their resultant cognitive functions as the product of evolution by natural selection. Considering human cognition from an evolutionary perspective can yield novel insights into the functioning of the human mind and those insights may, in turn, yield instructional insights (Sweller, 2003, 2004; Sweller & Sweller, 2006). In this chapter we will consider the two categories of knowledge introduced above that we have evolved to acquire, biologically primary and biologically secondary knowledge. How we acquire those two categories of knowledge and the consequent instructional implications will be analysed.

The distinction between biologically primary and biologically secondary knowledge was suggested by Geary (2007, 2008). By distinguishing between these categories of knowledge, Geary has provided a unique base for educational psychology. He differentiates between biologically secondary knowledge that is learnable and teachable and biologically primary knowledge that is learnable but not teachable because it is usually learned without being explicitly taught. In the process, he explains many otherwise puzzling findings. Indeed, his formulation has the potential to not only change instructional design but to change our view of ourselves.

The contrast between primary and secondary knowledge constitutes the core of Geary's treatment. We have evolved to assimilate biologically primary knowledge. In some ways, it can be seen as instinctive knowledge that we are programmed to acquire and so does not need to be taught. On the other hand, we also can assimilate biologically secondary knowledge; but because it is knowledge we have not had to deal with during our evolutionary history, it is different and acquired in a fundamentally different manner to biologically primary knowledge. Biologically secondary, unlike primary knowledge, needs to be explicitly taught within a culture. The secondary knowledge we acquire is largely dependent on the culture in which we develop. Since it is culture specific, it will alter from culture to culture. While secondary knowledge develops from primary knowledge, the characteristics of the cognitive processes associated with the two systems are in many respects quite different and those differences have instructional ramifications. We will begin by considering biologically primary knowledge.

Biologically Primary Knowledge

Humans have a wide repertoire of skills based on biologically primary knowledge. We sometimes take those skills for granted because they are universal, acquired effortlessly and frequently unconsciously, without explicit instruction. For example, we readily recognise and distinguish between human faces and recognise physical objects, learn how to interact with other humans, and learn to physically interact with our environment through movement, without explicit instructional programmes. Learning to listen and speak a first language is one of our most important biologically primary skills. We do not require curricula or learning and teaching programmes indicating how we should be taught our first language. The very concept of a curriculum devised to teach a first language to normally developing children is likely to be seen as peculiar. And yet, immeasurable amounts of information must be processed and stored in order for us to be able to listen and speak. For example, when learning to speak, we must simultaneously learn to manipulate and coordinate our lips, tongue, breath and voice in a large number of variations. We learn but are not taught this skill. There is no curriculum that anyone has devised to teach us how to talk and, indeed, most of us would have no conception of how to teach someone to speak their first language. We do not need to have such a curriculum because we have evolved to learn how to speak without being taught. Despite the immense amounts of information required in learning how to speak a first language, we experience no discernible cognitive load in acquiring the necessary skills in this or any other biologically primary area.

Why are the skills associated with these tasks so easily acquired despite their huge information content? We readily learn these skills because we have evolved to learn them over countless generations as a necessary condition of our biological survival. They constitute our biological rather than cultural inheritance and we expect most people to learn these skills irrespective of the culture in which they have developed. Geary (2007, 2008) categorised such instinctively acquired skills as biologically or evolutionary primary skills that require biologically primary knowledge.

Biologically primary knowledge is modular with every primary skill largely independent of every other skill. Each primary skill is likely to have evolved quite separately to every other primary skill, probably during a different evolutionary epoch. The manner in which we learn to recognise faces or the manner in which we learn a first language may bear little relation to each other. They are related only in that during two, quite different evolutionary epochs, we have evolved to acquire the knowledge required to learn to recognise faces and to speak. Because of this evolutionary history, both skills are acquired easily and effortlessly, without explicitly being taught.

We tend not to know we are acquiring primary knowledge and most primary knowledge is acquired when we are very young. We do not need to instruct people in the acquisition of primary knowledge. Membership of a functioning society is all that is required. Indeed, our ability to set up primitive societies is itself an example of biologically primary knowledge.

There are no definitive tests that identify biologically primary knowledge. The manner in which information is acquired provides the only available procedure that points to the presence of biologically primary knowledge. If we can acquire information easily and rapidly in an area without having to first consciously, actively learn and without explicit teaching, then that area almost certainly constitutes biologically primary knowledge.

Biologically primary knowledge provides a base for most aspects of human cognition. Because we have evolved to easily, rapidly and automatically store huge amounts of some categories of information in long-term memory, we are provided with a basic source for human ingenuity, creativity and skill. But biologically primary knowledge in itself, while essential, does not lead directly to those aspects of human cognition that we interpret as constituting intelligent behaviour. For example, while speaking is an example of biologically primary knowledge and we learn to speak easily and automatically by immersion in a culture, we also can consciously learn to speak in a new and different manner and can be explicitly taught to speak differently from the manner in which we grew up to speak. We may, for example, learn that certain grammatical constructions are either appropriate or inappropriate in our culture. We may be taught that it is appropriate to say 'It isn't here' but inappropriate to say 'It ain't here'. We also may be taught certain complex language skills associated with particular academic disciplines. Skills that require a substantial alteration in the expression of biologically primary knowledge are no longer biologically primary. They belong to biologically secondary knowledge.

Biologically Secondary Knowledge

Human culture is constantly changing, no more so than in recent times, with our stock of knowledge increasing exponentially. The nature of that new knowledge is quite distinct from the biologically primary knowledge discussed in the previous section. We have evolved to learn the motor and cognitive processes required to speak, for example, and will do so without explicit tuition. In contrast, while we require many aspects of biologically primary knowledge in order to learn to write, learning to write is a vastly different skill to learning to speak. We have not evolved to learn to write. We have only been able to write for a few thousand years, far too short a time to be influenced by biological evolution. Indeed, for most of the period after humans learned to write, only a tiny minority of people could write. It has only been with the advent of mass education in the last 100 years or so, and only in some societies, that most people have learned to write. The manner in which we have evolved to learn to speak has not and could not be recapitulated in learning to write. Accordingly, the instructional processes required to learn to write are vastly different from those required to learn to speak. The instructional processes differ because the cognitive system used to learn to speak is different from the system used to learn to write. Writing provides an example of biologically secondary knowledge rather than the biologically primary knowledge required to speak.

As well as the many different types of biologically primary knowledge we have evolved to acquire, each with its own acquisition system, we also have a system, probably unitary, for acquiring biologically secondary knowledge (Geary, 2007, 2008) required for cultural reasons but which we have not specifically evolved to acquire. In contrast to the ease with which we acquire biological primary knowledge, the acquisition of biologically secondary knowledge is effortful and conscious. While we will learn to speak just by immersion in a speaking society, we are unlikely to learn to write just by immersion in a writing society. Learning to write requires more than immersion. Being surrounded by people who speak provides a guarantee that most persons will learn to speak. Being surrounded by people who write provides no guarantee that a person will learn to write. Learning to write requires conscious effort and because acquiring secondary knowledge can be difficult, and because the importance of acquiring such knowledge is critical to modern societies, we have set up massive educational structures with the sole purpose of assisting learners to acquire secondary knowledge. Educational institutions exist in order to perpetuate and advance culture. While the acquisition of culture is dependent on biologically primary knowledge, culture itself does not consist of such knowledge. Rather, it consists of biologically secondary knowledge. We have not evolved to acquire most aspects of our culture automatically and unconsciously, especially advanced culture, in the way we acquire biologically primary knowledge. We require formal and informal institutions to acquire the biologically secondary knowledge that constitutes culture.

While we have not evolved to acquire any particular biologically secondary skill in the manner in which we have evolved to acquire particular primary skills, we have evolved the cognitive system that permits the acquisition of a possibly infinite range of secondary skills. That cognitive system will be discussed in detail in Chapters 2–4 of Part II.

Whether a skill requires some form of institutional support for its acquisition can be used as an informal guide to whether the skill relies largely on biologically primary or biologically secondary knowledge . Primary knowledge acquisition does not require institutional support while secondary knowledge acquisition does require such support. Every subject, every curriculum area from cooking to physics consists heavily of biologically secondary knowledge. How we acquire biologically secondary knowledge provides the major theme of this book.

Since the processes by which secondary knowledge is acquired are quite different to those required to obtain primary knowledge, we might expect the instructional processes also to differ. The fact that we do not acquire secondary knowledge automatically or unconsciously has instructional consequences. In Geary's (2007) words

(Geary's italics), '*most children will not be sufficiently motivated nor cognitively able to learn all of secondary knowledge needed for functioning in modern societies without well organized, explicit and direct teacher instruction.*' (p. 43). Simply leaving students to learn by constructing their own knowledge while immersed in an appropriate environment may be desirable or even unavoidable when dealing with the primary knowledge that we have evolved to acquire. Such procedures are not desirable when dealing with secondary knowledge that is culturally invented by humans. We have not evolved to specifically acquire such knowledge and so we require quite different and in some senses, 'artificial' techniques for assisting learners. As will be discussed in the next section, those techniques require highly explicit guidance.

Instructional Consequences

The division of biologically primary and secondary knowledge has instructional implications for both categories. With respect to primary knowledge, many of the general cognitive skills that are sometimes the subject of instructional procedures are skills that are basic and essential to human life. We are very likely to have evolved to acquire general cognitive skills as opposed to the more domain-specific skill which is associated with the subjects taught in educational institutions. As indicated above, if we have evolved to acquire general cognitive skills, they are biologically primary and are learnable but not teachable because they are automatically acquired. Attempting to teach biologically primary knowledge may be futile.

There are even more important instructional implications associated with biologically secondary knowledge. While general cognitive strategies constitute biologically primary knowledge, domain-specific knowledge taught in educational institutions constitutes biologically secondary knowledge. Secondary knowledge needs to be explicitly taught and is usually consciously learned, unlike primary knowledge. Expecting learners to acquire secondary knowledge via immersion may be just as futile as expecting biologically primary knowledge to be teachable (Sweller, 2008). The specific instructional consequences that flow from the characteristics of biologically secondary knowledge will be discussed in detail in Part IV. In this part, we will discuss more general instructional consequences associated with both primary and secondary knowledge, beginning with primary knowledge.

Instructional Consequences Associated with Biologically Primary Knowledge

There are a large range of general cognitive skills that are likely to be biologically primary, evolved activities. Our ability to engage in general problem solving, planning, decision making and thinking provide obvious candidates. We learn these skills but there is little evidence that they can be taught. Means–ends analysis is the most important, best-known, general problem-solving strategy discussed in the literature (e.g., Newell & Simon, 1972; Sweller, 1988). Several steps are required to use this general strategy irrespective of the problem domain. We must simultaneously consider the current problem state and the goal state, search for differences between these two states, search for legitimate problem-solving operators that can be used to reduce any differences found between the current and the goal state, and choose a problem-solving operator to apply to the current problem state. Once a problem-solving operator has been applied to a problem state, a new state is created. We now must check to see if the new state corresponds to the goal state. If it does, the problem is solved. If it does not, the procedure is used recursively until the goal is attained. This means–ends strategy will be described using an elementary algebra transformation problem.

Assume we are using a means–ends strategy to solve the algebraic problem, $a + b = c$, solve for a. We begin with the current problem state which also is the initial state, $(a + b = c)$. That state needs to be transformed in one or more moves into the goal state where the goal state consists of a isolated on the left-hand side of the equation. To accomplish this aim, we must search for any differences between the current problem state and the goal state. In this problem, there is only one difference. The equation has '$+b$' located on the left side. To solve the problem, we must eliminate '$+b$' from the left side. The next step required by a means–ends strategy is to search for legitimate problem-solving operators to eliminate '$+b$' from the left side of the equation. That step will satisfy the requirement to reduce the differences between the current problem state and the goal state. In the case of algebra, the rules of algebra provide the problem-solving operators. Subtracting the addend ($+b$) from both sides of the equation will eliminate $+b$ from the left side. Once this move has been made, we must check if the goal has been attained. In this case, the goal has been attained and so the problem is solved.

We use a general problem-solving strategy such as means–ends analysis whenever we must solve a problem for which we do not have domain-specific knowledge of a solution. For example, junior high school students beginning to learn algebra are likely to use the strategy as described above. Most readers of this book will not use a means–ends strategy to solve this algebra problem. After some exposure to algebra, a domain-specific strategy will be used. With sufficient experience of algebra, a person will instantly recognise the problem as one that requires subtraction of the addend from both sides. A search for differences between the given and goal states or a search for problem-solving operators that will reduce any differences found will not be necessary. Problem solvers will have learned to recognise the relevant problem states and know which solution move is appropriate for each state without searching for moves. They will immediately subtract b from both sides of the equation without engaging in a search for an appropriate move. Recognising problem states and their appropriate moves only occurs after considerable learning and only applies to particular, domain-specific problems. In contrast, a means–ends strategy is general because it can be applied to a large range of novel, unrelated problems that we might encounter. We only use the strategy when we are novices and do not have domain-specific knowledge that we can use to generate moves.

Evidence that novices use means–ends analysis while experts use domain-specific knowledge when solving problems comes from the substantial literature on expert–novice differences. For example, Larkin, McDermott, Simon, and Simon (1980a, b) found that novices, when solving physics problems, work backwards from the goal using a means–ends strategy while experts work forward from the givens using previously acquired knowledge. Sweller, Mawer, and Ward (1983) demonstrated the switch from a backward working, means–ends strategy to a forward working knowledge-based strategy. These results indicate that if we are aware of knowledge indicating a problem solution, we will routinely use that knowledge. In the absence of knowledge of appropriate problem-solving moves, we will use a means–ends strategy.

As far as we are aware, there are no successful examples in the problem-solving literature demonstrating improved problem-solving performance following the teaching of a means–ends strategy. We suggest it is unteachable because all normal humans have evolved to use the strategy. For survival, our ancestors needed to know how to use means–ends analysis. Without a means–ends strategy, we could not search for food, cross a river or find a route from point A to point B. We all use the strategy without explicit instruction because it is part of our repertoire of biologically primary knowledge.

All examples of general problem-solving strategies are likely to be equally unteachable for the same reason that means–ends analysis is unteachable. General cognitive strategies are very likely to uniformly consist of examples of biologically primary knowledge. The ease and automaticity with which we learn to use general problem-solving strategies without instruction provide evidence that they are acquired as primary knowledge. There are many examples of recommended general problem-solving strategies (see Polya, 1957); however, they cannot be taught to improve problem-solving performance because they consist of biologically primary knowledge which is acquired naturally. An example is provided by recommendations suggesting that when faced with a difficult problem for which we are unable to find a solution, we should think of a similar problem for which we know the solution moves (Polya, 1957). Teaching problem solvers to consider a similar problem is no more likely to be effective than teaching them to use a means–ends strategy. If we can think of them, we automatically generalise knowledge from previous, similar problems. Whenever we solve a familiar problem, we automatically treat it as though we know the problem and its solution even though it always differs in some respects from previous problems. If we know of a similar problem that can assist us in solving the current problem we will always use that similar problem because the knowledge that similar problems with similar solutions are useful is an example of biologically primary knowledge. If we cannot think of a similar problem, exhortations to think of a similar problem are pointless. Attempting to teach people to think of similar problems when solving unfamiliar problems is likely to remain just as unteachable in the future as it has in the past. We know of no randomised, controlled experiments indicating the effectiveness of such a strategy. Without such biologically primary, general problem-solving techniques we could not have survived and so we have evolved to assimilate them rapidly and easily without tuition.

A similar argument applies to all general cognitive techniques such as planning, decision making and thinking. We have evolved to engage in all of these techniques as part of our survival mechanism. Until clear bodies of evidence become available indicating that very general cognitive techniques are teachable as well as learnable, we should assume that general cognitive techniques consist of biologically primary knowledge that we acquire automatically. Some cognitive techniques are learned automatically and so cannot be taught.

What would constitute evidence for learnable/teachable general problem-solving strategies? Such evidence requires far transfer data from randomised, controlled experiments that alter one variable at a time. Test materials must be unrelated to learning materials to ensure that a general problem-solving strategy has been acquired rather than domain-specific knowledge. Anecdotal data does not constitute evidence. Nor does data from before/after tests without a control group, or a controlled experiment in which multiple variables are altered simultaneously. All of these techniques are compromised because any results obtained can be due to a variety of irrelevant factors. Far transfer tests are essential because if a general, cognitive strategy has been acquired, it should be usable and beneficial under novel conditions and transfer tests can be used to ensure that any effect found is not due to enhanced, domain-specific learning. To this point, there has been no sign of such a body of evidence in favour of teachable, general cognitive strategies becoming available. (A possible exception is considered in Chapter 3 in a discussion of brainstorming.)

Instructional Consequences of Biologically Secondary Knowledge

Biologically secondary knowledge is teachable but the manner in which we teach has been bedevilled by our failure to distinguish between primary and secondary knowledge. We have assumed that since the bulk of what humans learn outside of educational institutions is acquired effortlessly without direct, explicit instruction, the best way to improve instructional procedures is to eliminate explicit instruction. Constructivist, discovery and problem-based learning advocates have assumed that withholding information from learners should be beneficial because explicit information is not required for people to acquire much of the information we need to function in our societies (Kirschner, Sweller, & Clark, 2006; Mayer, 2004). Rather than showing learners how to best solve a problem, it is assumed that they learn more, or at least learn better, if they discover how to solve the problem by themselves, with minimal levels of guidance from instructors. This view assumes that learners need to learn how to construct knowledge for themselves and so explicit instructional guidance should be avoided in favour of having learners discover knowledge.

From a historical perspective, discovery learning should be seen as the precursor of a long line of indirect, inquiry-based teaching procedures that culminated in constructivist teaching. While the procedures have differing titles depending on the era of their popularity (discovery learning, problem-based learning, inquiry learning, constructivist learning amongst others) it is not possible to distinguish between them and they should be considered as essentially identical. All assume that information should be withheld from learners during instruction (Sweller, 2009a).

The reasons why constructivist teaching is assumed by many to be superior are not entirely clear because the reasons tend neither to be based on any obvious cognitive architecture nor on a body of data. Nevertheless, it seems possible to discern two categories of explanation. The first category assumes that withholding information from learners will, paradoxically, result in their acquiring that information better. The act of discovering information improves the quality of information according to this view. Discovered knowledge should be qualitatively better than directly taught knowledge (Bruner, 1961).

If this view was correct, then knowledge acquired during problem solving should be superior to knowledge acquired while studying worked examples. Evidence for this proposition is entirely absent. In fact, rather than providing support, the evidence is contrary to a discovery learning/constructivist position. Klahr and Nigam (2004) found no difference between the quality of knowledge of science learners who discovered a science principle as opposed to those who were explicitly instructed in the principle. The only difference was that those who were required to use a discovery approach took longer with fewer students learning the principle. Furthermore, evidence based on the worked example effect (Sweller & Cooper, 1985) is quite the reverse of what we should expect based on a constructivist, discovery learning viewpoint. The worked example effect occurs when learners learn more and are better at solving subsequent problems after studying worked examples rather than solving problems. That evidence will be discussed in detail in Chapter 8. Only when expertise develops does solving problems become a viable instructional technique, as discussed in Chapter 12.

The second argument why discovery learning/constructivist teaching procedures might be effective is less concerned with the acquisition of curricula information directly, but instead is concerned with learning to discover information in general. This view assumes that withholding information improves learners' ability to subsequently discover information. In other words, discovering information is assumed to be a general skill that needs to be taught as a useful technique for the acquisition of curriculum knowledge. Unless we are taught how to discover knowledge, we will not be able to find most of the knowledge we need.

It will, of course, be apparent from our previous discussion on the instructional consequences of primary knowledge that there is every reason to suppose that teaching people how to construct knowledge or giving them practice in constructing knowledge is likely to be futile. For survival, we have evolved to construct knowledge and so knowledge construction is a primary skill with all the characteristics of a primary skill. We learn the skill easily, automatically and without tuition. Of course, if learning to discover knowledge is defined as learning to use a library or the Internet, those skills do need to be taught but they should be taught directly and explicitly because they consist of biologically secondary knowledge. We have not specifically evolved to learn to use a library or the Internet. We have evolved to construct knowledge and so there is no point attempting to teach knowledge construction.

In summary, teaching students by having them discover the laws, rules, concepts and procedures of a discipline with minimal guidance by withholding easily presented information so that they can learn to construct knowledge is pointless if learners automatically construct knowledge. While the concepts and procedures of a discipline constitute secondary knowledge that needs to be taught, our ability to construct secondary knowledge is based on primary knowledge and so we do not need to be taught how to construct secondary knowledge. We merely need to be taught the relevant concepts and procedures, not how to acquire them. Furthermore, there is no evidence for the assumption that knowledge acquired by discovery is superior to knowledge acquired by explicit instruction. We automatically construct knowledge because it is an essential, evolved, primary skill that can no more be explicitly taught than recognising faces or listening to a first language. If so, empirical evidence for the effectiveness of constructivist teaching compared to direct instruction may never become available because primary skills are learned, not taught.

Conclusions

David Geary's formulation is interesting from a purely scientific perspective. It is critical from an instructional design perspective. If his views are valid, many of the currently, commonly used instructional procedures are utterly misguided and urgently need reform.

In this chapter, highly influenced by the work of Geary, we have suggested that knowledge can be divided into biologically primary knowledge that we have evolved to acquire and biologically secondary knowledge that has become important for cultural reasons. Primary knowledge is learned easily, automatically and unconsciously and cannot be taught. Secondary knowledge is culturally acquired knowledge that has become important in a particular culture. It is learned consciously and with effort and should be explicitly taught. Secondary knowledge is the domain of most of the curricula that can be found in educational institutions. Those institutions were devised specifically to teach biologically secondary knowledge because we have difficulty acquiring such knowledge without explicit tuition. It is quite misguided to treat biologically secondary knowledge as though it is primary knowledge.

Cognitive load theory and the remainder of this book are concerned in the most part with biologically secondary knowledge. Part II deals with those aspects of human cognitive architecture associated with processing biologically secondary information. This chapter used evolutionary theory to suggest that categories of knowledge differ depending on the extent to which we have evolved to acquire them. In discussing human cognitive architecture associated with biologically secondary information, a deeper use of evolutionary theory is required. The very machinery of evolutionary theory may be closely associated with the machinery of human cognitive architecture. It will be suggested in Part II that the information processing characteristics of human cognitive architecture recapitulate the information processing characteristics of evolution by natural selection. As a consequence, we can use the processes of evolution to throw light on how we learn, think and solve problems. And, of course, how we learn, think and solve problems is essential to instructional design.

Part II
Human Cognitive Architecture

Human cognitive architecture refers to the manner in which the components that constitute human cognition such as working and long-term memory are organised. The characteristics of human cognitive architecture when dealing with biologically secondary knowledge are considered in Chapters 2–4. While Chapter 1 in Part I indicated how biological evolution can be used to distinguish between important categories of knowledge, Chapters 2–4 of Part II use an evolutionary perspective in a quite different manner. In Chapters 2–4 the well-known machinery of biological evolution is used to throw light on what we suggest is the similar, analogous machinery of human cognition when dealing with biologically secondary information. Biological evolution requires a store of genetic information that determines the functions and activities of an organism in a particular environment. Those functions and activities are passed on to succeeding generations but can be altered by random mutations of the genetic material. If those mutations are adaptive for the species in the same or a new environment they are retained resulting in a change in the genetic information stored. If they are not adaptive, they are jettisoned. In this way, information is stored, transmitted and changed during evolution by natural selection.

This information processing system is not unique to biological evolution. The same processes are used to deal with secondary information by the human cognitive system. They belong to a category of systems that occurs in nature and so we will refer to them as natural information processing systems. These systems govern the activities of natural entities. Evolution by natural selection and human cognition are analogous because both provide examples of a natural information processing system.

Nature includes many information processing systems. Every living organism depends for its survival on an information processing system that allows it to deal with the various categories of information that the organism must deal with in its natural environment. These information processing systems vary in complexity and sophistication from relatively simple to immensely complex. We are concerned with the most sophisticated of those systems, biological evolution and human cognition. They have several definitional characteristics. First, sophisticated natural information processing systems are able to create novel information intended to deal with a variety of environments. Second, having created novel information and determined that it is effective, sophisticated natural information processing systems can remember that information for subsequent use or eliminate it if it is not effective. Third, these systems can use stored information to govern their activities. Fourth, they can disseminate effective information across space and time.

A sophisticated natural information processing system must meet these defining characteristics and, of course, it can be seen that the characteristics apply to human cognition. We do create novel information, have procedures for remembering that information, can use information to govern our activities and are able to disseminate information. While the characteristics apply to human cognition, it is not coincidental that they apply equally to evolution by natural selection. Evolution also creates, remembers, uses and disseminates information. Since both human cognition and biological evolution are sophisticated natural information processing systems that create, disseminate, use and remember information, it is plausible to conjecture that they both rely on the same basic information processing machinery to function. The operation of that machinery is based on a set of principles.

The components of natural information processing systems can be described in many ways but in this book five basic principles will be used: *the information store principle; the borrowing and reorganising principle; the randomness as genesis principle; the narrow limits of change principle;* and *the environmental organising and linking principle.* These principles will be shown to underlie both biological evolution and human cognition and so human cognition can be treated as an analogue of biological evolution. An application of these principles to human cognition provides us, in effect, with a cognitive architecture whose principles have already been established in evolutionary biological science as an integrated, natural information processing system. If the same principles can be applied to both human cognition and biological evolution, we potentially have a cognitive system that we know functions because evolution by natural selection is an established, functioning theory. In this manner, the established mechanisms of biological evolution can be used to throw light on the far less well-established mechanisms of human cognition. The five natural information processing system principles described in Chapters 2–4 will be shown to apply equally to biological evolution and human cognition. We will begin with the *information store principle.*

Chapter 2
Amassing Information: The Information Store Principle

Natural environments tend to be both highly complex and highly variable. The frequently immeasurable number of variables associated with natural environments tends to be in constant flux. Most animals and plants must survive in complex, variable environments dealing with day and night, summer and winter, drought and flood. Any natural information processing system must find a way to handle this complexity and variability. Nevertheless, despite the complex, variable environment in which a natural information processing system must function, it must be able to treat its environment as familiar and predictable. It must be able to ignore variability that does not matter to its functioning while responding to variability that does matter. In one sense, the manner in which this complexity is handled is straightforward. Immense complexity is handled by immense information stores. Natural information processing systems build sufficiently large information stores to handle most of the vagaries inherent in their environments.

How Natural Information Processing Systems Store Information

Evolutionary Biology

The manner in which the need for a large information store is met by evolutionary biology is well known. All genomes include a huge amount of DNA-based information that determines most biological activity (Portin, 2002; Stotz & Griffiths, 2004). The size of any genome must be large because organisms survive in complex, information-rich environments. A simple, small information store is unlikely to be able to deal with the complexity of any natural environment. A large and sophisticated store is needed to deal with the inevitable environmental variations it will face.

There is no agreed measure of genomic complexity or size. Nevertheless, all genomes consists of, at a minimum, thousands, or in many organisms, billions of base pairs that can be considered units of information. (There is no consensus on

J. Sweller et al., *Cognitive Load Theory*, Explorations in the Learning Sciences, Instructional Systems and Performance Technologies 1, DOI 10.1007/978-1-4419-8126-4_2, © Springer Science+Business Media, LLC 2011

what should be used as a measure of complexity but all measures yield very large numbers of units of information.) The genetic functioning of organisms and species rely on that large store of information. If all natural information processing systems require a large store of information, it follows that human cognition also must rely on an equivalently large store of information.

Human Cognition: Long-Term Memory

The role of long-term memory in cognition provides an analogical equivalent to a genome in evolutionary biology. Like a genome in biology, long-term memory acts as a very large store of information. The bulk of our normal, everyday activities are familiar. When we say something is 'familiar' what we really mean is that it is based on information in long-term memory. That information permits us to engage in activities from automatically recognising the huge number of objects we see from minute to minute to planning our routine daily activities. All depend on a huge, organised knowledge base held in long-term memory.

Storing biologically primary and biologically secondary information. It can be argued that much of the information stored in long-term memory consists of bio-logically primary knowledge. We have evolved to acquire enormous amounts of primary knowledge in order to survive and function in our world. For example, when we listen and speak, much of both the physical and social aspects of our activities are based on a massive store of primary knowledge held in long-term memory. Similarly, our ability to effortlessly navigate our physical world provides an indicator of knowledge stored in long-term memory. We see and recognise a large number of objects and faces and can engage in a wide range of physical activi-ties. Many of these activities can be learned without lengthy training and so are indicative of primary knowledge held in long-term memory.

Our primary knowledge base enables us to engage in many of the activities that we frequently consider to be easy and simple. In fact, in information processing terms, many 'simple' activities are anything but simple. They appear simple solely because we have acquired them as biologically primary skills and all biologically primary skills are seen as simple and easy. The enormous amount of stored infor-mation required to engage in most biologically primary activities can be seen from the difficulty we have in readily programming computers to mimic primary skills such as recognising voices. That difficulty arises from the large knowledge base required by these skills. We have evolved to rapidly acquire a large knowledge base but because of its size and complexity, an equivalent knowledge base can be very difficult to readily program into a computer.

As an example, consider a simple task such as going outside to pick a flower. Learning to go outside and pick a flower is not a task that requires a long period of training. Despite its simplicity, programming a computer to engage in a similar task would require an enormous expenditure of time and effort and indeed, as far as we are aware, such a task is beyond today's robot-connected computers. In reality, it is an immensely complex task that only appears simple to us because it is based on a huge, primary knowledge base held in long-term memory. We may contrast other tasks that computers are programmed to do. Compared to going outside and accomplishing a simple task such as picking a flower, it is much easier to program a computer to play chess at grandmaster level or to carry out complex mathematical operations. We see these tasks as immensely complex because they are based on secondary knowledge that we have not evolved to acquire.

The extent to which we are able to go outside and pick a flower or carry out mathematical operations are both determined by the amount of knowledge held in long-term memory. Nevertheless, the category of knowledge required by the two tasks is quite different. Picking a flower requires biologically primary knowledge that is quantitatively immense but easily acquired because we have evolved to acquire that knowledge. Complex mathematics requires secondary knowledge that we have not specifically evolved to acquire and so is much more difficult. The knowledge base is probably greater in the case of the flower-picking exercise even though we acquire a flower-picking knowledge base much more readily than mathematical skills. As indicated above, the evidence that going outside to pick a flower may require a larger knowledge base than even complex mathematical operations comes from the differential ease of programming a computer to accomplish both tasks. It is probable that the information associated with biologically primary activities may constitute the bulk of the knowledge we hold in long-term memory.

Evidence for the size and function of stored biologically secondary information. While most knowledge held in long-term memory probably can be categorised as primary, in absolute terms our secondary knowledge base is still immeasurably large. De Groot's (1965) and Chase and Simon's (1973) work on chess can be used to indicate to us the immense amount of secondary information held in the long-term memory store. Furthermore, that seminal work indicated for the first time that many higher-level cognitive activities that were assumed to rely minimally or not at all on long-term memory were largely driven by the contents of the long-term store.

The initial impetus for de Groot's work was the fact that chess grandmasters almost always defeat weekend players. He was concerned with finding the factors that almost invariably result in this outcome. What knowledge does a grandmaster have, in what activities does a grandmaster engage, to enable such dominance? There is a range of plausible hypotheses that, if valid, could provide an answer to this question. Indeed, several possible answers associated with problem-solving skill seem to have been intuitively assumed by most people who either played chess or thought about the factors that lead to chess skill.

One easily accepted plausible hypothesis is that grandmasters engage in a greater level of problem-solving search for suitable moves than weekend players. They may be particularly skilled at using means–ends analysis, for example. When using a means–ends strategy, grandmasters may search to a greater 'depth' than weekend players. That means instead of only considering the consequences of a small number of moves ahead they may consider a much longer series of moves. Considering the consequences of a longer rather than shorter series of moves should result in being able to choose better moves. Alternatively, chess grandmasters may engage in a greater search 'in breadth'. Whenever they had to make a move, they might consider a large range of alternative moves while a weekend player may only consider a small number of alternative moves. If a larger number of alternatives are considered we might expect a better move to be found than if only a smaller number of alternatives are considered.

In fact, de Groot found no evidence that grandmasters' superiority derived from either a greater search in depth or a greater search in breadth than weekend players. He found only one difference between different levels of players and that difference seemed to be quite unrelated to problem-solving skill. Rather, it was concerned with memory. De Groot showed chess players board configurations taken from real games for about 5 s before removing the pieces and asking the players to attempt to replace them in the configuration that they had just seen. The results indicated that masters and grandmasters were able to reproduce the board configurations that they were shown with a high degree of accuracy. In contrast, less-able players were far less accurate in replacing the pieces (see also, De Groot & Gobet, 1996).

De Groot obtained this result for chess board configurations taken from real games. He did not attempt to investigate if the same result could be obtained for pieces placed on a board in a random configuration rather than a real game configuration. Instead, Chase and Simon (1973) replicated de Groot's result but in addition ran exactly the same experiment placing the pieces on the board in a random configuration. The results were much different. For random configurations, there were no differences between more- and less-expert chess players. All players performed equally poorly on random configurations compared to grandmasters reproducing real game configurations. Only expert players faced with real game configurations performed well on this memory test. Less-expert players performed poorly on both real game and random configurations while expert players performed poorly on random configurations only.

In principle, these results are able to provide a full explanation of chess expertise without recourse to any other factors. Skill at chess is not based on an ability to think through a series of unique and ingenious chess moves. Expertise derives from learning to recognise many thousands of the board configurations that are found in chess games as well as learning the moves that are the most likely to be successful for the various configurations. This skill is acquired slowly over many years of consistent, continuous practice. That practice needs to be carried out with the explicit intention of improving performance, called 'deliberate practice' (Ericsson, Krampe, & Tesch-Romer, 1993). A chess grandmaster typically requires 10 years of deliberate practice before acquiring a high level of expertise.

Until de Groot's and Chase and Simon's work, the cognitive changes that occurred due to practice were essentially unknown. We now know what is learned during practice. According to Simon and Gilmartin (1973), chess grandmasters have stored in long-term memory tens of thousands of board configurations along with the best moves associated with those configurations. The source of chess-playing skill derives from that stored information rather than some mysterious thinking skill. Paradoxically, it is more likely that a less-skilled player must engage in complex thought because a less-skilled player does not have large numbers of board configurations and their associated moves stored in long-term memory. In the absence of stored knowledge, moves must be generated by problem-solving search. With the development of expertise, the need for problem-solving search activities is reduced. Instead, the best move at each choice-point becomes apparent without having to engage in search because that best move can be retrieved from long-term memory. Novices need to use thinking skills. Experts use knowledge.

This account of chess skill can be used to explain the phenomenon of simultaneous chess. In demonstration games, a chess grandmaster can simultaneously play and defeat a dozen weekend players. In the absence of a long-term memory explanation for chess skill, we would need to ask how anyone could possibly simultaneously devise multiple strategies for playing a dozen, complex, different games. The answer, of course, is that it is not possible, but nor is it required. Only the grandmaster's opponents must attempt to devise a strategy for their single game. The grandmaster can arrive at a board and irrespective of the progress of the game, look at the board configuration, immediately recognise it and recall the best move for that configuration. That process then can be repeated for the remaining boards. A novel game strategy does not need to be devised for each board. In contrast, the grandmaster's opponents do need to devise a novel strategy for their single game. In the absence of relevant information stored in long-term memory indicating the best move for each configuration, either a strategy or more probably random moves (see below) will be needed by less-knowledgeable players.

The findings associated with the game of chess are not, of course, unique. The cognitive processes associated with chess skill can be expected to apply to every area requiring biologically secondary knowledge. In particular, topics taught in educational institutions can be expected to have similar cognitive profiles as found in chess. In any biologically secondary area, we can expect the major, possibly sole difference between novices and experts to consist of differential knowledge held in long-term memory. Increased problem-solving skill should be directly caused by increased knowledge of relevant problem states and their associated moves rather than due to the acquisition of unspecified, general problem-solving strategies.

All of the readers of this book have skills similar to those exhibited by chess grandmasters. The only difference is that those skills are, for most people, in fields other than chess. If readers were asked to look at the last sentence for about 5 s and then replicate the very large number of letters that constitute that sentence, most could do so easily and accurately. Similar to the chess results, that skill disappears for randomly ordered letters. Replicating the letters of a sentence is in principle, no different to replicating the pieces from a chess board taken from a real game. The only difference is that educated people spend many years practicing reading while chess grandmasters spend many years practicing and studying chess. The cognitive consequences are identical.

As might be expected, findings similar to those obtained in chess have been obtained in many areas including understanding and remembering text (Chiesi, Spilich, & Voss, 1979), electronic engineering (Egan & Schwartz, 1979), programming (Jeffries, Turner, Polson, & Atwood, 1981) and algebra (Sweller & Cooper, 1985). These findings have important instructional implications that in conjunction with other aspects of human cognitive architecture discussed below have guided the instructional processes discussed in this book.

De Groot's findings not only have implications for instruction, they also provide us with vital information concerning the nature of human cognition and in the process have the potential to change our view of ourselves. De Groot's results provide us with some of the most important findings to be found in the field of human cognition. Humans may have a natural tendency to consider long-term memory as little more than fairly limited sets of isolated facts and incidents. Long-term memory can easily be considered to have a quite peripheral role in really important aspects of human cognition such as problem solving and thinking. De Groot's findings turn this view on its head. The function of long-term memory is vastly more important than simply enabling us to recall events, meaningful or otherwise, from our past. Instead, long-term memory is not only central to human cognition, but central to those aspects of cognition that are seen as representing the apex of the human mind. We require long-term memory for all higher-level cognitive activities such as problem solving and thinking. Expertise in such high-level cognitive processes is entirely dependent on the content of long-term memory. We are competent in an area because of information held in long-term memory. Furthermore, that information held in long-term memory may be the major reason for competence and skill.

Schema theory. Given the importance of information held in long-term memory, it is appropriate to analyse the form in which that information is held. Schema theory provides an answer. The theory became important with the work of Piaget (1928) and Bartlett (1932). Bartlett described an experiment that clearly indicates the nature and function of schemas. He asked one person to read a passage describing events from a foreign culture. That person then wrote as much of the passage as could be remembered. The remembered passage then was presented to a second person with the same instructions; the second person's written passage then was given to a third person etc. This process was repeated until a total of 10 people had read and recorded their memory of the previous person's passage.

Bartlett analysed the changes that occurred from passage to passage. He found two effects: levelling or flattening according to which unusual descriptions of events, such as descriptions of ghosts that appeared foreign to the readers tended to disappear; and sharpening, according to which descriptions of events that were familiar were emphasised. Descriptions of battles that appear commonly in Western literature and culture provide an example of features that were sharpened. What was remembered were not the events depicted in the original passage but rather, schematic representations of those events. Long-term memory holds countless numbers of schemas and those schemas determine how we process incoming information. What we see and hear is not determined solely by the information that impinges on our senses but to a very large extent by the schemas stored in long-term memory.

Schema theory became increasingly important in the 1980s, providing an explanation of aspects of problem-solving performance. A schema can be defined as a cognitive construct that permits us to classify multiple elements of information into a single element according to the manner in which the multiple elements are used (Chi, Glaser, & Rees, 1982). Most people who have completed junior high school algebra, for example, are likely to have a problem-solving schema that indicates that all problems of the form $a/b = c$, solve for a, should be solved in the same manner, by multiplying both sides of the equation by the denominator on the left side (b). Anyone who has acquired this schema will treat this and all similar problems requiring a similar solution as the same entity to be treated in the same way despite any differences between examples. With sufficient levels of expertise, all of the individual elements such as the pro-numerals and the mathematical symbols that constitute this and similar problems are treated as a single element by the relevant schema. As a consequence, any information that appears to correspond to this schema will be treated in an essentially identical manner. We will attempt to solve all problems such as the above algebra problem in a similar manner. In effect, the schema provides a template that permits us to effortlessly solve the problem.

The manner in which problem-solving schemas function provides us with immense benefits. We are able to solve problems that otherwise would be difficult or impossible to solve. Unfortunately, the same processes also have negative consequences that appear unavoidable. Sometimes, a problem will appear to be relevant for a particular schema but, in fact, is not relevant. Schemas held in long-term memory not only can render difficult problems easy to solve but can render simple problems very difficult to solve if the schema is erroneously assumed to provide an appropriate template. When we attempt to solve a problem by using an inappropriate schema because the problem looks as though it belongs to a particular category of problems but does not belong to that category, we have an example of *einstellung* or mental set (Luchins, 1942; Sweller, 1980; Sweller & Gee, 1978). Schemas stored in long-term memory may be essential for us to function but they also can prevent us from seeing what would otherwise be obvious.

Automation. Newly acquired schemas must be processed consciously and sometimes with considerable effort. With increasing practice schemas can be used with less and less conscious processing. Instead, they can be used automatically and largely without effort (Kotovsky, Hayes, & Simon, 1985; Schneider & Shiffrin, 1977; Shiffrin & Schneider, 1977). Our ability to read provides a clear example. Initially, when we are learning to read, we must consciously process each individual letter. With increasing practice, we acquire automated schemas for individual letters but still may need to consciously process the groups of letters that constitute words. With additional practice, word recognition becomes automated and even groups of familiar words can be read without conscious control. With high degrees of automation, conscious effort may only need to be expended on the meaning of text. Thus, competent English readers of this text not only have schemas for individual letters that permit the recognition of an infinite number of shapes, including hand-written letters, a large combinations of letters that form words, phrases and sentences also can be recognised automatically. The lower-level schemas for letters and words become increasingly automated with increasing competence and no longer need to be consciously processed because they have been automated. In contrast, beginning English readers are unlikely to have the same level of automation and will need much more effortful processing to fully understand the text.

Instructional Implications

The role of long-term memory in learning and problem solving provides us with a purpose and function for instruction. The purpose of instruction is to increase the store of knowledge in long-term memory. If nothing has changed in long-term memory, nothing has been learned. Instructional procedures that cannot describe what has changed in long-term memory run the risk that nothing has changed and nothing has been learned.

Not only do we know that an increase in knowledge held in long-term memory is central to learning, we now have a much better idea of what is learned and stored as a consequence of instruction. While we do store very domain-general concepts and procedures in long-term memory, these do not usually provide appropriate subject matter for instruction. General problem-solving strategies such as means– ends analysis must be stored in long-term memory but they cannot easily be the subject of instruction because they are acquired automatically and unconsciously as part of our biologically primary knowledge. Knowledge that can be the subject of instruction tends to be much more narrow. It is domain specific rather than domain general.

De Groot's work on chess indicated the astonishing extent of that specificity. We can learn the rules of chess in about 30 min and using those rules, we can theoretically generate every game that has ever been played and that ever will be played. Learning those rules is essential to chess skill but in another sense, it is trivial. Real chess skill comes from acquiring automated schemas. Good chess players must learn to recognise countless numbers of board configurations and the best moves associated with each configuration. Without that knowledge, knowing the rules of chess is largely useless. Exactly the same principle applies to learning in every curriculum area. For competence, we must acquire domain-specific schemas in curriculum areas that we wish to learn. While we need to learn the well-defined rules of mathematics and science or the more ill-defined rules associated with language-based disciplines such as literature or history, that knowledge will not take us very far. For real competence, we also must learn to recognise large numbers of problem states and situations and what actions we should take when faced with those states and situations.

De Groot's lesson should not be forgotten when designing instruction. In areas where we have not evolved to acquire knowledge, covered by most curriculum areas, knowledge consists of large numbers of domain-specific schemas that must be acquired. That knowledge provides a complete description of expertise. De Groot did not find that chess grandmasters had vastly superior repertoires of general problem-solving strategies, or indeed, cognitive, meta-cognitive, or thinking strategies. Furthermore, there is no body of literature demonstrating enhanced levels of these skills in expert chess players. We argue that such strategies are likely to be biologically primary and so do not need to be taught. Instead of general strategies, chess grandmasters had knowledge of chess board configurations and the best moves associated with those configurations. Differing levels of that knowledge are sufficient to fully explain differing levels of chess expertise. Domain-specific knowledge is also sufficient to fully explain expertise in curriculum areas. We must carefully consider whether many recently popular instructional techniques associated with inquiry, problem-based or constructivist learning procedures that do not emphasise domain-specific knowledge have any base in our cognitive architecture (Kirschner, Sweller, & Clark, 2006). Such techniques appear to proceed without reference to long-term memory or any of the other aspects of human cognition discussed in the next two chapters.

Conclusions

The information held in the long-term memory store is central to all facets of human cognition just as the information held in a genomic store is central to the information processes necessary for evolution by natural selection. The immense size of these stores is necessary to enable them to function in complex natural environments. A natural information store must be sufficiently large to enable it to respond flexibly and appropriately to a very large range of conditions. In the case of human cognition, our long-term memory store is sufficiently large to enable the variety of cognitive activities, both biologically primary and secondary, engaged in by humans. The next issue concerns how natural information stores are acquired. That issue is covered by the *borrowing and reorganising principle* and the *randomness as genesis principle*, covered in Chapter 3.

Chapter 3
Acquiring Information: The Borrowing and Reorganising Principle and the Randomness as Genesis Principle

How do natural information processing systems acquire information? The information store principle discussed in Chapter 2 indicates that in order to function in a complex environment, natural systems require a massive store of information that can guide activity. The manner in which that information is acquired is of immediate interest to anyone concerned with instructional design and instructional procedures. One of the critical functions of instruction, given the centrality of the information store, is to provide efficient and effective procedures for acquiring the information that is to be stored in long-term memory.

As was the case when determining the characteristics of the stores of information required by natural information systems, we can use evolution by natural selection to provide insights into the processes by which natural systems acquire information. Those processes can be applied analogically to human cognition. There are two basic processes used by natural systems to acquire information: a procedure for obtaining organised information from other information stores termed the borrowing and reorganising principle and a procedure for creating novel information termed the randomness as genesis principle. This chapter is concerned with these two principles.

The Borrowing and Reorganising Principle

The information store requires huge amounts of information. The vast bulk of that information is obtained via the borrowing and reorganising principle which applies equally to both evolution by natural selection and human cognition.

Biological Evolution

The manner in which information is acquired by a genome is well known. Reproduction, either asexual or sexual, provides the process by which almost all

J. Sweller et al., *Cognitive Load Theory*, Explorations in the Learning Sciences, Instructional Systems and Performance Technologies 1, DOI 10.1007/978-1-4419-8126-4_3, © Springer Science+Business Media, LLC 2011

the information held by a genome is obtained. In the case of asexual reproduction, an exact copy of a genome, apart from mutations, is transmitted to all descendents. During asexual reproduction a cell splits into two cells that are identical to each other and to the parent cell. In contrast, sexual reproduction is organised to ensure that the information held in a genome must, for structural reasons, differ from all ancestors. Information is borrowed equally from both male and female ancestors and combined to form a unique genome that not only differs from all ancestors but also from all current and future genomes with the exception of genetically identical siblings. In this manner, sexual reproduction simultaneously is able to superimpose variety, novelty and creativity on a process that otherwise involves exact transmission.

Asexual reproduction provides a biological example of borrowing without reorganising. Each descendant borrows its entire genome from its immediate ancestor without alteration. Sexual reproduction provides a biological example that includes both borrowing and reorganising. Information is borrowed from ancestors during sexual reproduction but it is reorganised during the borrowing process to create a novel information store. Each of our cells contains a mix of information from both our mother and father. That mix of borrowed and reorganised information results in the creation of a unique individual. We will consider analogical processes of borrowing and reorganising in human cognition as well as processes requiring borrowing alone.

Human Cognition

The analogy is relatively straightforward. Almost all of the secondary knowledge stored in long-term memory is borrowed from other people. This secondary knowledge is stored in the long-term memory stores of individuals and can be transmitted to other individuals. Our ability to receive such knowledge from others and to transmit it most likely depends on a biologically primary skill. It is an evolved skill that allows us to communicate that knowledge to each other. For example, while learning to read and write are secondary skills, the use of language in general and the need to communicate with other people do not need to be taught. We have evolved to communicate with other people and do so automatically as a primary skill.

There are several processes we use to communicate. Imitation (Bandura, 1986) can be central to many of the activities in which we engage. It is very probably a skill based on biologically primary knowledge. We are likely to have evolved to imitate other people and do so automatically without being taught. Our propensity to imitate is associated with considerable neurological evidence that has become available recently via the newly discovered mirror neuron system. While mirror neurons fire when we make a movement, interestingly, the same neurons also fire when we see other people make the same movement, when we think about a movement or even when we hear a sentence about a particular movement (Grafton,

Arbib, Fadiga, & Rizzolatti, 1996; Iacoboni et al., 1999; Tettamanti et al., 2005). Given these characteristics of the mirror neuron system, it may be plausible to suggest that this system is basic to our propensity and ability to imitate movements of other humans. Similar imitative mechanisms may also apply to other cognitive activities. Knowing how to imitate other people is not an activity that needs to be taught despite the complexity associated with the task. It is a biologically primary skill. Imitative activity occurs automatically in humans without instruction because it is biologically driven and essential for intellectual development. We have evolved our ability to imitate and that ability is used to acquire knowledge.

Not only is our propensity to imitate likely to be biologically primary, much of the knowledge that is acquired via imitation is primary knowledge and we are likely to acquire most of our primary knowledge through imitation. Nevertheless, imitation also is used in the acquisition of secondary knowledge. Any instructor in any educational institution who demonstrates a complex, novel procedure to students is relying on the human propensity to imitate. We assume that when we demonstrate something to learners that they will assimilate the knowledge associated with that demonstration. In other words, we assume that learners will imitate us. The act of imitation borrows information from the long-term memory of an instructor to be stored in the long-term memory of the learner.

The imitative process, of course, is rarely perfect. The learner already has information in long-term memory and the new information must be combined with previously stored information. A process of reorganisation will occur that will result in changes to the new information in a manner similar to the changes that occur during sexual reproduction. Those changes may be beneficial or may be detrimental and so all deviations from the original, imitated source must be tested for effectiveness. Beneficial changes from the original source should be retained while detrimental changes should be eliminated. If the changes are sufficiently detrimental, the learning episode will have failed. If the deviations from the source are neutral or even beneficial, the learning episode is successful.

Imitation is not the only way in which we obtain information from others. Nevertheless, it is basic and the other, more common techniques humans use to provide each other with biologically secondary information are essentially a derivative of imitation. Rather than showing people how to do something using the visual modality of observation associated with imitation, we can, in effect, 'show' people how to do something using the auditory modality of speech or its visual equivalent, written material. Thus, we not only imitate other people, we also listen and read. In an instructional context, our intention when listening or reading is to acquire the secondary knowledge held in the long-term memory of others. Almost all of the information we acquire in instructional contexts is obtained either by listening, reading or looking at diagrams and pictures. When we borrow information from others in an instructional context, we do so by listening to what they say, reading what they write or studying diagrams or animations that they have produced. In this way, information is borrowed from the long-term memories of others and assimilated into our long-term memory. As is the case for direct imitation, the transfer of information via procedures related to imitation is never exact. It usually is reorganised and combined with information already held in long-term memory. That transformation will either have a negative, neutral or positive effect. If it has a negative effect, the information will either have to be transformed further or jettisoned if meaningful learning is to occur. If the transformation has neutral or positive effects it can be stored in long-term memory. Of course, misconceptions also can be stored in long-term memory if it is not clear that they are misconceptions. Once stored, misconceptions can have negative consequences for extended periods unless they are corrected.

The evidence is strong that borrowed information is reorganised. The previous chapter on the information store principle indicated that knowledge in long-term memory is stored in the form of schemas. Those schemas are borrowed from other people and the process of schema acquisition usually involves some degree of reorganisation. Evidence for that process of reorganisation comes from the studies by Bartlett (1932) discussed in the previous chapter. As previously discussed we reduce or eliminate (flatten) those aspects of the information obtained from others that bear little relation to previous knowledge stored in long-term memory while emphasising (sharpening) those aspects of the new information that correspond with information previously stored. In this way, borrowed information is reorganised when it is combined with current knowledge in long-term memory to construct a new schema. The new schema that is constructed is likely to be different in informational content to the schema being borrowed.

The process of reorganisation has other characteristics that need to be discussed because they are central to the randomness as genesis principle, described below. If reorganisation results in novel information, it has an inevitable random component. Randomness is necessarily associated with all novel information that is created by an individual rather than transmitted from another person's long-term memory. When information, initially obtained from someone else's long-term memory is reorganised into a novel configuration, it is impossible for the individual to have prior knowledge indicating whether the reorganised configuration is going to be effective. There is no logical procedure available for determining the effectiveness of any novel alteration prior to the alteration actually being made. Once the reorganisation has been made, it must be tested for effectiveness but in the absence of prior knowledge, the effectiveness of any alteration cannot be determined prior to the reorganisation. Effectiveness only can be determined after the event by testing whether the change works as expected.

The logic of novelty whether due to reorganisation or due to other procedures (see below) dictates the processes by which creativity occurs. If knowledge concerning the effectiveness of a potential reorganisation is unavailable prior to a schema being stored in long-term memory, a random generate and test process is a concomitant of the reorganisation process. Reorganisation must be generated randomly and then tested for effectiveness with effective changes retained and ineffective ones jettisoned. It follows that quite different consequences flow from the 'borrowing' aspect and the 'reorganising' aspect of the borrowing and reorganising principle. The principle ensures that information borrowed with minimal reorganisation has a reasonable chance of being high in coherence and fidelity to the environment.

Its effectiveness should already have been tested by someone else, although we can never be certain when borrowing information from someone else. Information obtained from other people always has a risk associated with it even if it is borrowed without alteration. Nevertheless, we frequently can and do assume that borrowed information without reorganisation already has been tested for effectiveness by being used to good effect in its environment. The same can never be said of alterations made to that information through reorganisation. We do not and cannot know whether those changes are effective prior to the changes being made because they all have a random component. They will need to be tested for effectiveness after the changes have occurred.

Instructional Implications

The borrowing and reorganising principle provides the major procedure by which we obtain knowledge. It is central to instructional design and, indeed, central to cognitive load theory. If the principle is valid, the instructional implications are clear. We should provide learners with as much relevant information as we are able. Withholding information from students based on a version of a constructivist, discovery or problem-based learning theory has no justification. We have evolved to obtain information from others and are particularly adept at both providing and receiving information. It is difficult to find any aspect of our cognitive architecture that suggests learners have an advantage discovering information for themselves. Assisting learners to obtain needed information by the use of scaffolding such as providing information during problem solving should be beneficial. Providing them with that information directly and explicitly should be even more beneficial.

Conclusions

Because the borrowing and reorganising principle provides the major technique by which knowledge, both primary and secondary, is stored in the information store, it is both central and essential to a natural information store. Without this principle, large amounts of knowledge could not be acquired to be stored. For this reason, the later chapters of this book dealing with instructional procedures are largely concerned with techniques designed to facilitate the acquisition of information from diagrams or pictures and written or spoken information. Devising instruction, according to cognitive load theory, means devising instructional procedures that facilitate the borrowing of information held by instructors and provided to learners in spoken or visual form.

The borrowing and reorganising principle increases the probability that the knowledge held in an information store is likely to be effective. Borrowed information has already been organised and is likely to be appropriate for the environment for which it is intended because it has already been tested for effectiveness.

While borrowing information is the primary function of the borrowing and reorganising principle, the manner in which information is borrowed results in a degree of creativity. Nevertheless, the borrowing and reorganising principle is not an original source of novelty. New information can be created by reorganising previously stored information and in this way provide a degree of creativity. That creativity through reorganisation of old information differs from the creation of totally new information. The next principle has the creation of new information as its only goal.

Randomness as Genesis Principle

According to the borrowing and reorganising principle, information is borrowed from other, external sources. By what mechanisms is that information created in the first instance? While the borrowing and reorganising principle explains how information is communicated in natural systems, the randomness as genesis principle provides the mechanism by which it is initially created. It provides the creativity engine for natural information processing systems by using a random generate and test procedure. Accordingly, a random generate and test procedure is the ultimate source of all novelty in natural systems.

The suggestion that random generation is at the heart of human creativity may be a novel concept when applied to human cognition. Nevertheless, the suggestion that all genetic variation has randomness as its origin is both central and accepted virtually universally in biology. If our analogy is valid, there is every likelihood that human cognition, as a natural system, also will have randomness as a central facet in the creation of novel information. We will begin by considering the role of randomness in the creation of novelty in biology.

Biological Evolution

All genetic variation between individual organisms, including individuals belonging to the same or different species, can be traced back to a series of random mutations. We indicated above that sexual reproduction increases variation between individuals by ensuring the birth of unique individuals, but it needs to be recognised that the unique individuality of offspring has its direct causal differences in the male and female alleles that combine during reproduction. If conditions were such that male and female alleles were identical, then the reorganisation that occurs under the borrowing and reorganising principle could not occur. Sexual reproduction would not result in any more variation than asexual reproduction and so would be pointless because offspring would be identical to their parents. It is solely because of the differences between the genetic information obtained from both parents that offspring vary from their parents and theoretically, those differences can always be traced back to a series of random mutations.

In isolation, random mutation without tests of effectiveness would be useless. It is effective because each random mutation is tested for effectiveness. Adaptive mutations, those that are effective for survival and reproduction, are retained in the information store, the species genome in the case of biological evolution, for future use. The vast bulk of mutations are not adaptive. These mutations, that are not effective for survival and reproduction, are not stored in the species genome. Instead, they are eliminated.

Random mutation is the ultimate source of all variation and so all novelty in biology. The massive creativity demonstrated in all biological systems ultimately derives from random mutation. That creativity dwarfs anything humans are able to produce or to this point, even understand. We have massive research programmes attempting to understand biological systems created by random mutation. We could not, for example, create a factory able to convert vegetable matter into meat and other materials the size of a mouse. The processes of evolution by natural selection, along with the other principles associated with biological evolution, have, of course, been able to achieve just such an outcome via a long series of random mutations.

Based on biological evolution, the general process, random generate and test, is a powerful and critical aspect of natural information processing systems. The randomness as genesis principle describes an essential aspect of such systems. We might expect it to be equally central to processes used by human cognition when creating novel information.

Human Cognition

The role of random mutation in biology provides a particular example of random generate and test. Random generate and test during problem solving may play the same role in human cognition as random mutation plays in evolution by natural selection. Consider a person attempting to solve a novel problem and assume they neither have a complete solution to the problem in long-term memory nor are they able to access a solution provided by someone else. Where relevant knowledge is absent, the only possibility is to randomly attempt one of the possible moves. Testing the effectiveness of a move can be accomplished either mentally or physically. This process of testing the effectiveness of a move without having prior knowledge of the outcome of that move is a random generate and test procedure. It is unavoidable when knowledge is unavailable. Existing knowledge can be used to reduce the number of alternative moves that must be randomly tested but once knowledge is exhausted, a random generate and test procedure is all that remains.

Evidence for a random generate and test procedure. We argue that there are two categories of evidence for the use of random generate and test when solving novel problems. First, there is some empirical evidence. While solving a complex, novel problem, most problem solvers will arrive at many dead ends. Arriving at a dead end indicates that the previous move or series of moves was inappropriate.

Some dead ends may be due to misconceptions that have been stored in long-term memory. Nevertheless, it can be argued that many may be due to random generation of moves. Where misconceptions can be eliminated as a cause of problem-solving dead ends, there is currently only one clear explanation for dead ends with alternative explanations unavailable. We can expect moves generated randomly to result in many dead ends and it is difficult to find any other procedure that will have a similar result. Each dead end indicates that somewhere along the previous chain of moves at least one move was executed randomly to determine if it could lead to the solution. The greater the amount of previously stored knowledge is used to generate moves, the fewer dead ends can be expected to occur. Dead ends provide possible empirical evidence for the use of a random generate and test procedure during problem solving.

The second and possibly more important evidence for the use of a random generate and test procedure as a problem-solving strategy comes from a logical argument rather than from empirical evidence. We assume all problem-solving moves when solving novel problems are generated by (a) a random generate and test procedure, (b) knowledge held in long-term memory or (c) almost universally, some combination of (a) and (b). If these three alternatives are the only ones available, it follows that when solving a problem, at those points where knowledge is unavailable to distinguish between possible moves in terms of their likelihood of success, the only possible strategy available is a random generate and test procedure. If there are alternatives to knowledge and a random generate and test procedure as mechanisms for generating moves, they have not as yet been identified. Until alternatives are generated with evidence that they exist, we should assume that a combination of knowledge and random generate and test is the only available procedure for generating problem-solving moves.

It might be argued that problem-solving strategies such as analogical problem solving provide an alternative to knowledge and a random generate and test procedure. In fact, demonstrating that analogical problem solving can be decomposed into a combination of knowledge and random generate and test is quite straightforward. When using analogical problem solving, we must determine a suitable analogy. We will use our knowledge of problem-solving surface and deep structure to make the choice. Nevertheless, if the target problem is novel, we can never be certain that the analogy will work. Certainty can only come from knowledge. When we try to solve the target problem by analogy to a source problem, there is an inevitable random generate and test aspect. The analogy may be perfect but it also may be totally useless – a dead end. We can determine the effectiveness of the analogy only after we have tried it and acquired knowledge of its effectiveness. If it is effective, we can use that procedure subsequently. If it is not effective, we must go back to the drawing board. Choosing an analogy is a problem-solving move no different from any other problem-solving move. It requires a combination of knowledge and random generate and test.

A consequence of a random generate and test procedure. In the previous section it was indicated that we cannot know the outcome of choosing a source problem analogy that has random components until after the choice has been made and tested. This lack of knowledge is general and has structural implications. When a move is randomly generated, its outcome is unknown until after the move has been made, either mentally or physically. We only can determine the effectiveness of a random move after physically or mentally making that move. By definition, we do not have knowledge prior to making a random move that can indicate to us the consequences of making that move. It is only after randomly choosing a move that we can determine its effectiveness. If a move is effective we may retain it and continue the problem-solving process by choosing a subsequent move either by using knowledge if it is available or by randomly choosing another move. If a move is ineffective in helping us reach a goal because it either takes us further from the goal or because it results in a dead end, it is jettisoned. Effective moves can be stored in long-term memory for subsequent use. They become knowledge.

Knowledge as a central executive. The cognitive architecture used by cognitive load theory does not postulate nor need an independent central executive (Sweller, 2003). A central executive is a structure that organises and controls cognitive processes. During problem solving, knowledge indicates which moves should be made and when and how they should be made. In effect, knowledge held in long-term memory acts as a substitute for an independent central executive. In the absence of knowledge, a random generate and test procedure is used instead.

It can be argued that there is no conceivable central executive, apart from long-term memory, in the human cognitive system. Nevertheless, central executives are postulated in cognitive theories, with Baddeley's (1992) working memory theory providing the best example. We argue that an independent central executive dissociated from knowledge held in long-term memory results in an infinite regress of central executives. If knowledge held in long-term memory does not have the attributes normally attributed to a central executive, we are immediately faced with the question of how a knowledge-independent central executive determines its actions. We require another central executive governing the first central executive that in turn requires a third central executive, etc. The problem is eliminated by assuming that knowledge in long-term memory acts as a de facto central executive with both the borrowing and reorganising and the randomness as genesis principles explaining how knowledge is acquired.

The analogy with evolution by natural selection becomes particularly valuable at this point. Evolution does not require a central executive to function. If the analogy of human cognition to evolution is valid, human cognition does not require a knowledge-free, independent, central executive either. A combination of knowledge held in long-term memory and a random generate and test procedure is required for a functioning natural information processing system.

Creativity. Based on this analysis, the randomness as genesis principle is the source of creativity. It is uncontroversially the ultimate source of all variation and hence creativity in biological evolution. Random mutations are assumed to provide the bedrock of all genetic variation and hence the major source of the immense creativity demonstrated in biological systems and explained by evolution by natural selection. We suggest random generate and test during problem solving plays an identical role in human cognition. If so, random generate and test provides the ultimate source of all novel concepts and procedures invented by humans.

There may be objections to characterising creativity in terms of a random generate and test process. Nevertheless, even ignoring the analogy with evolution by natural selection, we argue that the rationale is compelling. Creativity, on any definition, requires a move into the unknown. If something is new, if it is an idea, object, concept or procedure that has not been produced before, its development cannot rely entirely on knowledge already held in long-term memory. It must go beyond current knowledge. Apart from the reorganisation that constitutes part of the borrowing and reorganising principle, how can we go beyond already stored knowledge? Any 'move' or process in which we engage must have a procedure by which it is generated. We know it can be generated randomly but if it is not generated randomly, what other procedure is available? Until an alternative procedure is described, we should assume that random generation is the sole available process. Human creativity may be just as reliant on random generate and test as is evolution by natural selection.

Why do individuals differ in creativity if at its source it consists of random generate and test? The answer lies in our knowledge base. The knowledge base held by individuals differs immensely. Random generate and test from a low knowledge base will lead to vastly different outcomes than random generate and test from a much higher knowledge base. If we know the properties of electricity and of materials through which electricity flows, we may have a chance of inventing a light bulb by randomly testing many different materials as suitable elements for a light bulb. If we do not know those properties, we have no chance of inventing a light bulb.

On this analysis, differences in domain-specific knowledge may go further in explaining differences in human creativity than any other factor. Furthermore, domain-specific knowledge, unlike general problem-solving strategies, is both learnable and teachable.

Instructional Implications

If differences in human creativity rely heavily on domain-specific knowledge, then attempts to enhance creativity by means other than increasing domain-specific knowledge are likely to be difficult. According to the randomness as genesis principle, we would need to encourage learners to engage in a process of random generate and test. Since random generate and test may have been part of human cognitive history for countless generations, it is likely to have heavier biologically primary than secondary components. If so, the possibility of teaching random generate and test may be severely restricted because we may automatically use the technique. The history of research into enhancing human creativity bears out this supposition (Sweller, 2009b). It is difficult to find successful examples of creativity enhancing procedures.

There may be one exception. The technique of brainstorming, invented by Osborn (1953), appears to encourage random generation. Brainstorming requires people to generate as many ideas as possible without reference to their possible usefulness until later. The technique has never been associated with any viable cognitive architecture as far as we are aware but since it appears to consist of random generation without testing, it may be possible to relate the procedure to aspects of the randomness as genesis principle. Asking people to brainstorm may be equivalent to asking them to randomly generate problem-solving moves.

There is some evidence that instructions to brainstorm do result in more usable ideas (Meadow, Parnes, & Reese, 1959) and so brainstorming may be an example of successfully teaching problem solvers to use a random generation procedure. Whether the technique can be useful in areas that are normally the subject of instruction remains to be seen. The bulk of the research on brainstorming has used idea-generation tasks such as 'Think of as many uses of a brick as you can'. Nevertheless, it seems reasonable to assume that brainstorming instructions also should be effective in educationally relevant areas such as mathematical problem solving and our research in such areas is currently obtaining promising results.

Conclusions

The borrowing and reorganising principle and the randomness as genesis principle provide the two basic, natural information processing system principles associated with the acquisition of information to be stored in an information store, either a genome in the case of evolution by natural selection or long-term memory in the case of human cognition. The two principles work together. Information can be communicated over time and space by the borrowing and reorganising principle. Natural information processing systems require very large information stores and the borrowing and reorganising principle provides an effective procedure that explains how such large amounts of information can be acquired. Most novel information originates from the randomness as genesis principle with some originating from the reorganising function of the borrowing and reorganising principle. Thus, together, the randomness as genesis and the borrowing and reorganising principles explain how information is created, transmitted and then stored in the information store – long-term memory in the case of human cognition.

We generate novel information during problem solving via a random generate and test process. At present, alternatives to random generate and test as a novel information generating process are not available. They will never become available if they do not exist. If so, the randomness as genesis principle may be the sole procedure available that can account for the generation of novel information by humans, just as it is the only procedure used by biological evolution to explain biological variation.

The reason for the primacy of random generate and test as a generator of novel information needs to be emphasised. If there is no logically possible central executive that can direct the creation of novel information, an alternative is required. Random generate and test provides that alternative. If a central executive not based on information held in an information store could be specified without an infinite regress of multiple executives, random generate and test would not hold its position of primacy. Random generation avoids an infinite regress and in addition, generates novel information. It may be a requirement of novelty in both human cognition and evolution by natural selection.

The information stored in either human long-term memory or a genome and communicated by the borrowing and reorganising principle is ordered and functional. It may appear paradoxical that order has random generation as its genesis and indeed that paradox has been an explicit source of rejection of evolution by natural selection as the source of biological diversity by those who seek other, non-scientific explanations of the existence of species. This paradox is resolved by the second part of random generate and test. If information were to be randomly generated without a test of its effectiveness, it would indeed be largely useless. Most of the novel information generated randomly by both evolution by natural selection and human cognition is, in fact, not adaptive. It is non-functional and cannot be used. When we attempt to solve a novel, difficult problem, most of our moves do not lead to a successful solution but rather, to dead ends, in just the same way as only a tiny percentage of genetic mutations are advantageous with most being deleterious. The immense power of random generation to lead to useable novelty only can become apparent if it is followed by a test of each outcome for effectiveness with effective processes retained and ineffective ones jettisoned. An outcome of usable, novel information only can occur if a test is added to random generation. Furthermore, in natural information processing systems such as human cognition, not only can random generation and test create novelty, it may be the only way of creating true novelty just as random mutation is the only way in which evolution by natural selection creates true novelty.

While the information store principle explains the need for natural information processing systems to store large amounts of information and the borrowing and reorganising and the randomness as genesis principles explain the processes that allow systems to acquire a large store of information tested for effectiveness, we also require procedures by which natural information processing systems interact with the external world. The borrowing and reorganising principle indicates that large amounts of information are obtained from the external world but the structures and processes by which that information is obtained need to be specified. The two principles discussed in the next chapter, the narrow limits of change principle and the environmental organising and linking principle, are concerned with the procedures by which natural information processing systems interact with their environment.

Chapter 4
Interacting with the External Environment: The Narrow Limits of Change Principle and the Environmental Organising and Linking Principle

The previous chapters indicated that when dealing with biologically secondary information, human cognition requires a very large information store in order to function. Long-term memory constitutes that store. The bulk of the information held in long-term memory is acquired by borrowing information from other people's long-term memories with smaller amounts of original information created by a random generate and test procedure. The ultimate purpose of this information, both borrowed and created, is to allow us to interact with the external environment. Chapter 4 specifies the required machinery.

In order to function, natural information processing systems need to interact with the external environment by obtaining information from the environment and by performing appropriately within an environment. The characteristics required by a natural information processing system to obtain information from the environment are collectively termed the narrow limits of change principle. The characteristics required for a system to perform appropriately within an environment are likewise collectively termed the environmental organising and linking principle. These two principles provide the links between natural information processing systems and their environments. They are central to cognitive load theory and lead directly to the instructional effects covered in the latter parts of this book. When dealing with human cognition, both principles are concerned with human working memory. When dealing with evolution by natural selection, they apply to the epigenetic system (Jablonka & Lamb, 2005; West-Eberhard, 2003) which plays an analogous role to human working memory. The epigenetic system is a chemical system that can affect the location and rate of mutations and that can turn genes on or off depending on environmental signals. Both working memory and the epigenetic system can be thought of as an interface between the information store and its external environment.

J. Sweller et al., *Cognitive Load Theory*, Explorations in the Learning Sciences, Instructional Systems and Performance Technologies 1, DOI 10.1007/978-1-4419-8126-4_4, © Springer Science+Business Media, LLC 2011

Narrow Limits of Change Principle

The randomness as genesis principle with its emphasis on random generate and test has structural consequences for the manner in which information is obtained from the external environment. By definition, randomly generated information is not organised and there are limits to the amount of unorganised information that a processing system can handle. Those limits can be readily demonstrated mathematically.

Assume the system must handle three elements of information where an element is anything that needs to be processed. By the logic of permutations, there are $3! = 6$ possible permutations of three elements and so the system needs to consider which of these six permutations are appropriate for its environment. Dealing with six possible permutations should not overwhelm the system. In contrast, assume that rather than having to deal with three elements of information, the system must deal with ten elements. There are $10! = 3,628,800$ permutations of ten elements, a number that any system may have considerable difficulty handling.

Given the combinatorial explosion that occurs with quite small increases in the number of elements that need to be considered, there are advantages to narrowing that number. To keep the number of permutations down to manageable levels, we might expect that the number of randomly generated elements that a natural information processing system can deal with is severely restricted. The narrow limits of change principle reflects this imperative when natural information processing systems obtain information from the external environment. The epigenetic system, in the case of evolution by natural selection, and working memory, in the case of human cognition, need to be structured in a manner that takes the characteristics of randomly generated information into account.

Biological Evolution

Knowledge concerning how genetic systems interact with the external environment and, more specifically, obtain information from the external environment is, in many ways, still rudimentary. We have used evolution by natural selection as a source analogue for human cognition because evolutionary theory and knowledge is, in most respects, considerably more detailed than knowledge of human cognition. When dealing with information obtained by natural information processing systems from the external environment, our relative knowledge levels tend to be reversed. We know more of how the human cognitive system obtains knowledge from the outside world than how the genetic system obtains its equivalent information. Nevertheless, we do have some knowledge concerning the flow of information from the external environment to the genetic system. This information flow and its consequent impact on biological evolution have analogies in human cognition.

In biological evolution, the pertinent processes are controlled by the epigenetic system, which plays a role similar to that played by working memory in human cognition. The epigenetic system provides an intermediary between the genetic system and the external environment. It controls the interaction between the

DNA-based genetic system and the environment external to the DNA. Considerably less is known of the epigenetic than the genetic system but it is generally assumed that they are distinct (Jablonka & Lamb, 1995, 2005; West-Eberhard, 2003) and act independently, although they commonly interact.

From an information processing perspective, the epigenetic system has two broad functions. First, it selectively processes and transmits information from the external environment to the DNA-based genetic system in a manner that can result in genetic changes. That function is of concern in the present section covering the narrow limits of change principle. The second, and as it happens, better elucidated function of the epigenetic system is to use environmental information to determine which parts of the genetic system will perform and which will not perform. That role of using environmental information to determine how the genetic system functions is dealt with under the next principle, the environmental organising and linking principle. In this section, we are concerned with how information from the environment can change the DNA code of the genetic system, covered by the narrow limits of change principle.

The epigenetic system can use the environment to influence where mutations occur. Depending on environmental conditions, mutations in some parts of a genome can be facilitated while mutations in other areas are inhibited. For example, in some organisms, stressful environments which can jeopardise the survival of the organism can lead to increases in mutations. Increased mutations in sections of a genome that code for products that assist an organism to survive in a new environment can increase diversity and therefore enhance the chances of survival of the species. As another example, the rate of mutation may be thousands of times higher than average in sections of a genome that might require high levels of diversity such as venom used to capture prey. Not only are mutations facilitated by the epigenetic system in locations that can assist survival, the epigenetic system also can ensure that those mutations are not repaired.

While the epigenetic system can determine where mutations occur and even the rate of mutation, it does not determine the nature of a mutation. The nature of a mutation is determined by random generation as discussed under the randomness as genesis principle. Because randomness is the ultimate generator of mutations, there are, as indicated above, severe limitations to the number of mutations that can occur. Successful mutations are rare even under conditions where the rate of mutation is increased by the epigenetic system. During reproduction, most genetic information is reproduced precisely. A substantial mutation event is unlikely to be adaptive because of the randomness of mutation. Random generate and test must be limited to small steps leading to the narrow limits of change principle.

Human Cognition

In human cognition, the structural consequences that flow from the randomness as genesis principle and lead to the narrow limits of change principle manifest themselves in the characteristics of working memory when dealing with novel information. We are only conscious of what is in working memory and for that reason working memory can be equated with consciousness. Evidence for the link between consciousness and working memory comes from our introspective knowledge of the contents of long-term memory. We are aware of the large amount of information held in long-term memory but we also are aware that at any given time, we are only conscious of a tiny portion of that information. That portion consists of any information from long-term memory that happens to be in working memory at a particular time. We are unaware of the remainder of the contents of long-term memory until they are transferred into working memory. Our conscious knowledge extends only to the very small amount of information held by working memory at any time and we are unconscious with respect to the remaining information held in long-term memory.

Working memory is the primary structure that processes incoming information from the environment. Using Atkinson and Shiffrin's (1968) architecture, information first is received and very briefly processed by the various modules of the sensory system, depending on whether its modality is visual or auditory. Then, some elements of this information are passed on to working memory where it can be consciously processed in conjunction with information held in long-term memory. If information processed by working memory is to be retained for any length of time, it needs to be passed to long-term memory for permanent storage. Once information has been stored in long-term memory, it can be returned to working memory and used to govern further behaviour, a process that will be discussed in detail under the next principle, the environmental organising and linking principle. In this section, dealing with the narrow limits of change principle, we are only concerned with how working memory deals with novel information originating in the environment and arriving in working memory via the sensory system rather than from long-term memory.

The characteristics of working memory when it deals with novel information originating from the environment have been extensively studied and are well known. Working memory has two prominent and in many ways surprising characteristics that are critical to anyone concerned with instructional design issues. The first characteristic of working memory when it deals with novel information is that it is very limited in capacity (e.g., Cowan, 2001; Miller, 1956) and the second characteristic is that it is very limited in duration (Peterson & Peterson, 1959). We will begin by discussing the capacity limitations.

Only a very limited number of items or elements can be processed in working memory. Items can most readily be understood as schemas, although that is not how they were originally conceptualised. While there is universal agreement that working memory when dealing with novel information is very limited in capacity, the exact limits have been open to some discussion, probably because those limits change slightly depending on testing conditions. Miller (1956) suggested that the limit was about seven items but more recently Cowan (2001) suggested about four items was a more representative figure. From an instructional perspective, the exact figure is probably irrelevant because the important point is that working memory is severely limited in its ability to store information.

In fact, when dealing with instructional considerations, the limitations of working memory are considerably narrower than is suggested by most measures of working memory capacity. Frequently, working memory capacity measures incorporate our ability to remember random collections of items such as words, digits or letters. Normally, in instructional contexts, we do not use working memory to store such items because we do not characteristically use working memory to store information of any kind. Instead, working memory is used to process items where processing requires organising, combining, comparing or manipulating items of information in some manner. The only storage normally required of working memory is maintenance storage of, for example, intermediate products of cognitive operations. For this reason, working memory does have a storage function as well as its primary processing function.

We are likely to be able to process far fewer items of information than we can store, depending on the nature of the processing. We suggest that no more than two to three items of novel information can be processed by working memory at a given time. If we are required to process any more items of novel information, our working memory processing system tends to break down. When processing novel information, the capacity of working memory is extremely limited. We suggest the reason for that limit is the combinatorial explosion that occurs with even small increases in the number of elements with which working memory must deal.

Most of us are intuitively aware of the storage limitations of working memory. We know, for example, that if we must remember a new number such as a telephone number that we are dialling that has more than about seven digits, we are unlikely to be able to remember that number and will need to return to the written version at least once while dialling. We may be less aware that if we have difficulty understanding an explanation or solving a difficult problem, that the reason is also due to the processing limitations of working memory. Those processing limitations should be a major consideration when designing instructions, as will be explained in the later chapters of this book.

The limitations of working memory are not restricted to its capacity. Working memory also is limited in duration. The temporal limitations of working memory were addressed by Peterson and Peterson (1959). Most novel information only can be held in working memory for a few seconds before being lost with almost all information lost after about 20 s. We can avoid this loss by rehearsal. If we constantly rehearse new material, it is refreshed and can be held in working memory indefinitely.

As was the case for capacity limitations, we can obtain an intuitive feeling for working memory's temporal limitations by considering what we do when dialling a new telephone number. If we are unable to dial the number immediately, we will rehearse it until it is dialled. We know that we must rehearse the number because if it is not rehearsed, it will be lost from working memory rapidly. Similarly, if we obtain information that must be processed as part of an explanation or problem, if it cannot be processed almost immediately, it will be lost to further processing later and that loss may severely compromise understanding or problem solving. Rehearsal also has the added advantage of assisting in the transfer of information to long-term memory.

Working memory's capacity and duration limits only apply to novel information obtained from the external environment via sensory memory rather than from long-term memory. These limitations do not apply to familiar information obtained from long-term memory. Working memory has dramatically different characteristics when dealing with familiar rather than novel information. These characteristics will be discussed under the next principle, the environmental organising and linking principle.

Working memory and the modality of information. While sometimes it is convenient to consider working memory as a unitary structure, it is more accurate to think of working memory as consisting of multiple processors that correspond to the modality of information being received. For example, the working memory processor that deals with auditory information is different from the processor that deals with visual information. There are instructional implications to be discussed subsequently that depend on the multi-channel characteristic of working memory.

Baddeley's theory is the best known, multi-channel working memory theory (e.g., Baddeley, 1992). He divides working memory into three components: a central executive, a visual-spatial sketchpad and an auditory loop. (More recently, he has added an episodic buffer to the model.) As we indicated in the previous chapter, we have doubts concerning the viability of a central executive because it leads to an infinite regress of executives and would prefer the role of a central executive to be allocated to long-term memory. In contrast, a division of working memory into partially independent auditory and visual components is not associated with the same issues concerning logical status and has considerable empirical support (Penney, 1989). We do seem to have different processors to handle visual and auditory information and those processors seem to be partially, although not wholly, independent. Both processors share the characteristics we discussed above with both having capacity and duration limitations. Under some circumstances, to be discussed in subsequent chapters, effective working memory capacity may be increased by using both processors. For this reason, the division of working memory into separate auditory and visual processors has important instructional implications.

Instructional Implications

There are many specific instructional implications that flow from the capacity and duration limitations of working memory and this book, through cognitive load theory and categories of cognitive load (Part III) and the cognitive load theory instructional effects (Part IV), is primarily concerned with those implications. In general terms, most students are novices and so most of the information provided to them is novel and must be processed by a limited capacity, limited duration, working memory. The same information usually can be presented in a variety of ways with a variety of activities required of learners. In other words, a variety of instructional designs can be associated with the same curriculum material.

Each form of presentation, each activity required of learners, will impose a working memory or cognitive load. (The two terms are used synonymously throughout this book.) That load will vary with variations in instructional design and so instructional designs should be chosen that reduce an unnecessary cognitive load. Given the limitations of working memory, one aim of instruction should be to reduce unnecessary working memory load and ensure that scarce working memory resources are directed to the essentials of the curriculum area and away from activities that are only required as part of an inadequate instructional design. Directing working memory resources to the intrinsic essentials of a curriculum area and away from extraneous aspects is the goal of cognitive load theory.

Conclusions

From an evolutionary perspective, our working memory limitations may seem counter-intuitive. Why was it necessary for humans to have evolved with such severe working memory limitations when faced with unfamiliar information? The current framework provides us with an explanation. The narrow limits of change principle that incorporates the limitations of working memory flows directly from the randomness as genesis principle. Random generate and test is a necessary aspect of dealing with novelty because when faced with novelty, we lack a central executive in working memory indicating to us how to organise new information. Therefore the absolute number of elements that we must organise becomes a critical factor. A small number of elements leads to only a small number of permutations with which we must deal. Small increases in that number of elements lead to millions of permutations that are effectively impossible to handle. There may be minimal benefit of a working memory that processes more than a very limited number of elements and so there was no reason for a large working memory to evolve. Given the limitations of working memory when dealing with novel information, we require instructional procedures that take into account the working memory load imposed during instruction, with an aim to reducing unnecessary load.

Working memory in human cognition has a genetic equivalent, the epigenetic system, which plays a similar role in evolutionary biology. Both structures permit natural information processing systems to process novel, environmental information that can eventually be stored in organised form in the information store – long-term memory in the case of human cognition, a genome in the case of evolution by natural selection. Once information is stored in organised form in an information store, it can be retrieved from that store by either human working memory or the epigenetic system. The characteristics of working memory when dealing with organised information from long-term memory or the epigenetic system when dealing with organised genomic information are very different to their characteristics when dealing with random information from the environment. Those characteristics are dealt with by the final principle, the environmental organising and linking principle, discussed next.

The Environmental Organising and Linking Principle

The four previous principles explain how natural information processing systems can obtain and store information either by creating it via a random generate and test process or by borrowing already created information, processing that information so that only useful information is selected for storage and then storing that information in an information store. The previous four principles explain how useful information is gathered and stored but the ultimate aim of a natural information processing system is not simply to store information. Rather, the ultimate purpose of a natural information processing system in storing information is to permit it to function in a natural environment.

The environmental organising and linking principle provides that final step and in doing so provides the ultimate justification for natural information processing systems. Without this principle, natural information processing systems would have no function because it is this principle that allows them to coordinate their activities with their environment. The environmental organising and linking principle allows massive amounts of stored information to be used to determine activity relevant to a particular environment.

Biological Evolution

The role of the environmental organising and linking principle in biological evolution is to permit organised information from a genome to be linked to the environment and so to ensure that activity is appropriate for the environment. As was the case for the narrow limits of change principle, the epigenetic system is central to the environmental organising and linking principle. While the narrow limits of change principle uses environmental information via the epigenetic system to focus mutations at particular times and particular locations, the environmental organising and linking principle uses the epigenetic system to marshal vast complexes of stored genetic information for specific activities that are relevant to a particular environment. The epigenetic system is used to link DNA-based information to the external world beyond the DNA.

The environmental organising and linking principle deals with previously organised information from the information store in a very different manner to how the narrow limits of change principle must deal with novel information. Accordingly, the characteristics of the epigenetic system when it deals with environmental information to influence mutations via the narrow limits of change principle are very different to its characteristics when it assembles genetic information in order to affect a particular outcome via the environmental organising and linking principle. The most obvious difference is that while there may be limits to the amount of novel information in the form of mutations that the epigenetic system can deal with, there may be no limits to the amount of previously organised, DNA-based genetic material that it can handle. Only very small amounts of novel information that might be a candidate for storage in the information store can be processed by the epigenetic system. In contrast, huge amounts of previously organised and stored information can be handled by the same system.

The role of the epigenetic system can be seen clearly in the manner in which genotype, or genetic characteristics, links to phenotype, or physical characteristics. It is the epigenetic system that controls that link. Phenotype is determined largely by having particular genes activated or silenced and it is the epigenetic system that determines whether a gene is turned on or off. Once activated by the epigenetic system, a series of chemical reactions result in the production of particular proteins and it is those proteins that determine a particular phenotype. All the steps of protein synthesis are controlled by the epigenetic system. The epigenetic system, in turn, is influenced by environmental conditions where the environment is everything external to the genome. Thus, the environment influences the epigenetic system that in turn influences which genes will be activated and which will be silenced. In this way, the environment determines phenotype or physical characteristics.

The importance of the epigenetic system as a conduit between the environment and the genome, or information store, can be seen in both the narrow limits of change principle and the environmental organising and linking principle. In the case of the narrow limits of change principle, the epigenetic system, triggered by environmental conditions, can determine where mutations occur and their frequency. In the case of the environmental organising and linking principle, the epigenetic system, again triggered by the environment, determines which stored genetic information will be used or ignored.

The characteristics of the epigenetic system in its two roles are very different. Mutations, even when accelerated, result in very small genetic changes. In contrast, the amount of genetic material that may be required to allow a particular phenotype to be expressed appears to have no limit. Huge amounts of genetic information may be organised by the epigenetic system to determine a particular phenotype. The epigenetic system is able to organise large amounts of information because the information is already organised in the genome. That organised information can be treated as a single, large block (a gene or several genes) that acts in concert determining phenotype.

An intuitive feel for the critical influence of the epigenetic system can be seen when one considers the variety of cells in the human body. All cells in the human body that contain a nucleus have an identical DNA structure despite physical differences that can be immense. A liver cell bears little relation in structure and function to a kidney cell. These differences are not due to genetic differences because both liver and kidney cells for a given individual have identical DNA. Factors other than DNA must cause the differences between the cells. The differences are due to environmental factors switching various genes on or off via the epigenetic system. Once triggered by the environment, massive amounts of DNA-based information can be used by the epigenetic system to determine the type of cell that will be produced.

Human Cognition

As was the case for the other principles, the environmental organising and linking principle plays a role in human cognition analogous to its role in biological evolution. In both biological evolution and human cognition, through the environmental organising and linking principle, information held in the information store is used to ensure that activity is appropriately coordinated with the environment. The relevant cognitive structure that governs that coordination is working memory, the structure that also is central to the narrow limits of change principle. While working memory is central to both principles, its properties when dealing with familiar information held in long-term memory are vastly different to its properties when it is used to acquire novel information.

When discussing the narrow limits of change principle, it was pointed out that working memory was severely limited in capacity and duration. The suggested reason for that limitation is that novel information from the environment cannot have a central executive to provide organisation. Instead, random generate and test acts as a substitute for a central executive and random generation must be limited in order to prevent combinatorial explosions.

Working memory, as well as receiving environmental information via the sensory system, also interacts with and receives previously stored, organised information from long-term memory that is used to coordinate activity with the environment. Stored information held in long-term memory is very different from information received from the environment. Stored information is organised, not random, and can be treated substantially differently. While random information must be limited to prevent combinatorial explosions, limitations on the amount of organised information that can be dealt with by working memory are unnecessary. Combinatorial explosions cannot occur because the manner in which the information is combined is already established. Consequently, the amount of organised information from long-term memory that can be dealt with by working memory has no known limits. Similarly, there are no known limits to the duration that information from long-term memory can be held in working memory.

The immense differences in the characteristics of working memory when dealing with information from sensory memory as opposed to information from long-term memory led Ericsson and Kintsch (1995) to postulate a new processor when working memory deals with organised information from long-term memory, that they called 'long-term working memory'. The most important characteristics of long-term working memory are that it has no obvious capacity or duration limits, in stark contrast to the severe limits of working memory when dealing with novel information. While in this book we will treat working memory as a single structure with different properties depending on whether it is dealing with information from the environment via sensory memory or with information from long-term memory, it makes just as much sense to consider two separate structures, working memory and long-term working memory. For present purposes, it makes no difference whether long-term working memory is treated as a subset of working memory or whether they are treated as two separate entities. The instructional implications are identical for both formulations.

Working memory obtains information from long-term memory in order to provide an organised link to the environment. The environmental organising and linking principle allows organised information to be transferred from long-term memory to working memory in order for that information to be used by working memory to coordinate activity in a manner that is appropriate for a given environment. Rather than working memory receiving information from the environment via sensory memory and processing that information for possible storage as occurs under the narrow limits of change principle, working memory receives environmentally appropriate information from long-term memory under the environmental organising and linking principle.

The analogy between biological evolution and the human cognitive system is particularly close at this point. The epigenetic system requires a trigger from the environment to turn specific genes on or off. Similarly, working memory depends on environmental cues to determine which information from long-term memory will or will not be retrieved and used. Environmental information is used by working memory as a trigger to use some information from long-term memory but ignore other information just as environmental information is used by the epigenetic system to determine which information from a genome will or will not be used. By using the environment as a trigger to select information from long-term memory, an appropriate coordination between the environment and activity is ensured in the same way as the epigenetic system ensures appropriate coordination between the environment and biological activity.

In this manner, information in long-term memory does not become active until it has been triggered by cues from the environment that induce working memory to choose one set of schemas over another. For example, we may have a schema held in long-term memory that permits us to recognise problems of the form $(a + b)/c = d$, solve for a. That schema lies dormant until we see this equation. Once seen, the equation acts as a cue triggering the schema that tells us what action to take.

In that sense, the environment informs us which of the multitude of schemas held by long-term memory are appropriate. Once environmental information triggers working memory to choose a particular set of schemas held in long-term memory, those schemas can be used to govern complex behaviour that is appropriate for that environment. In the same sense, once environmental information triggers the epigenetic system to activate a particular set of genes held in a genome, those genes can be used to govern complex behaviour that is appropriate for the environment. Thus, via the environmental organising and linking principle, information in long-term memory or a genome is chosen by working memory or the epigenetic system to determine activity in a given environment.

Under the discussion of the narrow limits of change principle, it was pointed out that when dealing with unorganised, novel information, there are evolutionary advantages to having a limited working memory. When dealing with organised, familiar information, there are equal evolutionary advantages in having an unlimited working memory. If we have a large number of complex, organised clusters of information (schemas) in long-term memory that are available for transfer to working memory, then we are likely to have a large number of environmental circumstances that we can deal with. For example, learning the layout of a locality enables us to easily and rapidly move around without getting lost. That knowledge has evolutionary advantages and those advantages are likely to increase with increases in the size of the locality with which we are able to become familiar.

Instructional Implications

As might be expected, the environmental organising and linking principle serves a critical function in education. A major purpose of education is to permit us to perform appropriately in our environment, requiring us to selectively access information from long-term memory. Without our ability to transfer large amounts of familiar information from long-term to working memory, there would be little purpose to education. The current activity of readers of this book provides a clear example. In a purely physical sense, readers are simply faced with an immensely complex page of squiggles. Those squiggles are important only because they act as an environmental trigger. We derive meaning from them because we have spent years or decades acquiring the information stored in long-term memory that permits us to connect those squiggles to the external world via the environmental organising and linking principle. The squiggles are used as a trigger by working memory to transfer schemas from long-term memory. Those schemas then can be used to derive meaning.

Conclusions

The environmental organising and linking principle provides the final step in permitting a natural information processing system to function in a given environment. It also provides the primary justification for a natural information processing system. In a very real sense, the previous principles only are necessary in order to permit the environmental organising and linking principle to function. It is this principle that ultimately allows us to perform in our environment. Without the environmental organising and linking principle, there would be no purpose to creating novel information through the randomness as genesis and narrow limits of change principles, no purpose to storing that information in an information store or transferring that information to other stores via the borrowing and reorganising principle. All of these principles and the processes they cover are required for the environmental organising and linking principle to serve its function of allowing a natural information processing system to function appropriately in its environment. We can function, both cognitively and biologically, in our complex world, because of the environmental organising and linking principle.

Summary of Structures and Functions of Human Cognitive Architecture

Part II has outlined a version of human cognitive architecture by describing five basic principles that together can also be used to describe a natural information processing system. Since human cognition can be considered a natural information processing system, those five principles provide us with a human cognitive architecture. In this section, that architecture has been used to indicate some general instructional recommendations. A series of specific instructional recommendations will be outlined in Part IV following an outline of cognitive load theory described in Part III. Cognitive load theory is based on the current cognitive architecture.

Human cognitive architecture can be considered to be a natural information processing system that has been generated by biological evolution. Biological evolution also can be considered to be a natural information processing system and so both systems are governed by the same underlying principles. Those principles can be used to specify the aspects of human cognitive architecture that are relevant to instruction, specifically those aspects that deal with biologically secondary knowledge. All five of the natural information processing system principles discussed above are required to specify how secondary or teachable knowledge is acquired and used while only a few of the principles are needed to indicate how biologically primary knowledge is acquired and used.

The information store principle is equally important when dealing either with primary or secondary knowledge. Both categories of knowledge must be stored in an information store in essentially the same way and, as far as we are aware, there is no evidence indicating that the store differs depending on the nature of the knowledge stored. Unless evidence becomes available suggesting different storage requirements for primary and secondary knowledge, we should assume that both categories of knowledge are held in the same store.

Much primary knowledge, such as language acquisition, probably is acquired through imitation, indicating that the borrowing component of the borrowing and reorganising principle is important in the acquisition of primary, as well as secondary knowledge. The reorganisation component of the principle may play a much more limited role in the acquisition of primary knowledge. Primary knowledge is modular in that we have evolved to acquire very specific categories of such knowledge that will automatically be acquired under appropriate environmental conditions. While borrowing may be central when acquiring primary knowledge, that borrowed information may undergo little if any reorganisation. Primary knowledge may undergo minimal reorganisation when assimilated to previously acquired schemas. In contrast, secondary knowledge can undergo substantial reorganisation when it is assimilated via the borrowing and reorganising principle. Usually, that reorganisation can be beneficial. Nevertheless sometimes, what a learner 'borrows' when listening or reading may bear little relation to the original information being presented leading to misunderstandings and misconceptions.

Both the randomness as genesis and narrow limits of change principles are critical to biologically secondary knowledge but may have no function in the acquisition of primary knowledge. We do not have to randomly generate and test novel primary knowledge because we rarely create such knowledge. Novel versions of a means–ends problem-solving strategy or novel ways of recognising faces do not have to be randomly generated and tested for effectiveness. We have evolved to only assimilate versions of such procedures that are effective.

If random generation is not required for the creation of primary knowledge, there is no need for a slow build-up of that knowledge in long-term memory. We are assured that primary knowledge is effective and there is minimal risk that the rapid acquisition of such knowledge will destroy the functionality of long-term memory. Primary information can be acquired quickly in large quantities without a need to test its effectiveness. Humans have evolved to acquire that knowledge precisely because it is effective and must be acquired for normal functioning. For this reason, primary knowledge is acquired much faster than secondary knowledge and it is acquired without conscious effort and largely without instruction.

The environmental organising and linking principle functions in tandem with the information store principle and so, like that principle, applies equally when dealing with primary or secondary knowledge. Just as occurs in the case of secondary knowledge, large amounts of primary knowledge, once acquired and stored in long-term memory, can be marshalled to deal appropriately with the environment. Primary knowledge, as occurs with secondary knowledge, is acquired and stored in long-term memory solely in order to generate activity appropriate to specific environments. The purpose of the environmental organising and linking principle when dealing with primary knowledge is identical to its purpose when dealing with secondary knowledge. In both cases, the principle permits a link between knowledge held in long-term memory and the external environment.

From this analysis, it can be seen that primary and secondary knowledge are stored and used in a similar manner but differ substantially in their acquisition. We have evolved to store and use biologically primary and secondary knowledge in a similar manner but we acquire the two categories of knowledge in a quite different manner using different acquisition systems. Those different acquisition systems allow large amounts of primary knowledge to be acquired rapidly and easily without mechanisms to test whether the knowledge is needed and effective. Primary knowledge always is needed and effective because we have evolved to need and use that knowledge. In contrast, we can survive without secondary knowledge and so that knowledge is acquired in a very different manner.

All five natural information processing system principles apply to secondary knowledge, including the mechanisms for acquiring that knowledge, because unlike the acquisition mechanisms for primary knowledge, we do not have mechanisms for automatically acquiring secondary knowledge. We need specific machinery for acquiring secondary knowledge and working memory supplies that machinery. For that reason, the principles most closely associated with working memory, the randomness as genesis and the narrow limits of change principles, are central to the acquisition of secondary knowledge but unimportant in the acquisition of primary information. Because of the critical importance of working memory in the acquisition of secondary knowledge, relations between working memory and long-term memory are central to secondary or teachable knowledge. When dealing with instructional issues, the relations between working memory and long-term memory should be carefully considered, including the transformed characteristics of working memory (or long-term working memory) when dealing with external information or information from long-term memory.

A major purpose of instruction is to increase usable knowledge in long-term memory. Learning is defined as a positive change in long-term memory and so if nothing has changed in long-term memory then learning has not occurred. From the perspective of our knowledge of cognitive architecture, the purpose of learning is to increase the effectiveness of the environmental organising and linking principle. The environmental organising and linking principle can be effective only if it has a large amount of useful information on which it can draw. Its potential to be functional depends on information held in long-term memory. The most effective way to increase information held in long-term memory is through the borrowing and reorganising principle and so it follows that instruction should emphasise this principle. Of course, the borrowing and reorganising principle can be used only if appropriate information is available in another person's long-term memory from which information can be borrowed. If information is not available for borrowing, either because another person is not available, either directly or indirectly through written or other sources, or even because the required information has not as yet been created, the only other solution is to create the information via the randomness as genesis principle. We create information very slowly because working memory is extremely limited when dealing with new information. The narrow limits of change principle ensures that the randomness as genesis principle works very slowly. All novel information, whether obtained through the reorganisation component of the borrowing and reorganising principle or through the randomness as genesis principle, is subject to the limitations of working memory.

These working memory limitations must be taken into account whenever we deal with the biologically secondary knowledge that is the subject of instructional procedures. Cognitive load theory is an instructional theory that uses this cognitive architecture as its base. Accordingly, the relations between working memory and long-term memory are critical to the theory. Categories of cognitive load are discussed in Part III.

Part III
Categories of Cognitive Load

Instructional design theories and processes can be anchored by the cognitive architecture described in the previous chapters. That architecture is vital. Without it, instructional design decisions occur in a vacuum and are based on ideology or on individual, personal experience. While personal experience can be valuable, there is no substitute for a viable, evidence-supported theory to guide decisions. Cognitive load theory, which includes the cognitive architecture described in the previous chapters, is intended to provide such a theory.

Human cognitive architecture provides a context that can be used to explain why some instructional procedures do or do not work. Based on human cognitive architecture, we can determine categories of instruction that are likely to be effective. We can, for example, hypothesise that very general learning and problem-solving strategies are likely to be biologically primary and so usually do not need to be taught because we have evolved to acquire those strategies easily and automatically from a very young age. The acquisition of biologically primary knowledge is too important and too urgent to be left to the system responsible for gradual, conscious and effortful acquisition of biologically secondary knowledge which begins functioning at a later age, including through exposure to formal education processes. If very general strategies are biologically primary and so do not need to be taught, teaching should be restricted to domain-specific knowledge that we have not evolved to acquire as biologically primary skills. We also might hypothesise on the basis of the cognitive architecture outlined in the previous chapters that teaching domain-specific knowledge should be direct and explicit because we have evolved to acquire knowledge from other people and direct, explicit teaching through use of the borrowing and reorganising principle provides an ideal procedure for obtaining knowledge from others. In addition and critically, from a cognitive load theory perspective, we might hypothesise that the limitations of human working memory when acquiring new information need to be considered when designing instruction.

These general suggestions flow from our current knowledge of human cognitive architecture. Of course, until rigorously tested, they remain no more than suggestions. When tested as hypotheses, supporting data can be used to advocate particular instructional procedures. Cognitive load theory has been used for this purpose. Based on the cognitive architecture described in the previous chapters, cognitive load theory suggests that the major purpose of instruction should be to increase advantageous biologically secondary knowledge held in long-term memory. Furthermore, information presented with that aim in mind needs to take into account the limitations of working memory when processing novel, secondary information. Information needs to be presented in a manner that attempts to reduce unnecessary processing and so cognitive load theory is heavily concerned with procedures for presenting novel information to learners in a manner that reduces an unnecessary cognitive load while increasing those aspects of cognitive load that lead to learning. Chapter 5 is concerned with the categories of cognitive load that instructional procedures can impose, while Chapter 6 is concerned with techniques for measuring cognitive load.

Chapter 5
Intrinsic and Extraneous Cognitive Load

Learners must process instructional information in working memory. The load imposed on working memory by that instructional information can be divided into categories depending on its function (Paas, Renkl, & Sweller, 2003, 2004; Sweller, van Merriënboer, & Paas, 1998; van Merriënboer & Sweller, 2005). Some of the working memory load is imposed by the intrinsic nature of the information and that load is called 'intrinsic cognitive load'. It is imposed by the basic structure of the information that the learner needs to acquire for achieving learning goals irrespective of the instructional procedures used.

Another category of cognitive load that requires working memory resources is imposed not by the intrinsic structure of the information but rather by the manner in which the information is presented or the activities in which learners must engage. In other words, as well as the nature of the instructional material, the nature of the instructional design used to present the material can impose a cognitive load that under many circumstances can be unnecessary. In the case of the instructional design, where the load is unnecessary and extraneous to the learning goals, it is called 'extraneous cognitive load'. This load is imposed solely because of the instructional procedures being used.

The cognitive load imposed by the intrinsic nature of the material (intrinsic cognitive load) and the manner in which the material is presented (extraneous cognitive load) both must be dealt with by working memory with resources allocated to both of these two sources of cognitive load. Resources devoted to the load imposed by the intrinsic nature of the material are germane to learning and so can be referred to as 'germane resources'. The term, 'germane cognitive load' is frequently used to refer to germane resources although it is probably inappropriate to use this term. Unlike intrinsic and extraneous cognitive load that are imposed by the nature and structure of the learning materials, germane cognitive load is not imposed by the learning materials. Rather, it belongs to a different category that can be better understood as working memory resources that are devoted to information that is relevant or germane to learning. Such information imposes an intrinsic cognitive load. In a similar manner, extraneous cognitive load, imposed by the instructional design used, must also be allocated working memory resources. Working memory resources devoted to information that is imposed solely by the instructional design can be referred to as 'extraneous resources' that must deal with extraneous cognitive load.

Additivity of Intrinsic and Extraneous Cognitive Load

Intrinsic and extraneous cognitive load are additive. Together, they determine the total cognitive load imposed by material that needs to be learned. That total cognitive load determines the required working memory resources needed to process the information with some resources dealing with intrinsic cognitive load (germane resources) and other resources dealing with extraneous cognitive load (extraneous resources). While resources are devoted to dealing with either intrinsic or extraneous cognitive load those resources come from the same undifferentiated working memory pool.

If the working memory resources required to deal with the load imposed by intrinsic and extraneous cognitive load exceed the available resources of working memory, the cognitive system will fail, at least in part, to process necessary information. Germane resources will be too low to deal with the intrinsic cognitive load imposed by the learning materials. Indeed, if the instructional design is particularly poor resulting in a very high extraneous cognitive load, there may be insufficient resources to even move beyond the barrier of the poor instructional design and begin to devote germane resources to intrinsic cognitive load. Learners may not even commence learning because the entire pool of working memory resources is needed to deal with the instructional processes used.

One aim of instructional design is to reduce extraneous cognitive load so that a greater percentage of the pool of working memory resources can be devoted to issues germane to learning rather than to issues extraneous to learning. Extraneous cognitive load should be reduced as far as possible, thus reducing working memory resources devoted to extraneous issues and increasing the availability of germane resources devoted to intrinsic cognitive load.

Element Interactivity

Levels of both intrinsic and extraneous cognitive load are determined by element interactivity. Interacting elements are defined as elements that must be processed simultaneously in working memory because they are logically related. An element is anything that needs to be learned or processed, or has been learned or processed. Elements are characteristically schemas. Most schemas consist of sub-schemas or sub-elements. Prior to a schema being acquired, those sub-elements must be treated as individual elements in working memory. After they have been incorporated into a schema, that schema can be treated as a single element in working memory. Thus, learning reduces working memory load by converting multiple lower-level schemas into a smaller number of higher-level schemas or even a single higher-level schema that can be treated as a single entity.

With respect to intrinsic cognitive load, some material can be learned one element at a time and so is low in element interactivity and low in intrinsic cognitive load. Such material requires few working memory resources. Other material has elements that cannot be learned in isolation. The elements interact and so they must be processed simultaneously rather than as single, unrelated elements because they cannot be understood as single elements. Such material is high in element interactivity and high in intrinsic cognitive load. High element interactivity material requires more working memory resources than material that is low in element interactivity until the interacting elements have been incorporated into a schema after learning.

Extraneous cognitive load also is determined by levels of element interactivity but, in this case, element interactivity that is unnecessary for achieving learning goals. Some instructional procedures require learners to process only a limited number of such elements simultaneously. In this case, element interactivity is low and extraneous cognitive load is low. Different instructional designs require learners to process a large number of elements simultaneously resulting in high element interactivity and a high extraneous cognitive load. The manner in which element interactivity influences intrinsic and extraneous cognitive load will be discussed next.

Element Interactivity and Intrinsic Cognitive Load

As indicated above, this source of cognitive load is intrinsic to the information that the learner must deal with (Sweller, 1994) and is entirely determined by levels of element interactivity. Element interactivity can be estimated for any information that students may be required to learn. We will begin with examples of low element interactivity information.

Acquiring a new vocabulary is a common necessity in many disciplines. Learning the new vocabulary of a second language provides an obvious example but acquiring a new vocabulary, to a greater or lesser extent, is likely to be a requirement of all areas. In chemistry for example, the symbols of each of the elements of the periodic table must be learned. For many vocabulary items of a discipline, each of the elements can be learned in isolation with no consequences for, and no relation to, any of the other elements that must be learned. For example, a chemistry student can learn that the symbol for copper is Cu quite independently of learning that the symbol for iron is Fe. Similarly, a second language student can learn that the translation of the English word 'cat' is the French word 'chat', independently of learning that the translation of the English word 'dog' is the French word 'chien'. In each case there are no logical or structural reasons why learning one relation should have any impact on learning other relations. As a consequence, these categories of relations do not need to be learned simultaneously. They can be learned independently at different times and without reference to each other because the learning elements do not interact. Learning these relations provides an example of low element interactivity material.

High element interactivity information consists of elements that are closely related to each other and so cannot be learned in isolation. The elements interact in a manner that renders learning individual elements in isolation meaningless. All relevant elements must be processed simultaneously in order to be learned in a meaningful fashion. For example, while we can learn chemical symbols in isolation, we cannot learn in isolation the various ways those symbols are manipulated in a chemical equation such as $MgCO_3 + H_2SO4 \rightarrow CO_2 + MgSO_4 + H_2O$. We need to consider the entire equation, including all of the elements that constitute the equation, whenever any manipulation occurs.

Indeed, equations in general, by their very nature are high in element interactivity. We can see the effect of high element interactivity by considering simple algebra equations. Assume someone is learning to solve equations of the form, $(a + b)/c = d$, solve for a. This equation includes a large number of interacting elements. The symbols of the equation such as a, b, $=,/$, etc. provide obvious elements but there are many more elements than the symbols. All of the relations between all of the symbols also constitute elements that must be processed when learning to solve equations. As an example, the symbol '/' and the symbol, 'c', have a particular relation that must be processed and understood in order to learn how to solve this problem. The relation between '/' and 'c' constitutes an element that must be learned. Furthermore, that element itself interacts with all of the other elements in the problem whether those elements consist of symbols or other relations between symbols. The number of interacting elements incorporated in the problem $(a + b)/c = d$, solve for a is large and because they interact all elements must at some point be considered simultaneously. Learning to solve algebra equations is a high element interactivity task because there are many elements that must be processed simultaneously.

A full understanding of high element interactivity material cannot occur without simultaneously processing all of the elements that constitute the task. We cannot, for example, process the '/' symbol in the previous equation, in isolation, without reference to the other symbols and relations between the symbols. We need all of the other symbols and relations to confer meaning on the '/' symbol. The equation only can be fully understood by processing all of the relevant symbols and relations simultaneously. Furthermore, to solve the problem, the symbols and relations must be related to the entire problem statement and its possible solution. Unless all of the interacting elements are processed simultaneously, high element interactivity material cannot be understood because considering individual elements in isolation tells us little of relevance to the problem and its solution.

The level of interactivity between elements of information that are essential for learning determines intrinsic cognitive load. If element interactivity is low, intrinsic cognitive load also will be low because only a small number of elements and relations will need to be processed simultaneously in working memory. At the extreme, individual elements can be learned independently of all other element and no element imposes a high working memory load resulting in a very low intrinsic cognitive load. In contrast, if the level of interactivity between essential elements is high, intrinsic cognitive load will also be high.

Task Difficulty

A low intrinsic cognitive load needs to be distinguished from levels of task difficulty. A task may have a very low intrinsic cognitive load imposing a very low load on working memory but still be very difficult. Learning the vocabulary of a second language provides a clear example. Natural languages have a great number of vocabulary items that need to be learned. Learning those vocabulary items can be a difficult, time-consuming task that frequently takes many years. The difficulty of the task is driven by the large number of items, not the complexity of the items. Each vocabulary item may be acquired with little working memory load if it is low in element interactivity and so imposes a low intrinsic cognitive load. Difficulty in learning some material such as second language vocabulary items derives from the many individual elements that need to be learned, and not from any difficulty associated with each element.

While a low element interactivity task is only difficult if there are many elements that must be processed sequentially as in the case of acquiring the vocabulary of a second language, a high element interactivity task may be difficult even if the number of relevant elements is relatively low. But the reason for task difficulty when dealing with high element interactivity material such as the algebra equation presented above is usually very different to the reason low element interactivity material may be difficult. A small number of elements, if they interact, can be very difficult to process in a capacity constrained working memory. A large number of interacting elements can be impossibly difficult for some people. The difficulty of learning novel, high interactivity material can derive from two unrelated sources. High interactivity material always is difficult because of element interactivity. It also may include a large number of elements, although the total number of elements does not contribute directly to element interactivity. Thus, some high element interactivity material can be difficult to learn not only because it may consist of a large number of interacting elements but also because it consists of many elements in absolute terms. Material that includes both a very large number of elements with many of those elements interacting will be exceptionally difficult to learn.

The total number of elements and the extent to which they interact can vary independently and so the total number of elements has no relation to the intrinsic cognitive load unless the elements interact. Learners may need to assimilate literally thousands of elements but face a relatively insignificant intrinsic cognitive load if low element interactivity allows individual elements to be processed independently of each other. The task of assimilating many elements is in itself difficult even if they do not interact, but processing any individual element is not difficult. In contrast, a relatively small number of interacting elements can impose an overwhelming intrinsic cognitive load because in order for the information to be understood, all elements need to be processed simultaneously and simultaneously processing several elements may exceed working memory limits. The resultant, excessive intrinsic cognitive load requires particular instructional strategies. Those strategies will be discussed in Part IV.

Understanding

Element interactivity can be used to define 'understanding' (Marcus, Cooper, & Sweller, 1996). Information is fully understood when all of its interacting elements can be processed in working memory. A failure to understand occurs when appropriate elements are not processed in working memory. Information is difficult to understand when it consists of more interacting elements than can readily be processed in working memory. Low element interactivity information is easy to understand because it can easily and appropriately be processed in working memory.

The relation between element interactivity and understanding can be seen clearly when we consider the language we use when dealing with low element interactivity information. Low element interactivity material does not have the term 'understanding' attached to it. Assume someone cannot tell us that Cu is the chemical symbol for copper. We assume that they either have not learned the symbol or have forgotten it and we will refer to their failure as a lack of knowledge or a failure of memory. It would be seen as peculiar to refer to the failure in the context of understanding. If someone cannot tell us that the chemical symbol for copper is Cu, we are unlikely to attribute the failure to a lack of understanding. The term is inappropriate in this context.

The contrast is marked when we deal with high element interactivity information. The term 'understanding' only applies to high element interactivity material associated with a high intrinsic cognitive load. It is never used when dealing with low element interactivity material that imposes a low intrinsic cognitive load. Consider a student who has failed to solve the problem $(a + b)/c = d$, solve for a. Similar to materials with low element interactivity, that failure is due to a lack of knowledge or a failure of memory. The student has never learned to solve this category of problems or has forgotten how to solve them but in this case, most people are likely to assume that a failure of understanding has occurred. Information is 'understood' when we are able to process multiple, interacting elements simultaneously in working memory. We fail to understand information when the number of multiple, interacting elements is too large to permit us to process all of the elements in working memory. In the case of the above algebra example, students may be unable to understand how to solve this problem if they are unable to process all of the pro-numerals, symbols and relations between them in working memory.

The distinction between learning with understanding and learning by rote can be explained by element interactivity. Learning by rote tends to have strong negative connotations while learning with understanding has equally strong positive connotations.

Both forms of learning can be explained by processes of element interactivity in working memory. While learning with understanding is reserved for high element interactivity information, learning by rote can be applied to either low or high element interactivity information. When dealing with low element interactivity information, we assume, correctly, that learning by rote is unavoidable because no other form of learning is available. If learning chemistry, we have no choice but to rote learn that the symbol Cu stands for copper. In contrast, high element interactivity material can be either rote learned or learned with understanding and so the differential connotations associated with learning by rote or learning with understanding apply. However, we need to understand the solution to the problem $(a + b)/ = c$, solve for a to enable us to create more complex schemas in this domain. We should not rote learn the solution.

The distinction between learning by rote and learning with understanding in element interactivity terms will be exemplified by considering a child learning the concept of multiplication. Multiplication can be learned in the same way as a new vocabulary with each multiplicative value stored in long-term memory. A child can rote learn that $3 \times 4 = 12$. There are several advantages to rote learning with a major one being an immense reduction in element interactivity and a commensurate reduction in working memory load. Rote learning that $3 \times 4 = 12$ is likely to require no more than five elements consisting of the five symbols that constitute the expression.

Understanding why $3 \times 4 = 12$ also requires knowing the outcome of the procedure but, in addition, it requires processing much more information in working memory and storing that information in long-term memory, resulting in a considerable increase in element interactivity. Rather than merely learning that $3 \times 4 = 12$, learners need to understand that the reason the answer to the multiplication is 12 is because 4 is added 3 times. Not only does $3 \times 4 = 12$, but $4 + 4 + 4 = 12$ and the fact that both arithmetic operations give an answer of 12 is not a coincidence. The multiplication equation means adding 3 lots of 4. To begin to understand the multiplication equation as opposed to merely rote learning it, the elements associated with $4 + 4 + 4 = 12$ must be added to, and interact with, the elements associated with $3 \times 4 = 12$. Element interactivity and its associated cognitive load must be substantially increased. Additional understanding along with additional element interactivity and working memory load occur when students learn that $3 \times 4 = 4 + 4 + 4 = 3 + 3 + 3 + 3 = 4 \times 3 = 12$. Learning relations between addition, subtraction, multiplication and division results in further understanding, further element interactivity and further working memory load. Many learners cease adding additional interacting elements beyond $3 \times 4 = 12$ because of the dramatic increase in element interactivity and cognitive load that is required when learning with understanding. This failure to go beyond the basic knowledge ($3 \times 4 = 12$) means that learners will not at this point learn the commutative law of multiplication ($a \cdot b = b \cdot a$) and how the commutative law might be applied to other numbers (e.g. $2 \times 5 = 5 \times 2$). Hence schema formation is limited by not learning further relations and connections within the multiplication system.

Based on this analysis, learning by rote and learning with understanding require the same qualitative processes. In both cases, information must be processed in working memory prior to being stored in long-term memory. The differences are quantitative, not qualitative. Learning with understanding always increases the number of interacting elements that must be processed in working memory. For all of us, under at least some circumstances, the increase in element interactivity and working memory load associated with understanding information may be too large to handle. Learning by rote without understanding may be the only viable option. Learning with understanding should always be the goal of instruction, but as instructors we need to understand that sometimes that goal will not be achievable. Rote learning may be the only available option, at least in the initial stages of learning.

From an instructional perspective, we can see that under some circumstances, it may not be possible for very high element interactivity material to be simultaneously processed in working memory because working memory limits may be exceeded. Such information cannot be understood, at least initially. An initial failure to understand does not mean the information cannot be processed. Processing can occur, individual element by individual element or by small groups of elements. We label such processing conditions as learning by rote. Rote learning may be unavoidable during the initial stages of learning very high element interactivity material (Pollock, Chandler, & Sweller, 2002). This issue will be explored further, in conjunction with empirical evidence, when discussing the isolated–interacting elements effect in Chapter 16.

Altering Intrinsic Cognitive Load

In one sense, intrinsic cognitive load cannot be altered because it is intrinsic to a particular task. If the learning task is unaltered and if the knowledge levels of the learners remain constant, intrinsic cognitive load also will remain constant. That constant or fixed cognitive load can be altered by changing the nature of the learning task. For example, it was pointed out above, that if interacting elements are taught as though they are isolated with each element treated as though it bears no relation to other elements, element interactivity and intrinsic cognitive load can be reduced. Of course, the reduction in intrinsic cognitive load only has been accomplished by changing the task. Learners no longer are taught the relations between interacting elements, a major component of intrinsic cognitive load. That may not matter during early learning, but for most subject matter full understanding including the relations between interacting elements is likely to be essential at some point. Reducing intrinsic cognitive load by altering the nature of what is learned may be an important instructional technique, but in most cases its utility is likely to be temporary.

Intrinsic cognitive load also will be reduced by the act of learning itself. Learning includes converting a group of interacting elements that are treated as multiple elements in working memory into a smaller number or even a single element. Almost any instance of learning provides an example. To people not familiar with the Latin alphabet and English, 'CAT' is likely to provide a complex set of squiggles that overwhelm working memory. To readers of this text, of course, with schemas for 'CAT', the interacting elements are buried in the schema and the intrinsic cognitive load is negligible. A major function of learning is to dramatically reduce element interactivity and intrinsic cognitive load by incorporating interacting elements in schemas. The resultant reduction in cognitive load frees working memory resources for other activities. In the present case of reading this text, because working memory resources are not devoted to decoding the text, they can be used to interpret the content, the ultimate aim of learning to read. Thus, learning through schema acquisition eliminates the working memory load imposed by high element interactivity information.

Apart from altering what is learned or the act of learning itself, intrinsic cognitive load cannot be altered. For a particular task presented to learners with a particular level of knowledge, intrinsic cognitive load is fixed.

It can be seen that the concept of element interactivity is closely tied to the overlapping definitions of elements and schemas. An element is anything that needs to be learned or processed while schemas are usually multiple, interacting elements. Schema construction consists of learning how multiple elements interact while schema automation allows those interacting elements to be ignored when using a schema. Once a schema has been constructed, it becomes another, single, element that does not impose a heavy working memory load and can be used to construct higher-order schemas. The interacting elements are embedded in a schema that can be treated as a single element in the construction of more complex schemas. While a written word consists of a complex set of interacting lines and curves that someone unfamiliar with the written English language may have difficulty interpreting or even reproducing, to a fluent reader those interacting elements are embedded in a schema that itself acts a single element.

Relations of Intrinsic Cognitive Load to Human Cognitive Architecture

Novel, unfamiliar information that needs to be learned is governed by the borrowing and reorganising, randomness as genesis and narrow limits of change principles. These principles describe how novel information is acquired. Once learned, information that needs to be used is governed by the information store and the environmental organising and linking principles. These principles describe how familiar, stored information is used to govern activity.

Learned, familiar information is treated quite differently from novel, yet-to-be-learned information. As indicated when discussing the narrow limits of change and the environmental organising and linking principles, the characteristics of working memory are very different when dealing with unfamiliar and familiar information. Those differences now can be considered from the perspective of the manner in which high element interactivity information is handled. Novel, high element interactivity information that is yet to be learned is likely to impose a high intrinsic cognitive load that may overwhelm working memory when it is being acquired via the borrowing and reorganising or randomness as genesis principles. That same information, once learned and stored in long-term memory as a schema with its interacting elements incorporated in the schema, can be retrieved from the information store using the environmental organising and linking principle. In contrast to the difficulty in processing the elements of that information when a schema is being constructed, once it has been constructed and stored in long-term memory, it can be retrieved as a single rather than multiple elements from long-term memory to govern activity. The multiple, interacting elements are embedded within a schema and it is that schema that is retrieved from long-term memory. Processing a single schema as a single element is likely to impose a minimal working memory load.

Element Interactivity and Extraneous Cognitive Load

Element interactivity is associated with extraneous as well as intrinsic cognitive load. Unlike intrinsic cognitive load that is imposed by the intrinsic nature of the information that learners must acquire, extraneous cognitive load is imposed on working memory due to the manner in which information is presented during instruction. Some instructional procedures require learners to process a large number of interacting elements many of which are not directly relevant to learning through schema acquisition. Other procedures, in presenting the same information for learners to acquire, substantially reduce this element interactivity. While detailed information concerning element interactivity associated with extraneous cognitive load will be presented in the chapters of Part IV, preliminary information will be presented in this section.

It may be recalled that based on the borrowing and reorganising principle, the acquisition of biologically secondary information is assisted by direct, explicit instruction. (We have evolved to acquire biologically primary knowledge without explicit instruction.) Let us assume that instead of direct, explicit instruction, problem solving is used as an instructional tool. Learners must acquire knowledge by discovering solutions to problems that they have been presented. Students might, for example, be learning mathematics by the common technique of solving problems. Solving novel problems for which a solution is not available in long-term memory requires the use of a means–ends strategy. As indicated in Chapters 7 and 8 on the goal-free and worked example effects, that strategy requires problem solvers to simultaneously consider the current problem state (e.g. $a + b = c$), the goal state (make a the subject of the equation), to extract differences between the current state and the goal state (the term '$+b$' is located on the left-hand side of the equation and needs to be eliminated) and to find problem-solving operators (rules of algebra) that can be used to eliminate the differences between the current state and the goal state (subtract b from both sides of the equation). The problem cannot be solved unless all of these elements are considered. Element interactivity is very high when using a means–ends strategy because the strategy necessarily involves processing several elements.

Furthermore, those elements cannot be considered in isolation. We cannot extract differences between a given problem state and a goal state without simultaneously considering the given state, the goal state, the differences between them and the problem-solving moves that might reduce those differences.

There are alternatives to using a high element interactivity means–ends strategy. Rather than having learners solve problems, they could be presented with worked examples that completely eliminate a means–ends strategy because learners are no longer engaged in problem solving. Whether learners engage in problem solving or in studying worked examples is under the control of instructors and so the high element interactivity associated with means–ends problem solving is an example of extraneous cognitive load that can and should be reduced. The consequences of using problem solving rather than worked examples will be discussed in detail in Chapter 8. There are many other examples of element interactivity resulting in a high extraneous cognitive load that will be discussed in the chapters of Part IV.

This argument is closely tied to the structures of human cognitive architecture. If instruction requires learners to engage in problem-solving search via the randomness as genesis principle, or if it includes other cognitive activities that are similarly unfavourable to schema acquisition and automation, then the effectiveness of that instruction will be reduced due to working memory limitations associated with the narrow limits of change principle. Problem-solving search along with a variety of other cognitive activities associated with some instructional procedures imposes a heavy extraneous cognitive load that can interfere with learning.

While it is never advantageous to increase extraneous cognitive load, it can be advantageous to increase intrinsic cognitive load. Increasing intrinsic cognitive load increases the amount of information that needs to be processed and learned, and providing working memory capacity is available that increase is likely to be beneficial (see the variability effect in Chapter 16). In contrast, an increase in extraneous cognitive load results in learners using scarce working memory resources for purposes other than learning. Since extraneous cognitive load normally is under the control of the instructor, it can be reduced by altering instructional procedures and without compromising understanding. Understanding is likely to be increased if a reduction in extraneous cognitive load frees working memory resources for schema acquisition and automation.

Instructional Implications

Total cognitive load, consisting of intrinsic and extraneous cognitive load, must not exceed working memory resources. If total cognitive load is too high, processing necessary information may become difficult and so learning may cease. For given learners and given information, intrinsic cognitive load cannot be altered. It can be increased or decreased by changing the nature of what is learned. If the intrinsic cognitive load is high, the level of extraneous cognitive load can become critical. Reducing extraneous load is much more important when intrinsic cognitive load is high than when it is low. A high extraneous cognitive load may not matter a great deal if intrinsic cognitive load is low because the total cognitive load may be less than available working memory resources. In other words, for material with a low element interactivity and therefore low intrinsic cognitive load, learners neverthe-less will be able to process the information. A less than optimal instructional design associated with low intrinsic cognitive load due to low element interactivity may therefore not interfere with learning. The total cognitive load still may be within working memory limits.

If intrinsic cognitive load is high, adding a high extraneous cognitive load to an already high intrinsic cognitive load may well result in an excessive total load. Under high intrinsic cognitive load conditions, instructional design issues may be important, unlike low intrinsic cognitive load conditions. Adding the high element interactivity associated with a high intrinsic cognitive load to the high element interactivity associated with a high extraneous cognitive load may exceed avail-able working memory resources. Devoting working memory resources to deal-ing with an inappropriate instructional design may not matter when intrinsic cognitive load is low. It may be critical when intrinsic cognitive load is high (see Chapter 15 on the element interactivity effect). As a consequence, most of the cognitive load effects discussed in the chapters of Part IV are concerned with conditions under which both intrinsic and extraneous cognitive load are high and so need to be reduced. Cognitive load theory has been concerned primarily, though not exclusively, with reducing extraneous cognitive load.

Conclusions

Cognitive load imposed by instructional materials can be divided into intrinsic and extraneous cognitive load. Equivalently, working memory resources can be divided into germane resources that deal with intrinsic cognitive load and extraneous resources that deal with extraneous cognitive load. This division has proved to be basic to the development of cognitive load theory. The primary, though not sole, aim of cognitive load theory has been to devise instructional procedures that reduce extraneous cognitive load and so decrease the working memory resources that must be devoted to information that is extraneous to learning. Working memory resources that no longer need to be devoted to dealing with extraneous cognitive load can instead be diverted to dealing with intrinsic cognitive load that is germane to the learning process.

Most of the cognitive load effects discussed in Part IV of this book are con-cerned with instructional procedures that reduce extraneous cognitive load. When dealing with extraneous cognitive load, it is always advantageous to reduce it and never advantageous to increase it. A smaller number of the cognitive load effects are concerned with altering intrinsic cognitive load rather than reducing extraneous cognitive load. It can be advantageous to increase or decrease intrinsic cognitive load depending on whether intrinsic cognitive load exceeds available working memory resources or under-utilises those resources. The cognitive load effects discussed in Part IV were all based on the assumption that extraneous cognitive load should be reduced while intrinsic cognitive load should be optimised. In order to describe ideal levels of cognitive load, we first need to discuss techniques for measuring cognitive load. The next chapter is concerned with this issue.

Chapter 6
Measuring Cognitive Load

Because of the centrality of working memory load to cognitive load theory, measuring this load has been a high priority for researchers. While it is possible to demonstrate support for the validity of the theory by predicting experimental outcomes, it is useful to additionally provide independent measures of cognitive load. In this chapter we describe the various methods used to measure cognitive load and how they have developed over the last 30 years.

Indirect Measures of Cognitive Load

In the early days of cognitive load theory, cognitive load was not directly measured. It was assumed based on the results of experiments examining the relation between problem solving and learning. Several techniques were used to indirectly assess cognitive load.

Computational Models

The initial research into cognitive load theory focused on the inefficiency of problem solving as a learning strategy. It was hypothesised that high problem-solving search led to a greater working memory load than low problem-solving search. In a series of experiments conducted by Sweller and colleagues in the 1980s, it was demonstrated that a learning strategy that required considerable problem-solving search led to inferior learning outcomes than a strategy that employed far less problem-solving search. To explain these results, Sweller (1988) argued that schema acquisition was impeded because using some problem-solving heuristics led to unnecessary problem-solving search that imposed a high extraneous cognitive load. In contrast, procedures that reduced problem-solving search were assumed to reduce cognitive load.

Theoretical support demonstrating that problem-solving search did increase cognitive load was indicated by computational models. Using production system

J. Sweller et al., *Cognitive Load Theory*, Explorations in the Learning Sciences,
Instructional Systems and Performance Technologies 1,
DOI 10.1007/978-1-4419-8126-4_6, © Springer Science+Business Media, LLC 2011

models to compare a high with a low search strategy, Sweller (1988) found that higher search required a more complex model to simulate the problem-solving process, corresponding to more information being held and processed in working memory. Similarly, Ayres and Sweller (1990) using a production system model to simulate the problem-solving solution of multi-step geometry problems provided evidence that a high search strategy required more working memory resources than a simpler strategy.

The indirect evidence provided by computational models has restricted their use as an indicator of cognitive load. Nevertheless, within a cognitive load theory framework, computational models were the first attempt to provide a degree of independent evidence that cognitive load was an important factor in instructional design. They were an important factor in the origins of cognitive load theory.

Performance During Acquisition

During this early period of cognitive load theory, performance indicators during the acquisition or learning phase were also used to support a cognitive load explanation of the observed effects. Without a direct measure, Chandler and Sweller (1991, 1992) argued that instructional time could be used as a proxy for cognitive load. It was theorised that if students were required to learn a topic using a strategy that raised cognitive load, then this increase in cognitive load would impact on performance during the learning phase. Not only would future performance be affected as indicated through test scores, but also performance during acquisition. Early studies supported this argument (see Owen & Sweller, 1985; Sweller, Chandler, Tierney, & Cooper, 1990; Sweller and Cooper, 1985). Evidence was also found that error rates were higher during acquisition under conditions of expected high cognitive load (see Owen & Sweller, 1985; Sweller & Cooper, 1985). Increased cognitive load may impact negatively on both learning time and acquisition task accuracy.

Error Profiles Between Problems

Error rates also have been used to identify differences in cognitive load *within problems*. Ayres and Sweller (1990) showed that students often make errors at particular points when problem solving in a geometry domain due to the high working memory load at those points. In a later study, Ayres (2001) demonstrated that error rates varied on mathematical tasks that required sequential calculations. High error rates corresponded to locations where decision making was at its greatest intensity with many variables needing to be considered. Although these two studies investigated problem solving and not instructional procedures, they provided additional evidence that error rates could be used to determine working memory demands.

Subjective Measures of Cognitive Load

Initially, theoretical considerations of cognitive load were used to predict instructional effectiveness, supported mainly by indirect measures of cognitive load, such as error rates and learning times, indicated above. As cognitive load theory developed and more instructional effects were identified, the need for more direct measures of cognitive load became apparent. For example, Chandler and Sweller (1991) and Sweller and Chandler (1994) commented on the absence of a direct measure of cognitive load. The impasse was broken by Paas (1992) who provided a major breakthrough by developing a subjective measure of cognitive load.

A Subjective Measure of Mental Effort

Based on a previous instrument developed by Bratfisch, Borg, and Dornic (1972), Paas (1992) reasoned that learners are able to introspect the amount of mental effort invested during learning and testing and this 'intensity of effort' may be considered to be an 'index' of cognitive load (p. 429). Paas, Tuovinen, Tabbers, and van Gerven (2003) later refined the definition of mental effort as 'the aspect of cognitive load that refers to the cognitive capacity that is actually allocated to accommodate the demands imposed by the task: thus, it can be considered to reflect the actual cognitive load' (p. 64).

Using a 9-point Likert scale ranging from very, very low mental effort (1) to very, very high mental effort (9), learners were asked to rate their mental effort at various points in the learning and testing cycle. In comparing instructional procedures that were hypothesised to raise or lower cognitive load, Paas (1992) found a match between self-rated mental effort and test performance. Learners who were presented an instructional design hypothesised to impose a low cognitive load had superior learning outcomes and rated their mental effort lower than students who were presented a design hypothesised to be high in cognitive load.

A follow-up study by Paas and van Merriënboer (1994) replicated the findings of Paas (1992). Furthermore, Paas and van Merriënboer (1994) also collected physiological measures through spectral analysis of heart rate. However, in contrast to the self-rating scale, the physiological measures were unable to detect differences between treatment groups and could only differentiate between mentally inactive and active periods. Subjective ratings were found to be more sensitive and far less intrusive than the physiological measure. The 9-point scale was also found to be highly reliable (see Paas, van Merriënboer, & Adam, 1994).

A Subjective Measure of Difficulty

The success of these early trials of subjective measures led others to adopt the subjective scale as a measure of cognitive load. However, many researchers, instead of using the term *mental effort*, asked learners to rate how *difficult or easy* they found the learning task. For example, in a series of experiments, Marcus, Cooper, and Sweller (1996) demonstrated that subjective measures of difficulty varied significantly according to the level of element interactivity of a task. In addition, Ayres (2006a) found that subjective measures of difficulty could detect variations in element interactivity within tasks.

The simple subjective rating scale, regardless of the wording used (mental effort or difficulty), has, perhaps surprisingly, been shown to be the most sensitive measure available to differentiate the cognitive load imposed by different instructional procedures. It has been used extensively to determine the relative cognitive load imposed by the various instructional procedures discussed in Part IV. Paas et al. (2003b) documented over 25 studies that used a subjective measure of cognitive load between 1992 and 2002. There have been many more since.

Variations in Subjective Ratings

Van Gog and Paas (2008) indicated that mental effort and difficulty may be distinct constructs with ensuing consequences. Some preliminary research investigating differences between the two scales supports this view (Ayres & Youssef, 2008). Asking a student how difficult he or she found a task differs from asking how much effort was invested in completing the task. Although the two measures are often correlated, difficulty does not always match effort. For example, very difficult problems may be so demanding for some learners that they are unable to make any realistic effort.

As well as potential differences in what is measured, van Gog and Paas (2008) also identified the time when mental ratings are collected as a further variation. Paas and van Merriënboer (1994) used mental effort measures collected after learners had solved test problems. In contrast, many other researchers have collected the data after the acquisition (instructional) period has been completed. The two strategies will not necessarily be comparable and may yield different results. Some of those differences will be considered below when discussing efficiency measures.

Consistency of the Subjective Measures

Despite these differing procedures, subjective measures of difficulty or mental effort have been surprisingly consistent in matching performance data predicted by cognitive load theory (see also Moreno, 2004; van Merriënboer, Schuurman, De Croock, & Paas, 2002) with few discrepancies or contradictions. However, in some studies, no statistically significant differences were found between subjective measures in spite of group treatment differences on performance tests (see Cuevas, Fiore, & Oser, 2002; Hummel, Paas, & Koper, 2004; Kester, Kirschner, & van Merriënboer, 2005).

There have also been studies where there is a cognitive load difference based on subjective measures but no group treatment effect on performance tests (Homer, Plass, & Blake, 2008; Van Gerven, Paas, van Merriënboer, Hendriks, & Schmidt, 2003). In Kalyuga, Chandler, and Sweller (2004), each of three experiments produced a different result: a cognitive load difference with no test effect; a cognitive load difference and a corresponding test effect; no cognitive load difference but a test effect. It is feasible, that under some specific conditions and materials, the expected match will not occur. Of course, when considering any statistically determined effect, there inevitably will be failures to match. The correlation between subjective rating scales and test performance cannot be perfect. Notwithstanding that occasional inconsistency, subjective measures have had a profound influence and provided a useful tool in providing evidence in support of cognitive load theory.

Efficiency Measures

Building on the Paas (1992) self-rating scale, Paas and van Merriënboer (1993) developed an *efficiency* measure, which combined mental effort with task performance indicators. Paas and van Merriënboer reasoned that it was important to consider the cognitive costs of learning. Even though two different instructional methods might produce the same learning outcomes, the effort that went into achieving these levels of performance was an important consideration. If one instructional strategy produces the same performance as another strategy but with fewer cognitive resources expended, then that first strategy is more efficient. Efficiency (E) was calculated using the following formula:

$$E = \left(Z_{Ptest} - Z_{Etest}\right)/\sqrt{2}$$

where Z_{Ptest} represents the standardised (Z scores) test scores, and Z_{Etest} the standardised mental effort scores collected after the testing period. The formula is based on the mathematical calculation of the perpendicular distance from a point to a line (in this case $y = x$). Differences in efficiency can be depicted by a simple graphic representation (see Fig. 6.1). When Z-scores for performance and mental effort are equal, the value of E is zero, depicted in Fig. 6.1 by the diagonal line ($y = x$). All points on this line equate to $E = 0$, whereas points above the line ($E > 0$) represent efficient learning and points below the line ($E < 0$) inefficient learning. Paas et al. (2003b) further explained that *high-instructional efficiency* results from high task performance and low mental effort (zone H in the diagram), whereas *low-instructional efficiency* results from low task performance and high mental effort (zone L in the diagram).

In a review of the efficiency measure, van Gog and Paas (2008) documented that in the period 1993–2007, over 30 cognitive load theory–related studies used an efficiency measure. However, as indicated above, van Gog and Paas (2008) also pointed out that there have been variations in the way in which mental ratings have

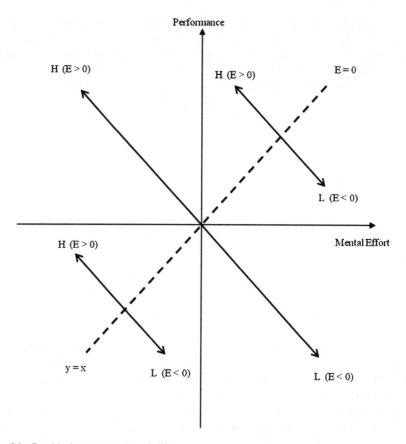

Fig. 6.1 Graphical representation of efficiency

been collected and those variations affect the efficiency measure because mental ratings are integral to the formula for efficiency. Van Gog and Paas argued that these different approaches measure different types of efficiencies. Using mental effort ratings collected after test performance, measures the *learning* consequences of acquiring cognitive structures such as schemas, whereas using the post-acquisition measures, indicates training efficiency.

We agree that learning efficiency may be a good indicator of schema acquisition and automation. If learners have acquired new schemas and can use them with less effort, then schema acquisition can be considered robust, even if the instructional method was more demanding. Nevertheless, instructional efficiency has an important role as it shows how efficient the learning process was, a key consideration of the cognitive load effects discussed in Part IV. Knowing how difficult or easy it was to follow an instructional design is critical to cognitive load theory. Despite these differences in approaches, both calculating the efficiency of training and the efficiency in using learned information in a test are important and can provide vital information relevant to instructional design.

Issues with Calculating Efficiency

Despite its wide-scale use, Hoffman and Schraw (2010) have identified some concerns associated with the calculation of instructional efficiency. In a review of efficiency, Hoffman and Schraw categorised Paas and van Merriënboer's original model as a *deviation* model, because it is based on the difference (discrepancy) between standardised scores of performance and effort. They argued that it is difficult to interpret the meaning of subtracting two variables that are conceptually different from each other. They made the point that it is similar to subtracting *z*-scores of an individual's intelligence and weight. It can be difficult to know what exactly the resultant scores indicate.

Hoffman and Schraw also noted that as *z*-scores are norm-referenced, the efficiency measure can only be based on group data and consequently cannot be used for comparing individual efficiency. On the other hand, they also suggested that provided differences in overall treatments are being compared, problems with comparisons of individual efficiency are not an issue. As will be shown in Part IV, most of the studies conducted under the umbrella of cognitive load theory focus entirely on overall group differences, therefore individual comparisons have not been an issue. As an alternative to the deviation model, Hoffman and Schraw described the advantages of two other methods (1) the *likelihood* model, based on a ratio of performance and subjective rating (e.g. the scale used in Kalyuga and Sweller, 2005; Kalyuga, 2008b; see Chapter 13 for more details) and (2) the *conditional likelihood* model, based on ratios of probabilities.

Hoffman and Schraw do not discount the deviation model, arguing that different models suit different research goals. If the aim is to investigate the difference between performance and effort score ranks then the deviation model of Paas and van Merriënboer has merit. Nevertheless, based on the Hoffman and Schraw analysis, a ratio of performance and subjective rating (the *likelihood* model) is very simple to calculate and can be used to determine individual efficiency measures. Those individual measures can easily be combined to provide the group efficiency that is essential when comparing overall treatment effects. We expect future research to make greater use of likelihood models.

Measuring Cognitive Load Through a Secondary Task

The subjective measures described above have been the most frequent instrument used to measure cognitive load. However, the traditional method of assessing working memory load is to use a secondary task (see Britton & Tesser, 1982; Kerr, 1973) in combination with a primary task (*dual-task methodology*). A secondary task requires learners to engage in an additional cognitive activity that is secondary to the primary task of learning or problem solving. For example, as well as learning how to solve a class of mathematics problems as the primary task, learners may be asked to respond in a particular way to a specific sound as the secondary task. If the primary task imposes a heavy cognitive load, performance on the secondary task deteriorates. In contrast, a lower cognitive load on the primary task can result in improved performance on the secondary task.

Usually, the secondary task is quite dissimilar and requires less working memory resources than the primary task; however, Sweller (1988) created an alternative to this format. Sweller reasoned that asking students to learn through problem solving involved two processes: (1) solving the problem, the primary task and (2) learning from the experience, the secondary task. In other words, when learners treat solving the problem as the primary task, this may interfere with learning about the problem, which students treat as the secondary task. The more complex the problem, the less might be learned about it. Empirical evidence based on a specific secondary task consisting of remembering the givens and the solution of a preceding problem supported this argument. Instructional processes intended to reduce the cognitive load associated with solving a problem increased the amount of information that was remembered about the previous problem.

In a more traditional use of a secondary task, Marcus et al. (1996) investigated element interactivity, and in particular how a diagram can reduce element interactivity compared with the same information presented as text only. In this study, two types of secondary tasks were used, with a learning episode constituting the primary task in each case. In one experiment, the secondary task was recognising a tone presented at random during the learning episode. On hearing the tone, learners had to respond to it by pressing a foot pedal. Response time was used as a measure of how cognitively demanding the primary task was, indicating cognitive load. In a second experiment, the secondary task was remembering two-digit numbers that were presented during learning episode. In this case, accuracy of recall of the secondary task was used as a measure of cognitive load. For both types of secondary measures, significant results were found matching the learning outcomes. Using diagrams and low element interactivity materials led to better learning outcomes and stronger performance on secondary tasks. Hence a cognitive load explanation was supported.

Chandler and Sweller (1996) also used a dual-task methodology to show that the secondary task, recalling a letter, was affected by the instructional mode. For this secondary task, two separate letters, prompted by tones, were presented 8 s apart on a computer screen during acquisition. Learners were required to recall the first letter while remembering the second letter. Results indicated that the superior learning strategy intended to reduce cognitive load resulted in higher scores on the secondary task. Furthermore, significant differences were only found for instructional strategies and secondary measures when learning materials were high in element interactivity. For materials that were low in element interactivity, more working memory resources were available to overcome inefficient learning strategies and so performance on secondary tasks was not affected. On problem-solving tasks, in contrast to learning tasks, Halford, Maybery, and Bain (1986) and Ayres (2001) used a secondary task method to demonstrate that high element interactivity is associated with a correspondingly high working memory load.

Brünken, Steinbacher, Plass, and Leutner (2002) required learners to monitor the change of colour of a letter that was positioned above the main instructional presentation. When the letter changed colour, learners were required to press a key on the computer keyboard. Reaction times in this secondary task were used as a measure of cognitive load. The secondary task results indicated that cognitive load was lowest for the best-performing learning approach, again supporting the cognitive load theory predictions.

In the previously described study, the secondary task was visual. In a follow-up study, Brünken, Plass, and Leutner (2004) investigated the impact of an audio secondary task. Using an argument based on the assumption that audio and visual materials are processed in different subsystems of working memory (see Baddeley, 1986), Brünken et al. (2004) reasoned that different modes (audio or visual) of secondary tasks will detect variations of cognitive load in different working memory channels. More specifically an auditory secondary task will identify differences in cognitive load in the auditory channel. This hypothesis was tested using the same learning materials as Brünken et al. (2002), but with a changed secondary task. Instead of recognising a colour change, a single tone (sound) was randomly inserted into the learning materials. Reaction times were then used to identify differences in cognitive load. As predicted, learning materials that included auditory information used more resources in the auditory working memory channel than learning material with no auditory component. These two studies (Brünken et al., 2002, 2004) demonstrated that the modality of the secondary task is an important consideration.

Van Gerven, Paas, van Merriënboer, and Schmidt (2006) also used a secondary task while investigating audio-visual instructional materials. In this study, the secondary task was detection of illumination of a jukebox button positioned in front of the learning material. In this study, an audio-visual format was compared with a purely visual presentation, and the impact of age investigated. Learning results indicated that young learners performed better than elderly learners but no effect was found due to the modality of the material. The secondary task mirrored these results: young learners had quicker reaction times than the older learners. Further, subjective measures of cognitive load (difficulty) were also collected, showing significant age and modality differences. Interestingly, even though no effect due to modality was found on test performance, the subjective measure found the dual-mode presentation to be rated easier than the single mode. It appeared that under these conditions, the subjective measure was more sensitive to cognitive load variations that the secondary task.

Cognitive load theory research has made far less use of secondary tasks than of subjective measures as an indicator of cognitive load. Ease of use probably provides the major reason for this differential use of the two measures. Subjective measures can be obtained easily and quickly. They can be used when testing learners individually or in whole classes without specialised equipment. In contrast, secondary tasks require much more planning and, depending on the nature of the secondary task, may require equipment. They can interfere with normal classroom practice to a much greater extent than subjective measures.

Nevertheless, there are advantages to using secondary tasks. The main advantage is that they can provide an almost continuous measure of cognitive load during a task, whereas subjective measures only indicate total cognitive load after a task has been completed. Physiological measures, discussed in the next section, potentially can provide an even more accurate measure of instantaneous cognitive load.

As far as we are aware, efficiency measures have not been calculated using secondary tasks. There is no reason why they should not be calculated. All of the efficiency measures discussed by Hoffman and Schraw (2010) can be just as easily calculated using secondary tasks as using subjective ratings, once a cognitive load value has been established.

Physiological Measures of Cognitive Load

Paas and van Merriënboer (1994) compared a subjective measure with spectral analysis of heart rate, concluding that the subjective measure showed more potential. Few, if any, follow-up physiological studies were conducted by cognitive load theory researchers in the following decade. However, in more recent times, there has been a re-emergence of interest in these measures. Cognitive papillary response is one strategy that has been tested. Van Gerven, Paas, van Merriënboer, and Schmidt (2004), citing the work of Kahneman and Beatty (1966), argued that pupil size could be related to memory load. Using a series of tasks that required differences in memory load, support was found for the suggestion that pupil dilation increased according to increased levels of memory load. However, it was also found that the papillary response strategy could have age limitations, as elderly participants did not show this correlation on some cognitive tasks.

Commentators have advocated using techniques such as functional magnetic resonance imaging (fMRI, see Paas, Ayres, & Pachman, 2008; Whelan, 2007) and electroencephalography (EEG, see Antonenko, Paas, Grabner & van Gog, 2010) to measure cognitive load. This interest coincided with the development of more sophisticated technologies. Evidence has started to emerge that physiological methods may have considerable merit. For example, Antonenko and Niederhauser (2010) collected both subjective and EEG measures in a study that investigated learning with hypertexts. A mental effort scale was used as the subjective measure and the EEG captured alpha, beta and theta brain wave rhythms. Performance scores indicated that using *hypertext leads* (introductory text linking nodes together) resulted in better learning outcomes than using hypertext without leads. Whereas no between-group differences were found for the mental effort measure, alpha, beta and theta measures were significantly lower in the hypertext lead groups. It was concluded that hypertext leads lowered cognitive load, but only the EEG measure was sensitive enough to show this difference. In discussing the failure of the subjective method, Antonenko and Niederhauser argued that an advantage of the EEG method was that it reflected various types of load, such as instantaneous, peak, average, accumulated, as well as overall load, whereas the subjective measure could measure only overall load. (For more information on temporal aspects of cognitive load see Xie & Salvendy, 2000.)

Van Gog, Rikers, and Ayres (2008) also discussed the advantages of an instantaneous measurement of cognitive load. Van Gog et al. distinguished between *online* methods, such as eye tracking and heart-rate monitoring that can be collected during learning and testing, and *offline* data, such as subjective measures that can only be collected after an activity has been completed without disrupting the task. Over the last few years, research into cognitive load theory and multimedia instructional environments have used eye tracking to gain further insights into cognitive processes (see van Gog & Scheiter, 2010). Some evidence has also emerged that eye tracking can be used to measure fluctuations in cognitive load. Underwood, Jebbert, and Roberts (2004) found that different combinations of text and pictures required different levels of cognitive processing, which were matched by corresponding variations in eye fixations. Overall, it has been argued that longer eye fixations reflect more cognitive processing. Consequently, eye-tracking data has significant merit, as it not only indicates where the learner focuses attention, but also for how long, thus implying corresponding variations in cognitive load.

Another online strategy that has shown potential is the use of indicators of language complexity. While not physiological in nature, speech complexity shares many characteristics of physiological measures, including the ability to be used online, simultaneously with learning and testing tasks. Khawaja, Chen, and Marcus (2010) reasoned that as task difficulty increases, lexical density of speech decreases. This effect was demonstrated in a study with bushfire incident management teams. As bushfire tasks became more challenging, including the occurrence of unexpected events, the speech patterns of the operating teams changed, becoming less dense according to task complexity. Hence measures of language complexity are potentially another useful online indicator of cognitive load.

After an inauspicious start, indicators of cognitive load that can be used as an alternative to subjective measures, such as physiological indicators, are garnering considerable current research interest. Some techniques are promising but it is still too early to determine whether the current research emphasis will result in solid results. In the past, physiological measures have proved insufficiently sensitive to indicate the differences in cognitive load generated by the instructional designs used by cognitive load theory. It remains to be seen whether the current attempts to find sufficiently sensitive physiological measures will prove successful.

Measuring the Different Types of Cognitive Load

Following the identification of different categories of cognitive load (see Sweller, van Merriënboer, & Paas, 1998), theoretical predictions based on cognitive load became more sophisticated. Instead of just using total cognitive load to argue why an instructional design would, or would not, be effective, researchers started to differentiate between categories of cognitive load in formulating their hypotheses.

Hence, in the last decade there has been much interest in obtaining individual measures of different types of cognitive load.

Theoretically, assuming that intrinsic and extraneous cognitive load add to the total cognitive load, it is a simple matter to distinguish between intrinsic and extraneous cognitive load by experimental means. In an instructional experiment, if intrinsic cognitive load is kept constant but extraneous cognitive load is varied between instructional conditions, any differences in cognitive load measures as indicated by subjective rating scales must be due to extraneous cognitive load. Similarly, by keeping extraneous cognitive load constant and varying intrinsic cognitive load, any measured differences must be due to differences in intrinsic cognitive load. Ayres (2006a) used this logic in one of the first attempts to measure intrinsic cognitive load.

Using problem-solving tasks Ayres (2006a) asked students to complete a set of algebraic problems requiring consecutive computations. As students had already received instruction on these tasks previously with no additional instruction provided, Ayres reasoned that extraneous cognitive load due to instructional factors was constant. In a previous study, Ayres (2001) found that students exhibited specific error profiles according to the location of the computations. Some computations were higher in element interactivity than others, leading to greater error rates at those points. In the Ayres (2006a) study, as students completed each problem they were asked to rate 'how easy or difficult' they found each computation. Results indicated a consistent match between the difficulty ratings and the error patterns. Through their subjective ratings, students were in effect able to identify significant differences in element interactivity (intrinsic cognitive load) within problems. It was also found that students with more domain-specific knowledge were better at identifying differences in intrinsic load through their ratings than those with less knowledge. Most likely expertise enabled students to reflect more deeply on the internal processes involved in each computation and rate load more accurately as a result. Even though students with high levels of domain-specific knowledge made few errors, they were still able to differentiate element interactivity levels. In this study, there was no attempt to provide separate measures of different categories of cognitive load. Rather, extraneous cognitive load was kept constant and so any differences in load could be assumed to be due to intrinsic load.

DeLeeuw and Mayer (2008) used a mixed approach consisting of subjective measures and a secondary task to investigate if different instruments could measure intrinsic, extraneous and germane cognitive load separately. DeLeeuw and Mayer argued that intrinsic cognitive load could be manipulated by increasing the number of explanatory sentences in a multimedia lesson and extraneous load by varying redundant material consisting of the same spoken and written text. Performance on transfer tasks was considered a measure of germane cognitive load. Three measures of cognitive load were collected: response time to a secondary task consisting of a background change of colour during the lesson, subjective mental effort rating collected during the lesson and subjective difficulty ratings collected after the lesson. Over two experiments it was found that the secondary task was most sensitive to manipulations of redundancy (extraneous load), mental effort ratings were most sensitive to changes in sentence complexity (intrinsic load) and difficulty ratings were most sensitive to differences in transfer success. Students who scored high on the transfer test were assumed to have invested more germane effort, while those who scored low, less germane effort.

These findings indicate that different measures can tap into different processes and show varying sensitivities. However, there may be some doubt whether the three measures used can distinguish different types of cognitive load. It is not clear why a secondary task should be more sensitive to extraneous cognitive load than mental effort ratings or why mental effort ratings should be particularly sensitive to intrinsic cognitive load. Furthermore, we doubt whether transfer performance is necessarily a measure of germane load. In addition, it needs to be noted that according to the current formulation, germane cognitive load is merely a reflection of the amount of load imposed by intrinsic element interactivity and so does not independently contribute to the total load. Nevertheless, it is interesting that these different measures yielded different results depending on the nature of the manipulation. Very few other studies (for other examples see Cierniak, Scheiter, & Gerjets, 2009b; van Gerven et al., 2003) have used both subjective ratings and secondary task measure of cognitive load in the same study.

In trying to measure different aspects of cognitive load some researchers have been influenced by a multidimensional scale called the *NASA Task Load Index* (*NASA-TLX*, Hart & Staveland, 1988). The NASA-TLX consists of six subscales that measure different factors associated with completing a task: (1) mental demands (How much mental and perceptual activity was required?), (2) physical demands (How much physical activity was required?), (3) temporal demands (How much time pressure occurred?), (4) performance (How successful do you think you were in accomplishing the goals of the task set by the experimenter?), (5) effort (How hard did you have to work – mentally and physically – to accomplish your level of performance?), and (6) frustration level (How insecure, discouraged, irritated, stressed versus secure, content and relaxed did you feel during the task?). An overall measure of mental load is achieved by combining the six subscales.

In a recent reflection on its use, Hart (2006) points out that the NASA-TLX scale has mainly been used in studies that have focused on interface designs and evaluations, including the impact of automation and decision aids. Furthermore, consistent with its original design for aviation use, many studies have focused on air traffic control and other aeronautical activities. In contrast, cognitive load theory researchers have focused on learning environments and often modified the instrument by selecting only some of the subscales, as well as changing the wording of the items. In an attempt to measure the different cognitive load categories, Gerjets, Scheiter, and Catrambone (2006) selected three items from the NASA-TLX (see also Gerjets, Scheiter, & Catrambone, 2004). They were 'task demands' (how much mental and physical activity was required to accomplish the learning task), 'effort' (how hard the participant had to work to understand the contents of the learning environment), and 'navigational demands' (how much effort the participant had to invest to navigate the learning environment). Gerjets et al. (2006) argued that each of these items could correspond to intrinsic, germane and extraneous load, respectively.

Results from a study that manipulated the complexity of worked examples indicated that there was broad agreement with the test performance data. In other words, groups with the highest learning outcomes reported lowest cognitive load. However, there was no collaborating evidence that the three measures corresponded to different types of cognitive loads as proposed.

In the search for more differentiated measures of cognitive load, there has also been a tendency to align the wording of the items with the notion of what the different types of load represent. For example Cierniak et al. (2009b, p. 318) used items such as 'How difficult was the learning content for you? How difficult was it for you to learn with the material? How much did you concentrate during learning?' The choice of wording was intended to link 'learning content' with intrinsic load, and to link 'learning with the material' with extraneous load. It was argued that concentration reflects attention to the learning-relevant processes and therefore represents germane load. In this study, significant matches were found between the cognitive load measures and the performance data.

However, sometimes matches between test performance and the cognitive load measures do not coincide with theoretical predictions. Gerjets, Scheiter, Opfermann, Hesse, and Eysink (2009) used further variations of wording. Students were asked to rate the 'difficulty of the domain' (intended intrinsic load) and 'how much effort they made in understanding the examples' (intended germane load). For extraneous load two items were used: 'differentiate between important and unimportant information', and 'rate the difficulty of dealing with the environment'. However, this study did not find the expected match between the cognitive load measures and learning outcomes.

The above inconsistencies in psychometric attempts to measure different types of cognitive load are not unexpected. Psychometric distinctions between categories of cognitive load require learners to indicate whether the cognitive load that they are experiencing is due to a particular category of cognitive load. We doubt learners, particularly novice ones, are capable of making the required distinctions. For example, when attempting to learn some new concepts, learners may be able to accurately indicate the extent to which they are finding the task difficult. They may be much less accurate in attributing their difficulty to the intrinsic nature of the material or the manner in which the material is being presented. In most cases, unless they are aware of relevant, alternative instructional procedures such as the ones discussed in Part IV of this book, learners may have no conception of how the instructional procedures could change. If learners are not familiar with instructional design principles, they are not in a position to indicate whether the level of difficulty they are experiencing is due to an inadequate instructional design or due to the natural complexity of the information with which they are dealing. Under these circumstances, psychometric procedures designed to indicate whether cognitive load is due to one category rather than another are likely to fail (Kirschner, Ayres, & Chandler, 2011).

There is an alternative to psychometric measurement of the categories of cognitive load. Randomised, controlled experiments that vary one category while keeping the other constant provide a good indicator of the independence of intrinsic and extraneous categories of cognitive load and simultaneously indicate the relevant instructional consequences. Since relative intrinsic or extraneous cognitive load can be determined experimentally as discussed in Part IV, our inability to determine the effect of categories of cognitive load using psychometric means is not critical.

Summary

This chapter has outlined the main methods used by researchers to measure cognitive load. It has described how in the early stages of cognitive load theory, indirect methods such as error rates, time on task and computational models were used to provide evidence that various instructional effects could be explained by fluctuations in cognitive load. These indirect measures, used in conjunction with performance test scores, strengthened the theory. A significant move away from indirect measures occurred when Paas (1992) proposed a single-scale subjective measure of mental effort. This measure and its derivative (the difficulty scale), as well as measures of instructional efficiency, have been used in scores of studies and have been invaluable tools in the development of cognitive load theory. In most instances, the subjective measures have provided collaborating evidence in support of all cognitive load theory effects. Nevertheless, subjective rating scales do not provide real-time, concurrent data. They only provide an indicator of cognitive load after the event and so cannot be used to determine changes in cognitive load during learning or problem solving. An alternative measure that is able to provide concurrent data is the use of a secondary task.

Secondary tasks have been used less frequently than subjective rating scales because they tend to be more intrusive and require more complex experimental conditions and, frequently, more complex equipment. The advantage of secondary tasks, that is their ability to measure cognitive load during learning and problem solving, is also a disadvantage. They can be difficult to use. In contrast, subjective rating scales can be presented immediately after a learning or problem-solving episode and usually require no more than about 30 s to administer. Nevertheless, secondary tasks have been used successfully in cognitive load theory research to show predicted variations in cognitive load. Other simultaneous and continuous methods of determining cognitive load such as eye tracking and physiological methods such as the use of EEG data have started to emerge as potential measures but are still in the early phase of testing and yet to be proven effective.

In summary, a number of methods have been used to measure cognitive load. The subjective scale of mental effort or difficulty has had the most use and has been very successfully employed. One of its great strengths is that it is easy to use and is very unobtrusive. In contrast, attempts to subjectively measure the different types of cognitive load have been much less successful. Whereas we need to distinguish the categories of cognitive load, we seriously doubt whether psychometric techniques can meaningfully differentiate these constructs, especially when studying the learning of novices. The alternative, to use appropriate experimental designs, has repeatedly proven to be successful. Part IV discusses the results of such experiments.

Part IV
Cognitive Load Effects

The theory outlined in the previous three parts has been developed incrementally over a 30-year period. It has had a single, over-riding goal – the generation of novel, instructional procedures. The ability to generate instructional procedures provides the ultimate criterion of cognitive load theory's success or failure.

Part IV describes the instructional procedures generated by the theory. Each procedure flows from a cognitive load effect where an effect is an experimental demonstration that an instructional procedure based on cognitive load theory principles facilitates learning or problem solving compared to a more traditional procedure. The use of replicable, randomised, controlled experiments is essential to this process. Each effect discussed in Part IV has been demonstrated on multiple occasions by numerous researchers. Each demonstration consists of, at a minimum, a control condition in which learners are taught in a conventional fashion and an experimental condition that varies from the control condition on one factor and one factor only. Participants are randomly allocated to either the control or experimental condition. Most commonly, there are two phases to each experiment. During an acquisition or learning phase, learners are taught according to either a conventional, traditional procedure or according to a new procedure generated by cognitive load theory. A second phase, the test phase, follows in which all learners are presented a common test to see if there are any differences in learning outcomes. If statistical analyses on the test results demonstrate that learning has been facilitated by the new procedure, a new cognitive load effect has been demonstrated and a superior instructional procedure generated. All of the effects described in Part IV are based on this procedure or more sophisticated variants.

The generation of novel, effective instructional designs has two major consequences. First, and most obviously, we have a new, better way of organising instruction. Second, the ability of a theory to generate instructional procedures inevitably strengthens the theory. While no theory can ever be final, complete or entirely valid with all theories requiring, at the very least, revision and ultimately replacement, the ability of a theory to produce practical implications provides one of the strongest forms of validation available. Cognitive load theory has produced many instructional applications and those applications are discussed in Part IV.

Chapter 7
The Goal-Free Effect

The *goal-free* effect was the first instructional effect investigated within a cognitive load theory framework. Goal-free problems occur when a conventional problem with a specific goal is replaced by a problem with a non-specific goal. For example, in high school geometry, a typical problem will ask students to calculate a specific angle, such as angle ABC. In contrast, goal-free problems will not require students to specifically calculate this angle, but use a more general wording such as 'calculate the value of as many angles as you can'. This particular wording of the problem will still allow students to calculate the targeted angle of the conventional problem (angle ABC), but students are free to calculate as many other angles as they can, and are not required to focus on one ultimate goal. Goal-free problems are sometimes called *no-goal* problems, and the *goal-free effect* is sometimes referred to as the *goal-specificity effect*. Consider an example taken from the domain of geometry. The goal-free effect occurs when students, having solved goal-free problems with an instruction to 'calculate the value of as many angles as you can' during acquisition, demonstrate superior learning outcomes to students who have solved the equivalent, conventional problems that include a goal such as 'calculate the value of angle ABC'.

The origins of the goal-free effect partly originate from some of the early work on expertise. When novices solve a conventional problem, they will frequently work backwards from the goal to the givens using a means–ends strategy (Larkin, McDermott, Simon, & Simon, 1980a, b; Simon & Simon 1978). For example, when novices are faced with a geometry problem requiring them to find a value for angle ABC, they tend to focus on the goal and work backwards using means–ends analysis, trying to find a set of connections to the givens. In contrast, experts, using schemas held in long-term memory, know the solution and are more likely to work forward from the givens to the goal. Their schemas tell them that for this problem with these givens and this goal, this is the best set of moves.

Working backwards using a means–ends strategy requires knowledge of the goal. If we do not know the goal, we cannot work backwards from it. We can only work forwards from the givens. Furthermore, we cannot reduce differences between the goal and the givens if the goal has not been identified for us. All we can do is work forward, considering one move at a time. Why should the elimination of a means–ends strategy be beneficial?

As indicated in Chapter 5, the means–ends strategy used by novices is an effective method of solving a problem but imposes a heavy cognitive load. Problem solvers are required to simultaneously consider the problem givens, the goal, the differences between the givens and the goal and the problem-solving operators that might reduce those differences. Each of these elements interact, resulting in very high levels of element interactivity. Furthermore, if the aim of problem-solving instruction is to learn to recognise problem states and the best moves associated with each state, the high levels of element interactivity associated with means–ends analysis constitute an extraneous cognitive load that should be reduced. Working memory may be overwhelmed by a means–ends strategy, reducing or even preventing learning.

In contrast, by creating a goal-free environment, learning is not dominated by strategies to connect a goal to the givens. Instead, the learner is focused only on the present problem state and how to get to any other state. By emphasising the current state and any move that can be made from the current state, the load on working memory is reduced leaving more capacity for learning. In terms of element interactivity, instead of having to consider givens, the goal, possible differences between the givens and the goal and operators that might reduce those differences, goal-free problem solving just requires problem solvers to consider the givens and any possible move. The reduction in interacting elements can result in a reduction in extraneous cognitive load and so enhance learning.

With respect to the cognitive architecture described in Part II, goal-free problem solving by reducing working memory load (narrow limits of change principle) increases the amount of relevant information that can be transferred to long-term memory (information store principle). Once stored in long-term memory, the environmental organising and linking principle allows that information to be used to solve subsequent problems.

Support for a cognitive load explanation of the goal-free effect was provided by Sweller (1988) who used a computational model to obtain a priori information concerning cognitive load (see Chapter 6). Firstly, using the computational model to simulate cognitive processes, Sweller demonstrated that a means–ends strategy to solving simple kinematics problems required significantly more inputs and computations than a goal-free approach. Secondly, Sweller reasoned that asking students to learn through problem solving involved two processes: solving the problem and learning from the experience. If more cognitive resources were required to solve the problem using a conventional rather than goal-free approach, fewer resources would be available to learn under a conventional approach leading to the superiority of goal-free problem solving. In an experiment using trigonometry materials, Sweller compared a conventional goal approach with a goal-free approach. Over a set of problems, the goal-free group gained more knowledge about the structure of the problems than the goal-specific group. Together, the computational model and empirical data provided further understanding of the goal-free effect and supported the cognitive load explanation.

Empirical Evidence for the Goal-Free Effect

During the early development of cognitive load theory, means–ends analysis was hypothesised as a major impediment to efficient learning. Research by Mawer and Sweller (1982) and Sweller, Mawer, and Howe (1982) found that means–ends analysis did not promote rule induction or acquisition of specific procedural schemas. Although problems could be solved by using simple heuristics, little learning occurred. Preventing or reducing means–ends analysis during problem solving could be achieved by removing the goal. A study by Sweller and Levine (1982) using puzzle problems showed that students would learn more if the problem goal was removed than if the problem goal was retained. Sweller and Levine showed that problem solvers who were aware of the location of a maze problem's goal made more errors than problem solvers who did not know the goal's location. The maze could be solved by using a simple rule. Over a series of experiments, Sweller and Levine showed that the more learners knew about the goal, the less they learned about the problem structure including the solution rule. Sweller and Levine argued that those with a goal were prevented from acquiring this information because of their focus on using means–ends analysis. A further study by Sweller (1983) using maze problems and the Tower of Hanoi puzzle demonstrated that means–ends analysis also prevented transfer effects.

Following these findings using puzzle problems, Sweller, Mawer, and Ward (1983) broadened the research to school-based curricula. Firstly, Sweller et al. demonstrated the advantages of a goal-free approach using simple physics problems. In this experiment, the goal group were given traditionally worded problems such as 'find the distance travelled by the racing car', whereas the goal-free group were instructed to 'calculate the value of as many variables as you can'. Results indicated that the goal-free group more readily switched to a forward-working strategy rather than continuing to use means–ends analysis on subsequent problems. Students in this goal-free group also used equations differently to the goal group. Instead of simply writing down the equations, a feature of the goal group, the goal-free group wrote down the equations with completed substitutions of the given values. The ability to write down equations and simultaneously substitute into them provided evidence of a reduction in cognitive load. Sweller et al. also found similar differences in strategy use with geometry problems.

Further evidence for the effectiveness of a goal-free approach came from Owen and Sweller (1985) using trigonometry problems. A conventional textbook approach simply asks mathematics students to calculate the length of a side of a geometric figure. To carry out this calculation, students may first have to find the length of another side acting as a subgoal. The problem solution may require two steps whereby the subgoal has to be calculated before the goal can be found. To turn this problem into a goal-free format, it only is necessary for the instructions to be modified to: 'Calculate all the unknown sides in the diagram'. The advantage of the goal-free approach is that students can start calculating values immediately without first finding a specific solution path by working backwards from the goal. Students do need prior knowledge of the trigonometric ratios (tangent, sine and cosine) to solve goal-free problems in this domain, but such problems do not impose the additional working memory load associated with a search for solution paths that a specific goal demands. All students have to do is find a side that fits a trigonometrical equation where the other variables are known. Once the initial calculations are made, further calculations can be made using the newly calculated values. The elimination of the interacting elements associated with searching for a solution path can substantially reduce extraneous cognitive load.

In the Owen and Sweller (1985) study, one group of students who completed goal-free problems during a learning acquisition phase were compared with a goal group who completed conventional problems with a specific goal. Total acquisition time was kept constant. Results indicated that during acquisition, the goal-free group calculated twice as many sides as the goal group, but with a significantly reduced error rate. On a post-acquisition test, where both groups were given conventional test problems, the goal-free group was five times as accurate as the goal group. Furthermore, it was found that students in the goal-free group were better able to transfer their knowledge to structurally different problems.

Trigonometry problems of the type discussed above are classified as transformation problems because they have an initial state, a goal state and a set of operators to transform the givens into the goal state (Greeno, 1978). Many problems requiring geometrical figures have these features and are also likely to be solved using means–ends analysis by novice learners in the domain.

Ayres and Sweller (1990) obtained direct evidence from verbal protocols of high school students that means–ends analysis was used with transformation problems in geometry. Furthermore, they found that students made significantly more errors calculating the subgoal angle compared with the goal angle. This finding provided direct evidence that locating and calculating the subgoal using means–ends analysis was more demanding on working memory than calculating the goal. A later study by Ayres (1993) showed that a goal-free approach alleviated this problem associated with the subgoal. Ayres constructed a geometry problem set in which it was only possible to calculate two angles, a goal angle and a subgoal angle. A goal group (find a value for angle X) was compared with a goal-free group (find as many unknown angles as possible). Because of the structure of the problems, both groups could only find the same angles and the problem space was identical. However, results indicated the goal-free group made significantly fewer errors than the goal group. By preventing means–ends analysis, goal-free students were able to adopt a different problem-solving strategy in a short space of time.

Bobis, Sweller, and Cooper (1994) collected further information on the goal-free effect in the geometry domain with primary-school students. In learning paper folding tasks, students were given a sheet of paper and instructions on how to fold the paper into a particular geometric shape. Students were either provided no further help (goal-free) or a physical model of the final desired shape (goal group). It was predicted that the physical model would be equivalent to having a goal. Results indicated that the goal-free group learned the paper folding steps significantly better than the group who were provided with the finished model. It may be assumed that the presence of the finished model enticed the students to work backwards from the final state using means–ends analysis.

Ayres (1998) conducted a further study in the mathematics domain by using problems that required consecutive uses of the Pythagorean theorem. A two-step trigonometry problem was used in which a subgoal had to be calculated before a side, acting as the goal, could be calculated. Results again indicated that the goal-free approach facilitated learning compared to conventional problems.

Paas, Camp, and Rikers (2001) investigated how goal specificity interacted with age. Using maze-tracing problems, Paas et al. compared a goal-free strategy (invisible goal) with a goal strategy (visible goal) using younger adults (mean age of 20 years) and older adults (mean age of 72 years). The younger adults outperformed the older ones, but the goal-free strategy was found to be helpful for both groups. On such performance characteristics as the number of steps to solution and time taken, the goal-free groups were superior to the goal groups. An important interaction was also observed indicating that use of a goal-free strategy decreased the performance difference between the two age ranges. In the goal condition, a large difference was found between the two age ranges, but this difference narrowed in the goal-free condition. This result suggests that a goal-free approach may be even more useful for older rather than younger adults. Paas et al. argued that working memory capabilities decrease with age, and thus using goal-specific strategies like means–ends analysis with its heavy demands on working memory may be particularly deleterious. In contrast, a goal-free approach allows more working memory resources to be directly devoted to learning.

Miller, Lehman, and Koedinger (1999) used an interactive game called Electric Field Hockey that simulated the movement of an electrically charged particle. Three different strategies were compared: (a) a goal-free condition where students were asked to 'experiment' and 'learn to understand the game's properties in any way you feel fit'; (b) a goal condition where students played a game where they had to reach a specific goal, which became progressively more difficult over a series of trials; (c) a specific-path condition which had the same task as the goal condition, but in which a worked example of a solution path was shown.

On relevant tests of physics principles simulated by the game, results indicated that both the goal-free and specific-path groups outperformed the goal group, but there was no difference between the former two groups. Thus, a goal-free effect was demonstrated along with a worked example effect (Chapter 8) in which worked examples proved superior to conventional problems. As will be shown in Chapter 8, worked examples are a highly effective alternative to problem solving with a fixed goal.

Alternative Explanations of the Goal-Free Effect

A Dual-Space Explanation

In a set of studies, Vollmeyer, Burns and colleagues also obtained a goal-free effect, but have provided an alternative explanation for the effect, based on dual-space theory. Simon and Lea (1974) proposed that a problem space can be divided into a *rule* space in which hypotheses and solution rules are formulated and tested and an *instance* space in which problem-solving moves are made. Vollmeyer, Burns, and Holyoak (1996) argued that different types of goals could encourage different types of strategies. Setting a specific goal may encourage use of a non-productive strategy such as means–ends analysis that does not emphasise a search for rules because it involves searching the instance space only. In contrast, a non-specific goal encourages a search for rules and hypotheses in the rule space. In other words, it was argued that goal specificity generates different types of strategies and not differences in cognitive load.

This formulation is plausible and also compatible with cognitive load theory. The reason learners search an instance space and ignore a rule space during means–ends analysis is, according to cognitive load theory, because working memory is fully occupied in searching the instance space leaving no resources available to search the rule space. If the rule space is not searched, rules cannot be learned. During goal-free problem solving, an emphasis on the rule space rather than the instance space eliminates this problem because working memory resources are directed to the rule space. A superiority of goal-free over conventional problem solving is the net result.

Vollmeyer et al. (1996) extended the research on the goal-free effect to a biology-based, complex, dynamic system, using a computer-driven simulation to construct a biological environment. A cover story indicated that there was a tank containing four types of sea creatures (crabs, prawns, lobsters and sea bass), which were affected by four input variables (temperature, salt, oxygen and current). The outputs of the system, the number of each species, were governed by various relationships with the input variables. The main task was for students to discover the rules governing these relationships. According to Vollmeyer et al., this biology lab task could be approached in two different ways. Either students could try to bring the system to a particular goal state by manipulating the input variables in order to reduce the difference between the current output state and the goal state (a means–ends strategy), or they could apply hypothesis testing to try to discover the rules of the system. Two groups were formed to align with these strategies. The students in the conventional, or goal group, were told that they had to manipulate the system to get a specific goal, whereas the goal-free group were told to explore the system. Test results indicated that the goal-free learners spent less time during acquisition, but scored higher on post-acquisition tasks, including transfer. Furthermore, goal-free students were more likely to use a strategy that varied one input variable at a time – an essential method in scientific research.

Vollmeyer and Burns conducted two further studies linking a dual-space argument to the goal-free effect. In the first study, Vollmeyer and Burns (2002) used hypermedia materials to extend the research into a very different type of learning environment. In this study, students had to learn about the cause of World War I. Participants in the goal group were required to focus on 20 specific events and dates while exploring the provided hyperlinks. The goal-free group was free to explore the hyperlinks without reference to those events. Tests of various types of knowledge revealed a significant goal-free effect with the goal-free group learning more facts, making more inferences and having a better understanding of the main theme.

In their second study, Burns and Vollmeyer (2002) collected verbal protocols in order to find more conclusive evidence in support of a dual-space explanation. In this study, they used a linear system of inputs and outputs similar to Vollmeyer et al. (1996), but the system simulated the control of water quality and was less complex. They again demonstrated the goal-free effect. The protocol analysis found that students in the goal-free group who were operating within a rule space tended to emphasise hypothesis testing, whereas the goal group who were operating within an instance space were more goal-orientated.

Geddes and Stevenson (1997) also used a dual-space theoretical argument in a goal-specificity study. Using a task designed by Berry and Broadbent (1984) participants were required to interact with a computer-generated person. The main aim of the task was to try to get the person to reach a required attitude state like 'very polite'. A chain of interactions would be required before the state was reached. Underlying this interaction was a particular pattern that the students had to discover to reach the desired state. In a three-group design, a goal group was told specifically to get the person to a certain state, a goal-free group was told to identify the pattern that generated the person's reaction and a dual-goal group was told to both shift the person to a certain level and identify the pattern, thus incorporating elements of both other groups. Over a series of trials, the goal-free group outperformed both of the other groups on test problems and questions of declarative knowledge. It was clear from the fine-grained analyses conducted in this study that the two groups with a specific goal did not learn the rule guiding the computer's behaviour. Geddes and Stevenson concluded that a specific goal leads to a focus on an instance space with inadequate use of the rule space.

Osman (2008) used the complex dynamic control task on water quality developed by Burns and Vollmeyer (2002) to not only investigate the goal-specificity effect, but also to examine differences between learning by observation and learning by action. During a learning phase, students either observed the manipulation of various inputs and their corresponding outputs, or directly manipulated the inputs themselves. In a 2 (goal or goal-free) × 2 (observation or action) design, Osman replicated the findings of Burns and Vollmeyer, showing that the goal-free groups scored higher during the learning phase and on post-acquisition tests targeting knowledge of procedural control and causal structure. Interestingly, no difference was found between the groups who learned by observation and those who learned by action. A goal-free advantage was obtained irrespective of whether learners solved problems themselves or observed the moves made by someone else either solving a conventional problem or solving a goal-free problem. This result suggested that with such complex dynamic control tasks, observation is just as effective as learning 'by doing'. Osman also concluded from the collected evidence about acquired procedural and declarative knowledge that hypothesis testing within a rule space was more likely to generate knowledge in this domain than the procedural tasks associated with controlling the inputs within an instance space.

In conclusion, studies testing the hypothesis that the goal-free effect is a consequence of problem solvers attending to an instance space rather than a rule space have provided some evidence in favour of this hypothesis. Nevertheless, it can be argued that an emphasis on the instance space prevents attention to the rule space. This argument leads directly to a limited working memory explanation proposed by cognitive load theory. Our limited working memory, according to this argument, prevents us from attending to both an instance and a rule space simultaneously.

An Attentional Focus Explanation

Trumpower, Goldsmith, and Guynn (2004) used an attentional focus explanation to explain the goal-free effect. They argued that under goal-free conditions, attention is more focused on the current problem state and possible moves. As a result, a number of local relations are acquired based on learning the relationships between any given state and the variables (givens and knowns) that allow progress to the next state. In contrast, with a specific goal, the focus is on trying to link the current state with the final goal state, leading to knowledge about how the variables link with the goal state, but not about how the variables relate to each other. Consequently, a goal-free approach is more likely to lead to knowledge about local relations rather than just relations with one goal.

To test this hypothesis in the learning domain of statistics, Trumpower et al. (2004) measured structural knowledge, which is the knowledge about the interrelationships between the domain concepts (based on the work of Goldsmith, Johnson, & Acton, 1991). To measure structural knowledge, participants were asked to rate the relatedness of pairs of statistical concepts. A computer algorithm was then used to calculate a network representation of each participant's structural knowledge. Through the analysis of these networks it was possible to ascertain whether problem solvers formed more links with the goal state or generated more local relations. Experimental results indicated a goal-free effect. On the structural knowledge indicator, the goal-free group made more local links and less goal links than the goal group.

Both the theory and results described by Trumpower et al. (2004) are interesting. It is plausible to suggest that the goal-free effect is caused by problem solvers establishing local links rather than links to the goal. Cognitive load theory has assumed that learners are more likely to acquire schemas under goal-free than conventional goal conditions. Schemas allow learners to recognise problem states along with the best moves associated with each state. Acquiring local structural knowledge is very similar to the process of schema acquisition. Acquiring links to the goal is likely to interfere with local structural knowledge because of our limited working memory. If we are acquiring links to the goal, we may have insufficient working memory resources to simultaneously attend to local links. We assume that limitations in attentional resources can be explained by the limited capacity of working memory. In other words, a limited working memory capacity and limited attentional resources constitute different terminology for the same constructs.

A Subjective Measure of Cognitive Load and the Goal-Free Effect

Ultimately, whether the goal-free effect is due to a reduction in extraneous cognitive load or due to other possibly related factors can be determined by measuring cognitive load. Most studies of the goal-free effect have not collected direct measures of cognitive load. As an exception, the production system model used by Sweller (1988) provided a priori, indirect measures of cognitive load. Many of the other cognitive load effects described in the following chapters have been extensively investigated using cognitive load measures. However, most of the studies of the goal-free effect were conducted prior to the systematic use of subjective measures of cognitive load (see Chapter 6). One exception was a study by Wirth, Künsting, and Leutner (2009) who used subjective measures of cognitive load based on the NASA-TLX instrument (task load index, Hart & Staveland, 1988). The main aim of the Wirth et al. study was to investigate the goal-free effect on tasks that either had problem-solving goals or those that had learning goals. In the case of specific problem-solving goals, it was argued that they generated a pure problem-solving strategy, whereas non-specific goals generated a learning strategy. However, if there are specific learning goals indicated, a learning strategy will be triggered regardless of goal-specificity. Using a computer-based science learning tasks, the same materials were developed that emphasised either problem-solving or learning goals under conventional goal or goal-free conditions. Results indicated a goal-free effect for learning goals but not for problem-solving goals, as predicted by the researchers. Perhaps more importantly, cognitive load measures indicated that the goal-specific groups experienced greater cognitive load than goal-free groups. This finding supports a cognitive load interpretation of the goal-free effect.

Conditions of Applicability

The evidence described in this chapter suggests that presenting goal-free rather than goal-specific problems creates an effective learning environment. Goal-free tasks are effective because they reduce means–ends problem-solving strategies and the extraneous cognitive load associated with trying to achieve a specific goal. Further, they facilitate rule induction and the acquisition of schematic knowledge because learners are able to focus on more localised relations connected to a particular problem state instead of referring to a goal. Reference to a goal may be critical during problem solving but not during learning. The various studies described in this chapter indicate that a goal-free strategy is effective in transformation problems with a limited problem space that involves only a limited number of possible moves. In situations with a more extensive problem space, goal-free problems are less likely to be useful because of the large number of possible moves available. Many of those possible moves may not be important resulting in learning that is less relevant to actual instructional goals.

Instructional Implications

Research on the goal-free effect has clear implications for instruction. Under a number of conditions, using goal-free problems represents a very effective alternative to problem solving with a fixed goal. Conventional problem solving, particularly for novices in a domain, should be avoided because of the extraneous cognitive load created by search strategies such as means–ends analysis. A significant advantage of using goal-free problems is that conventional goal-specific problems can easily be adapted to a goal-free format simply by removing reference to a specific goal and providing a simple instruction such as: 'find all of the unknowns you can'. Goal-free problems, when used appropriately, may provide significant benefits.

Conclusions

The goal-free effect was the first effect generated by cognitive load theory, following early work with mazes and other puzzle problems. Although a very simple and highly effective method to counteract the negative influence on learning of using search-based problem-solving strategies such as a means–ends analysis, the goal-free effect has been overshadowed by the worked example effect that similarly reduces the use of search-based problem-solving strategies during learning (see Chapter 8). Nevertheless, in a limited number of domains, usually involving transformation problems and focused on mathematics and science concepts, a goal-free strategy has significantly improved learning outcomes, including transfer. Provided the problem space is fairly constrained, eliminating the interacting elements associated with irrelevant search and unnecessary rule induction, a goal-free strategy may be a very useful technique to facilitate learning.

Chapter 8
The Worked Example and Problem Completion Effects

A *worked example* provides a step-by-step solution to a problem. The following is an example from algebra:

Make a the subject of the equation, $(a+b)/c = d$.

Solution

$$(a+b)/c = d$$
$$a+b = dc$$
$$a = dc - b$$

Learners can be presented this worked example to study. Alternatively, they can be asked to solve a problem. Learners asked to solve a problem are just presented the first line of the above worked example, 'Make a the subject of the equation, $(a+b)/c = d$'. The worked example effect occurs when learners presented worked examples to study perform better on subsequent test problems than learners asked to solve the equivalent problem.

The worked example effect flows directly from the cognitive architecture discussed in the initial parts of this book. Worked examples can efficiently provide us with the problem-solving schemas that need to be stored in long-term memory using the information store principle. Once stored in long-term memory, we can use the stored schemas to solve related problems using the environmental organising and linking principle. Those schemas are borrowed from the long-term memory of the provider of the worked example by way of the borrowing and reorganising principle. Worked examples impose a relatively low working memory load (narrow limits of change principle) compared to solving problems using means–ends search. While all the necessary, intrinsic interacting elements are encapsulated in the information contained within a worked example, solving a problem by means–ends search adds the additional elements associated with the randomness as genesis principle. That principle unnecessarily adds problem-solving search to the interacting elements, thus imposing an extraneous cognitive load. Together, these various mechanisms of cognitive load theory suggest that for novice learners, studying worked examples should be superior to solving the equivalent problems. There is a wealth of evidence supporting this hypothesis collected by researchers from around the globe.

J. Sweller et al., *Cognitive Load Theory*, Explorations in the Learning Sciences, Instructional Systems and Performance Technologies 1, DOI 10.1007/978-1-4419-8126-4_8, © Springer Science+Business Media, LLC 2011

Atkinson, Derry, Renkl, and Wortham (2000) observed there is no precise definition of a worked example but there are a number of common features found across the different types. Most worked examples include a problem statement and procedure for solving the problem. By studying a worked example, students are able to learn key aspects about the problem and use those aspects to solve other problems. As Atkinson et al. (2000) further remark 'In a sense, they provide an expert's problem-solving model for the learner to study and emulate' (p. 181). A number of different synonyms have been applied to worked examples such as learning from examples, example-based learning, learning from model answers and studying expert solutions.

Basic Empirical Evidence

Worked examples are not a recent innovation as teachers, particularly in mathematics and science, have used them extensively over a long period of time. However, as will become evident below, there are optimal ways of presenting worked examples. A traditional textbook approach in mathematics and science, when learning new concepts and procedures, is to present some initial worked examples and then ask students to practice what they have learned in a more extensive exercise including unfamiliar problems. Typically, under some conditions, students may only be shown further worked examples after failing to find solutions to some of the problems. Frequently, worked examples are not even used when students fail to solve a problem. Under such circumstances, learners are still required to spend a significant time on problem solving. As described in Chapter 7, problem solving via means–ends analysis requires problem solvers to process a large number of interacting elements and can create an extraneous cognitive load that inhibits learning. Even though some exposure to worked examples is used in most traditional instructional procedures, worked examples, to be most effective, need to be used much more systematically and consistently to reduce the influence of extraneous problem-solving demands.

Research into worked examples has a long history. Atkinson et al. (2000) reported that as far back as the 1950s, researchers used learning-by-example strategies to investigate the processes involved in concept formation. Whereas cognitive load theory researchers have also focused on concept or schema formation, many of their studies have explicitly compared worked example approaches to learning with a problem-solving approach. These comparisons have led to the identification of the worked example effect.

Worked Examples in Mathematics and Related Domains

Early evidence for the worked example effect came from studies involving the learning of mathematics. Sweller and Cooper (1985) used algebraic manipulation problems (e.g. for the equation $a = af + c$, express a in terms of the other variables) to show that worked examples required less time to process than solving the equivalent, conventional problems during acquisition, and led to quicker solutions times and lower error rates on similar test problems. The experimental design used in this study, which became a blueprint for many following studies, directly compared a worked example group with a conventional problem-solving group. Initially, both groups of high school students (Year 9) were presented a limited number of worked examples of the new material to be learned, in this case, solutions to algebra manipulation problems. This introductory phase was followed by the main learning acquisition phase. For the worked example group, students were presented a set of problem pairs consisting of a worked example to study and then immediately after, a similar problem to solve. This example–problem pair format was repeated several times with different problems to form the acquisition problem set. The conventional group was presented the same problem set but was required to solve all the problems, as students were not given any worked examples to study during this phase. In this design, the worked example group was asked to solve half the number of problems that the conventional group had to solve, but was also asked to study worked solutions to the other half. Following acquisition, both groups were presented a set of test problems to solve without the inclusion of any worked examples.

While Sweller and Cooper (1985) found improved test performance by the worked example group on problems similar to the acquisition problems, they failed to find evidence of transfer. The worked example group did not have an advantage over the conventional group on dissimilar problems. In a follow up study, Cooper and Sweller (1987) set out to investigate the conditions under which worked examples could facilitate transfer. They ran a series of experiments using both algebra manipulation problems and word problems to test the hypothesis that in order for transfer to take place, automation of problem-solving operators is necessary.

Rule or schema automation allows a procedure to be used with minimal working memory resources (Chapter 2). For example, we may be able to multiply out a denominator in a fractional algebraic equation automatically without actively thinking about the process. In contrast, when first learning to multiply out a denominator, we may need to consider the process every time we use it. Automation means working memory resources are available for other activities during problem solving. If we are presented with a novel problem that requires a denominator to be multiplied out, we can devote working memory resources to finding a solution rather than attempting to recall how the relevant rule works. In this manner, if worked examples facilitate automation more than solving the equivalent problems, transfer should be facilitated resulting in transfer effects.

However, automation takes place slowly and therefore requires substantial acquisition time, which the previous Sweller and Cooper (1985) study did not provide. In contrast, the Cooper and Sweller (1987) experiments provided extra learning time, enabling the worked example group to demonstrate significant transfer effects compared with the conventional group. Cooper and Sweller concluded that in any complex domain, significant acquisition time is required to automate the required problem-solving operators to demonstrate transfer. Worked examples were found to accelerate this process compared with a problem-solving approach.

A later study by Carroll (1994) found that worked examples were particularly helpful for students with a history of low achievement in mathematics and those identified as learning disabled. Pillay (1994) extended the research into the use of worked examples in mathematics by showing the advantage of using worked examples over problem solving when learning 2D and 3D mental rotations. Paas (1992) using statistics problems and Paas and van Merriënboer (1994) using geometry problems found strong evidence for the worked example effect. Paas' (1992) work will be discussed in more detail when discussing the completion effect in this chapter while Paas and van Merriënboer's (1994) work will be discussed further in Chapter 16 when discussing the variability effect.

Worked Examples and Ill-Structured Learning Domains

The bulk of research on the worked example effect has used well-structured problems from mathematics or science domains rather than ill-structured problems requiring natural language, humanities or other areas related to artistic endeavours. A well-structured problem is one in which we can clearly specify the various problem states and the problem-solving operators (e.g. the rules of algebra) required to move from one state to another. Ill-structured problems do not have clearly specified problem states or problem-solving operators. 'Discuss the meaning of this passage' provides an example of an ill-structured problem.

It has been suggested by some (e.g. Spiro & DeSchryver, 2009) that the worked example effect cannot be obtained using ill-structured problems. In fact there are theoretical reasons to suppose that the cognitive activities involved in both solving and learning to solve ill-structured problems are identical to those required to solve well-structured problems (Greeno, 1976). The cognitive architecture discussed in the previous parts does not distinguish between well-structured and ill-structured problems and there is no reason to suppose we have a different architecture to deal these differing categories of problems. We must acquire schematically based knowledge that allows us to recognise problem types and the categories of solution moves to solve particular categories of problems irrespective of whether the problems are well structured or ill structured. The solution variations available for ill-structured problems are larger than for well-structured problems but they are not infinite and experts have learned more of the possible variations than novices. Of course, the ultimate test is whether the worked example effect can be obtained using ill-structured problems.

In a review of worked examples, Renkl (2005) made a number of insightful comments and recommendations on future research into worked examples. One point made was that they could be 'relevant only to a limited range of domains' (p. 241). Renkl argued that they seem to be particularly suited to skill domains where algorithms can be applied, i.e. well-structured problems. He commented further that in areas such as writing a text or interpreting a poem, the essential strength of worked examples in showing solution steps may not be present. As indicated above, the vast majority of the experiments described so far in this chapter have used algorithmic-based domains such as mathematics, science and computing. Nevertheless, in recent years, an increasing amount of research has been conducted within a cognitive load theory framework in more ill-defined domains. For example although not directly testing the worked example effect (there were no problem-solving groups), Owens and Sweller (2008) demonstrated that music instruction could be effectively formatted using worked examples. Similarly Diao and Sweller (2007) and Diao, Chandler, and Sweller (2007) used worked examples in the domain of second language learning.

Three studies of particular note have demonstrated the worked example effect in ill-defined problem areas. Firstly, Rourke and Sweller (2009) required university students to learn to recognise particular designers' styles from the early Modernist period using chair designs. It was found that a worked example approach was superior to problem solving in recognising these designs. Furthermore the worked example effect extended to transfer tasks in the form of other designs, based on stained glass windows and cutlery.

Secondly, in two experiments, Oksa, Kalyuga, and Chandler (2010) presented novices (Grade 10 students) with extracts from Shakespearean plays. One group was given explanatory notes integrated into the original text, whereas a second group had no such notes. Results indicated that the explanatory notes group outperformed the unsupported group on a comprehension task and reported a lower cognitive load. The design of the Oksa et al. experiments does not fit the traditional worked example alternation format of study–solve problem pairs because these experiments were part of a wider study on the expertise reversal effect (see Chapter 12). Nevertheless, half of the students were provided model answers or interpretations to key aspects of the text. Those model answers are equivalent to problem solutions. In contrast, students with no explanatory notes were required to make their own interpretations, an activity equivalent to problem solving. The fact that the model answers resulted in more learning than requiring students to make their own interpretations in this very ill-structured domain provides strong evidence that the worked example effect is applicable to ill-structured problem domains.

Thirdly, Kyun, Kalyuga, and Sweller (in preparation) also demonstrated the worked example effect in learning English literature. More- and less-knowledgeable Korean university students for whom English was a foreign language were used in another study on the expertise reversal effect (Chapter 12). During the learning phase, half of the students were presented conventional essay questions that they were asked to answer. The other half of the students were presented the same questions along with model answers that they were asked to study, followed by similar questions that they had to answer themselves. All students then were asked to answer retention, near and far transfer tests. The less-knowledgeable students in the worked example group were rated by markers as having performed better on the problems of the learning phase. Even though there were no significant effects for transfer tests, for the retention test, the worked example group performed significantly better than the conventional problem-solving group. Again, the worked example effect was demonstrated using an ill-structured problem.

Worked Examples in Non-Laboratory-Based Experiments

The early research into worked examples described above was conducted under controlled laboratory-style conditions. Evidence also emerged that a worked examples approach could be implemented effectively on a much wider scale and under everyday classroom conditions. In a longitudinal study with Chinese students, Zhu and Simon (1987) showed that worked examples could be successfully substituted for lectures and other traditional mathematics classroom activities over a prolonged period. They found that a mathematics course that was traditionally taught in 3 years could be completed in 2 years with enhanced performance using a comprehensive strategy based on worked examples.

   Although not as extensive as the Zhu and Simon study, other studies have also been conducted within realistic learning settings. For example, a critical aspect of the Ward and Sweller (1990) study was that students studied worked examples during homework as part of a normal class. Carroll (1994) also administered a similar homework procedure. In both cases, a worked example effect was found.

Worked Examples and the Alternation Strategy

In most of the studies described above worked examples were presented in an example–problem pair format. During acquisition, pairs of similar problems were presented as the main learning vehicle. This methodology of pairing by studying a worked example and solving a similar problem was first adopted by Sweller and Cooper (1985). They created this alternation strategy on motivational grounds. It was assumed that students would be more motivated to study the worked example if they knew that they had to solve a similar problem immediately afterwards. Sweller and Cooper were concerned initially that students would not necessarily process the information in a worked example at a sufficient depth to assist schema acquisition if each worked example was not followed immediately by a similar problem to solve, and therefore created the study–solve strategy, that other researchers adopted.

   To test the effectiveness of the alternation strategy, Trafton and Reiser (1993) completed a study that included blocked practice and alternating practice. Two types of blocked practice were included: study a set of several examples and then solve a similar set of problems, or solve a set of problems and then solve a set of similar problems. In addition, there were two types of alternating practice: Study an example and then immediately solve a similar problem, or solve a problem and immediately solve a second similar problem. Trafton and Reiser found that for an example to be most effective, it had to be accompanied by a problem to solve. The most efficient method of studying examples and solving problems was to present a worked example and then immediately follow this example by asking the learner to solve a similar problem. This efficient technique was, in fact, identical to the method used by Sweller and Cooper (1985) and followed in many other studies.

It was notable that the method of showing students a set of worked examples followed later by a similar set of problems to solve led to the worst learning outcomes.

The Problem Completion Effect

The worked example effect is related to several other important instructional effects. Some of those effects were discovered while studying the worked example effect. The split-attention, redundancy, modality, expertise reversal, guidance fading and variability effects will be discussed in other chapters but the problem completion effect will be discussed in this chapter because it is closely related to the worked example effect.

One early concern about the use of worked examples was that they led to *passive* rather than more *active* learning. Would learners attend to and study the worked examples in enough depth or would they simply gloss over them? Furthermore, evidence had emerged that students may only study worked examples in depth if they find difficulty in solving conventional problems (Chi, Bassok, Lewis, Reimann, & Glaser, 1989). These issues suggest that learners may need to know that they have a similar problem to solve in order to fully process the example. As previously discussed, the paired alternation strategy (study an example–solve a problem) was developed to address this issue. Another strategy to ensure learners paid sufficient attention to the worked examples was to provide learners with completion problems (van Merriënboer & Krammer 1987). A completion problem is a partial worked example where the learner has to complete some key solution steps. The algebra worked example presented at the beginning of this chapter can be converted to a completion problem by only demonstrating the first step and then requiring learners to work out the second step themselves, as the following example indicates:

Make a the subject of the equation, $(a+b)/c = d$.

Solution

$$(a+b)/c = d$$
$$a+b = dc$$
$$a = ?$$

Van Merriënboer (1990) conducted the first extensive study on completion problems within a cognitive load theory paradigm using an introductory computer-programming course. Over a period of ten lessons, students followed either a conventional strategy in which they were asked to design and code new computer programs or a completion strategy that required the modification and extension of existing computer programs. It was found that the completion group was superior at subsequently constructing new programs, providing an example of the completion effect.

Van Merriënboer and de Croock (1992) also conducted a similar study with computer-programming content. A generation (conventional) group was compared with a completion group in learning about programming techniques. Results indicated superior learning by the completion group. When using a completion strategy, the presentation of new information and programming practice were linked to incomplete programs and learners were only required to complete the partial solutions, whereas the generation strategy presented both model programs and generation assignments. Although the model programs could be considered as worked examples, the experimental design was such that students did not necessarily need to study them immediately. Data indicated that the conventional group frequently had to search for examples while solving their problems. In this learning domain, computer programs are very complex; consequently asking students to generate new programs may cause a high working memory load, which is intensified by the need for learners to search for, and refer back to, equally complex model programs, thus creating a high extraneous cognitive load. Extraneous cognitive load is reduced by presenting learners with appropriate worked examples prior to problem solving so that they do not have to search for examples while problem solving. These two studies (van Merriënboer, 1990; van Merriënboer & de Croock, 1992) illustrated that worked examples that have many solution steps may themselves generate additional extraneous load, but it can be offset by using completion problems.

Paas (1992) expanded this research by comparing three groups (conventional problem solving, worked example and completion problems) in learning about elementary statistical concepts. Results indicated that both the worked example and completion groups had superior outcomes to the conventional group on both near and far transfer tasks, and also required less mental effort. A later study by van Merriënboer, Schuurman, de Croock, and Paas (2002a) found that completion problem superiority may be limited to far transfer effects, although it was also demonstrated that a conventional condition created more cognitive load and was less efficient than a completion approach.

To explain the effectiveness of completion problems, Sweller (1999) argued that the inclusion of an element of problem solving could ensure that learners consider the problem in sufficient depth to attend to key information. By avoiding full problem solving, working memory is not overloaded. In order to complete the problem, the learner must attend to and process the worked-out part and then respond to the incomplete steps. Completion problems are a hybrid, including elements of both a worked example and a problem to be solved (Clark, Nguyen, & Sweller, 2006). The completion effect was the first alternative to the standard format for worked examples.

Critiques of the Use of Worked Examples

The worked example effect has been criticised with the suggestion that it only is obtained because of the use of an inappropriate control group (Koedinger & Aleven, 2007). Under problem-solving conditions testing for the worked example effect, students usually are asked to solve problems without any kind of support. In contrast, computer-based, problem-solving tutors frequently provide support when learners fail to solve a problem by indicating appropriate steps. In this manner, an equivalent of worked example steps may be presented after or during problem-solving failure rather than prior to a problem being presented for solution. It can be argued that this type of supported problem solving may constitute a more appropriate control group for worked examples.

It is true that most studies demonstrating the worked example effect have used problem-solving control groups with little or no support. Learners were simply required to solve problems after a limited introduction to a new topic with no support while solving the problem. In defence of this procedure, these conditions mirror common practices in educational institutions as well as being recommended by problem-solving advocates. One merely has to inspect any commonly used textbook in mathematics or science and peruse the long lists of problems presented to learners with minimal numbers of worked examples to obtain an indication of commonly used procedures. Students are required to learn by solving large numbers of problems.

As it happens, even if problem solving is supported in a computer-based environment, studying worked examples is still superior. Schwonke, Renkl, Krieg, Wittwer, Aleven, and Salden (2009) found that the worked example effect was still present in a well-supported problem-solving domain using a computer-based, cognitive tutor. Studying worked examples provides one of the best, possibly the best, means of learning how to solve problems in a novel domain.

Other criticisms of the use of worked examples have tended to be more ideologically driven. Constructivists in particular tend to consider worked examples to be a form of knowledge transmission, devoid of active learning and devoid of much-valued problem-solving experience. Of course, whether learning is active is unrelated to the physical activity of learners. One can be just as mentally active when studying a worked example as when solving a problem. It is the cognitive consequences of the activity that matters. Based on the borrowing and reorganising principle (see Chapter 3), activity that results in the acquisition of information from others is a very efficient way of learning and should not be down-played. Worked examples reduce extraneous cognitive load and can substantially increase the effectiveness of learning. As Kirschner, Sweller, and Clark (2006) pointed out, the use of discovery learning and problem solving during learning have a very weak research and theoretical base in contrast to the use of worked examples.

Conditions of Applicability

There is substantial evidence that learners, particularly those in the initial stages of cognitive skill acquisition, benefit more from studying worked examples than an equivalent episode of problem solving. Nevertheless, we need to remember that worked examples are effective because they reduce extraneous cognitive load. It is all too easy to assume that worked examples are effective because they are worked examples. A badly structured worked example presented to learners may be no more effective or even less effective than solving the equivalent problem. If extraneous cognitive load is not reduced compared to problem solving, the use of worked examples will not be effective.

The conditions under which worked examples are effective depend on the characteristics of the material and the characteristics of the learner. All of the effects discussed in the following chapters are concerned with the manner in which instruction should be presented to particular categories of learners. Many of those effects apply directly to the use of worked examples as well as other forms of instruction. In particular, the split-attention, modality, redundancy, expertise reversal, guidance fading, element interactivity, self-explanation and imagination effects apply to worked examples as well as other forms of instruction. The factors associated with these effects all need to be considered when constructing worked examples and will be outlined in the following chapters.

Instructional Implications

The research on the worked example effect has some very clear implications for instruction. Asking students to problem solve, particularly those learning new concepts and procedures (novices in the domain), creates an extraneous cognitive load that is detrimental to learning. Instead there should be a systematic process of using worked examples in the sense that worked examples should be programmed to include the alternation strategy (or a guidance fading strategy discussed in Chapter 13) and consist of extensive practice prior to solving sets of problems unaided.

Critics of cognitive load theory have tended to treat worked examples as a form of passive learning. Studying worked examples can be passive but passivity can be easily avoided. The use of example–problem pairs provides a simple technique that avoids passive learning, as do completion problems and guidance fading. As the weight of research evidence has become more compelling, worked examples have become more prominent in education communities. For example, a recent US Department of Education document recommended an emphasis on worked examples (Pashler et al., 2007).

Conclusions

In over 25 years of cognitive load theory–based research the worked example effect has been shown to be very robust. Compelling evidence indicates that learners have a decided advantage in studying worked examples rather than solving equivalent problems.

Arguably, the worked example effect is the most important of the cognitive load theory effects. It has certainly been the most widely investigated. While the effect originated from cognitive load theory, the theory itself subsequently has been influenced by findings associated with the comparison of studying worked examples or solving problems. For example, the emphasis on the borrowing and reorganising principle in the current, evolutionary version of cognitive load theory relies heavily on the existence of the worked example effect. Furthermore, the effect can be difficult to explain by theories that place an emphasis on discovering or constructing information as opposed to obtaining that information from instructors (Kirschner, Sweller, & Clark, 2006).

The worked example effect has given rise to many other cognitive load theory effects, discussed in some of the subsequent chapters. The next chapter considers the split-attention effect, an effect that is critical to the effectiveness of worked examples.

Chapter 9
The Split-Attention Effect

The split-attention effect arose from the worked example effect following the discovery that worked examples with a particular format were relatively ineffective (Tarmizi & Sweller, 1988). Worked examples are valuable because they reduce extraneous cognitive load compared to solving the equivalent problems but, of course, it is unlikely that all worked examples, irrespective of their structure and function, will be equally effective. Indeed, some worked examples are likely to be ineffective because their format itself imposes a heavy extraneous cognitive load. Split-source worked examples fall into this category.

Split-attention occurs when learners are required to split their attention between at least two sources of information that have been separated either spatially or temporally. Figure 9.1a provides an example. From a cognitive load theoretical perspective, each source of information must be essential to an understanding of the overall content to be learned and must be unintelligible in isolation. For maximum learning to occur, all disparate sources of information must be mentally integrated. However, by requiring learners to integrate several sources of information that are separated in space or time, extraneous cognitive load is created. For example, switching from one source of information in order to attend to another requires information to be maintained in working memory while searching and processing interacting elements in the linked source. In this manner, presenting information in a split-source format unnecessarily increases element interactivity resulting in an increase in extraneous cognitive load. Under many split-attention conditions, working memory resources are likely to be diverted away from schema formation in order to deal with the extraneous, interacting elements, leading to a loss of learning. Consequently, to prevent the learner experiencing split-attention, the different sources of information need to be physically integrated, or synchronised in the case of temporal split-attention, by the instructional designer. Figure 9.1b provides an example. In this fashion, considerable extraneous load can be avoided.

The split-attention effect occurs when an instructional strategy based on integrated materials leads to better learning outcomes than one based on split-source materials. Multiple sources of information that require learners to split their attention in order to learn are replaced by, and experimentally compared with, a single, integrated source. In general, an integrated format leads to a more effective learning

J. Sweller et al., *Cognitive Load Theory*, Explorations in the Learning Sciences, Instructional Systems and Performance Technologies 1, DOI 10.1007/978-1-4419-8126-4_9, © Springer Science+Business Media, LLC 2011

a Find ∠ EFB

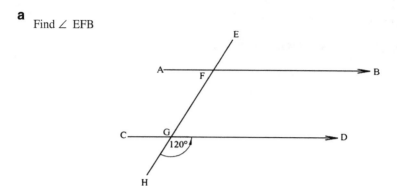

∠ GFB = 120° (corresponding angles between parallel lines AB & CD)

∠ EFB = 60° (angles on a straight line sum to 180°)

b Find ∠ EFB

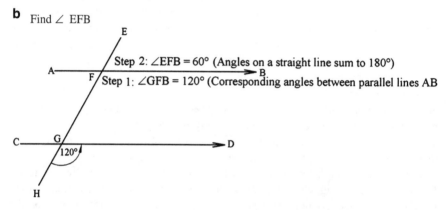

Fig. 9.1 (**a**) Split-attention format of a geometry worked example. (**b**) Integrated format of a geometry worked example

environment than a split-attention format. Much of the research into this effect has used multimedia materials because multimedia, by its definition, involves more than one information source (see Ayres & Sweller, 2005). For example, multimedia materials may include pictures or diagrams with text, or different forms of text (spoken or written). As noted by Sweller (1999), 'cognitive load theory does not distinguish between text and diagrams, text and text, or diagrams and diagrams as contributors to a split-attention effect' (p. 98). In the case of a diagram and written text (two sources of information), integration can be achieved by embedding the written text within the diagram. In the case of a diagram and spoken text, the narrative should be temporally aligned with the diagram. In both situations, integration is achieved.

The split-attention effect closely accords with human cognitive architecture. Providing information to learners uses the borrowing and reorganising principle to increase information in long-term memory (the information store). If that information is presented in split-source form, learners must search for referents.

Search always involves the randomness as genesis principle and imposes a working memory load due to the narrow limits of change principle. That search can be reduced by physically integrating multiple sources of information, reducing unnecessary interacting elements and so reducing extraneous cognitive load. The increased information stored in long-term memory then can be used to solve subsequent problems according to the environmental organising and linking principle.

The following two worked examples (see Fig. 9.1) illustrate the materials that can be used to demonstrate the split-attention effect. Figure 9.1a shows a worked example of the solution to an elementary geometry problem presented in a split-source form. Angle HGD is given as 120° and the problem solver is required to find angle EFB. Although there are several, alternative, possible solution paths, the worked example provides a two-step solution written below the diagram. As a first step, angle GFB is found using the 'corresponding angle between parallel lines theorem' (120°). Secondly, angle EFB (the goal angle) is found using the 'angles along a straight-line theorem' (60°). This example is categorised as using a split-source format because the solution is presented below rather than within the diagram, and neither the diagram nor the text can be understood in isolation as a solution to the problem. The worked solution requires the learner to read each statement and then examine the diagram to determine the correspondence between the lines and angles referred to in the statement and the diagram. This process of coordinating the statements with the diagram requires a search of the diagram to find relevant lines and angles. To conduct that search, both sources of information, the diagram and the statements, may need to be re-visited on several occasions with information from both retained in working memory. These mental processes increase the load on working memory resulting in an extraneous cognitive load due to the format of the information.

In contrast to the conventional, split-source format of a worked example in Fig. 9.1a, the integrated worked example, shown in Fig. 9.1b, requires reduced search for referents and reduced temporary storage of information because each solution step is embedded at an appropriate location within the diagram. Each solution step is positioned in close proximity to the relevant angles and lines referred to by the statement. The steps are numbered to make it easy for the learner to follow the correct sequence. In this physically integrated format, extraneous cognitive load can be significantly reduced compared to the split-attention format of Fig. 9.1a. It can be hypothesised that learners studying the integrated format of Fig. 9.1b will learn more than learners studying the split-attention format of Fig. 9.1a, demonstrating the split-attention effect.

Various Categories of the Split-Attention Effect

The split-attention effect has been obtained in a wide variety of circumstances using many different types of materials studied by many different categories of learners. Nevertheless, there is a set of requirements common to all circumstances in which split-attention occurs. The most important of these is that the multiple sources of information must be unintelligible and unlearnable in isolation. If, for example, a diagram provides all of the information needed to learn, integrating any additional text into the diagram will not be beneficial. Under these circumstances, the text should be eliminated, not integrated (see Chapter 11 on the redundancy effect). The split-attention effect only occurs when the two or more sources of information must be processed together in order to understand the information being presented. With that proviso, there are many different forms of the split-attention effect.

Worked Examples and the Split-Attention Effect

The initial research into many cognitive load effects was conducted using learning materials from mathematics and the sciences. The split-attention effect was no exception. The initial research was conducted by Tarmizi and Sweller (1988), who originally aimed to extend the findings of the worked example effect (see Chapter 8) to geometry materials, as at that time, the effect had only been demonstrated using algebra content (Cooper & Sweller, 1987; Sweller & Cooper, 1985). Initially, Tarmizi and Sweller found that neither worked examples nor guided solutions (partial worked examples) in geometry were any better than conventional problem-solving strategies. Tarmizi and Sweller reasoned that the split-attention format conventionally used in geometry and seen in Fig. 9.1a could explain the failure of geometry worked examples. The worked examples used had adopted the common presentation format found in mathematics textbooks with the written solution steps below the diagram. Tarmizi and Sweller then successfully tested an integrated approach similar to that depicted in Fig. 9.1b, demonstrating that studying worked examples was superior to conventional problem solving, provided diagrams and solution steps were physically integrated.

Following the success of the physical integration procedure in geometry, the split-attention effect was also found with coordinate geometry worked examples (Sweller, Chandler, Tierney, & Cooper, 1990). Although closely related to theorem-driven geometry, coordinate geometry has a greater reliance on formulae. However, historically, worked examples in this domain also separate the written text and formulae from the relevant diagrams. The study of Sweller et al. (1990) showed that worked examples had no advantage over conventional problem solving when they were constructed in a split-source presentation format, but had a significant advantage if they were structured according to an integrated approach.

Ward and Sweller (1990) demonstrated the split-attention effect when teaching students how to solve kinematics problems. In this highly mathematical domain based on formula manipulation, no worked example effect was found if problem solutions were presented in a traditional textbook format. Although diagrams are not necessarily involved in such problems, several different formulae are usually separated spatially both from each other and more importantly, from the problem statement. In these types of problems, a number of numerical values for velocity,

a A train moving from rest reaches a speed of 15 m/s after 5 seconds. What is the acceleration of the train?

$u = 0$ m/s

$v = 15$ m/s

$t = 5$ secs

$v = u + at$

$a = (v - u) / t$

$\quad = (15 - 0) / 5$

$\quad = 3$ m/s^2

b A train moving from rest (u) reaches a speed of 15 m/s (v) after 5 seconds (t) [$v = u + at$, $a = (v - u) / t = (15 - 0) / 5 = 3$ m/s^2]. What is the acceleration of the train?

Fig. 9.2 (**a**) Example of a split-attention format in dynamics. (**b**) Example of an integrated format in dynamics

distance and acceleration indicated in the problem statement have to be substituted into appropriate equations. In a conventional kinematics worked example, the problem statement containing the values for variables, and the equations into which the values must be substituted, are separated, resulting in split-attention between the problem statement and the equations used in the solution. Figure 9.2a provides an example.

As can be seen in Fig. 9.2a, in order to understand the substitutions of values into the formula, the problem statement either needs to have been memorised, a difficult task, or it needs to be constantly referred to while considering the equations with substituted values. Having to refer to both an equation and a physically separated problem statement in order to understand a worked example provides a classic example of a split-attention situation.

The approach taken in Fig. 9.2b integrates the equation into the problem statement. The substitution of values is made exactly when the terms are first indicated, and even before the entire problem statement is presented. Learners do not have to search for relations between the equations and the problem statement because those relations are made explicit in the physically integrated worked example. Working memory resources are not wasted in searching for appropriate referents in the problem statement or the equations because the referential connections are made explicit in the example.

By adopting this strategy, Ward and Sweller were able to demonstrate not only a worked example effect but also a split-attention effect. They compared three approaches: a conventional problem-solving strategy, a split-attention worked example strategy and an integrated worked example strategy. Test results indicated superior performance for the integrated worked example group compared with the other two groups that did not differ.

The studies described above were conducted with worked examples demonstrating procedural mathematical steps. As can be seen, a wide variety of worked examples from diagrammatic Euclidean geometry to formulae-based areas such as kinematics may require re-formatting in order to eliminate split-attention. However, many instructional techniques include explanatory text (spoken or written) combined with diagrams, other sources of text or even text associated with actual hardware as occurs when manuals are used to provide information about operating machines. All of these materials tend to be presented using split-attention formats with or without the inclusion of worked examples. These versions of the split-attention effect will be discussed in the following sections.

Diagrams and Written Explanations

The first study to examine the effectiveness of explanatory notes within a split-attention context was conducted by Sweller et al. (1990). In addition to their previously described results demonstrating the importance of reducing split-attention in coordinate geometry worked examples, they also found that the most effective format used to provide explanations during initial instruction was to integrate explanatory notes into a diagram at the closest point of reference. An example of this format is shown in Fig. 9.3.

Instead of writing explanatory notes below the diagram, the notes can be labelled and embedded into the diagram, as can be seen in Fig. 9.3. In this example, where the learners are required to plot a point on the *x*–*y* axis, the explanation is positioned alongside the actual point. Accordingly, there is only a limited amount of problem-solving

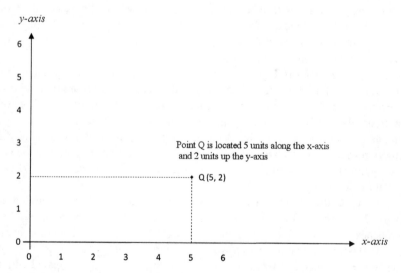

Fig. 9.3 Example of integrated explanatory text in coordinate geometry

search for referents required as the learner's attention is focused on the relevant mathematics rather than on attempting to mentally integrate the text and diagram. Physical integration provides a substitute for mental integration that is kept to a minimum by the integrated format. Instead, more working memory resources can be concentrated on schema acquisition that is germane to learning rather than dealing with unnecessary search and integration processes that are extraneous to learning.

Sweller et al. (1990) tested the relative effectiveness of the format demonstrated in Fig. 9.3 in which explanatory notes were fully integrated into the diagram. In one experiment, they demonstrated that physically integrated explanatory notes were more effective than writing the notes below the diagram in a split-source format. A second experiment combined initial, integrated explanatory notes (first phase) with integrated worked examples (second phase) and compared them with a strategy that provided split-source notes (first phase) and split-source worked examples (second phase). Again, the integrated format proved superior to the split-source format. In this experiment, group differences were consistently large, with the integrated format requiring less time to study the initial explanations (first phase), less time to study the worked examples (second phase) and less time to complete the test problems. Despite the reduced time on task, a clear advantage for physically integrated formats was found on both similar test problems and a transfer problem.

Sweller et al. (1990) extended their experiments to include the domain of numerical control programming. In learning these tasks, students were required to write programs to control industrial machinery. There is a connection to coordinate geometry, as control of the movement of machines such as lathes is dependent upon the Cartesian coordinate system. Nevertheless, compared with elementary coordinate geometry, such programming tasks are much higher in element interactivity. In this experiment, conducted with trade apprentices, an integrated group again outperformed a split-attention group on test problems and required far less time during acquisition. It is notable that the explanatory notes in this study were extensive, requiring multiple procedural steps.

Purnell, Solman, and Sweller (1991) found a split-attention effect in geography, a domain heavily dependent upon diagrams and tables that are usually linked with explanatory text. In a series of four experiments, students were required to read maps either in an integrated or a split-source format in which descriptions were placed below the map. Results indicated that the integrated approach led to superior recall of the items detailed on the map but also led to superior inferences being made about these items. Chandler and Sweller (1991), using electrical apprentices learning about the installation of electrical wiring, also successfully demonstrated the split-attention effect. Integrating diagrams of electrical circuits with explanatory text proved superior to a conventional format that separated diagrams and text.

Mayer (1989) found that students learning about hydraulic braking systems were disadvantaged if the explanatory text was placed below an illustration of the system. However, an integrated approach where the words were positioned next to the part of the picture to which the text referred, resulted in much better transfer test outcomes. In further work, Mayer, Steinhoff, Bower, and Mars (1995) conducted a series of experiments in which students learned how lightning works. Students in an integrated strategy group received a booklet where each illustration was positioned next to a paragraph of explanatory text. In addition, each illustration had a caption that contained keywords from the relevant paragraph of text. In contrast, students in a split-attention strategy group received a booklet where the explanatory text appeared on a separate page to the illustrations with no captions. Students in three different experiments performed better on transfer tasks if they received the integrated booklets. Moreno and Mayer (1999) collected further evidence using computer-based animations to teach students about lightning formations. In this experiment, they demonstrated the split-attention effect without radically separating units of information onto different pages as Mayer et al. (1995) had done. For the separated group, the on-screen text was placed at the bottom of the screen beneath the corresponding diagram, while the integrated group's text was placed near the relevant section of the diagram. Again, students in the integrated group performed best on transfer tasks. In a later study Austin (2009) replicated these results.

Later studies have extended research into the split-attention effect to other learning domains. Rose and Wolfe (2000) found the effect with undergraduate accountancy students. Using two sources of information, a decision aid for calculating tax liabilities and instructions on calculating tax, an integrated format was found to be more effective than dual screens (each source on a separate screen) or a split-screen (same screen but physically separated sources). In a similar study Rose (2002) replicated these results. Ayres and Youssef (2008) found the split-attention effect using economics materials. In this study, undergraduate students were required to learn about the supply and demand curve. The effect was greatest on questions that required diagrammatic knowledge.

Pociask and Morrison (2008) found the effect in teaching complex orthopaedic physical therapy skills in a realistic classroom setting. In this study, novice physical therapy students were shown a number of procedures for localising various forms of patient pain. Test results suggested that the integrated format led to superior learning as measured by written and psychomotor tasks as well as physical therapy performance, with reduced cognitive load. However, it should be noted that this study included redundant material making it difficult to interpret the precise cause of the effect. Studies by Cierniak, Scheiter, and Gerjets (2009a, 2009b), used very detailed instructions to explain the structure and physiological processes involved in the human kidneys. Text for both split-attention and integrated modes were very dense. A split-attention effect was found, indicating again (see also Sweller et al., 1990) that the effect could be found when the computer screen was filled with many lines of explanatory text related to diagrams.

These experiments conclusively demonstrated the advantages of placing essential information needed to understand a diagram on the diagram itself. For diagrams and text that cannot be understood in isolation, extraneous cognitive load is increased if learners must search for connections between the two sources of information due to a split-source presentation. That search process with its heavy working memory demands can be largely eliminated by integrating text into a diagram.

Multiple Sources of Text

As well as integrating diagrams and explanatory notes, Sweller et al. (1990) also investigated the integration of two sources of text. Using Numerical Control (NC) Programming, they integrated two sources of explanatory information. One set of instructions concerned the physical movements of a machine that was required to cut a metal sheet in a particular way and the second set concerned the numerical control statements that would program the machine to accomplish the requisite operations. For example:

1. The first manual instruction stated: *To commence cutting, move along the carriage towards the head-stock for 16 mm.*
2. The corresponding NC instruction read: *A straight line cut is to be made: The NC command for a straight line cut is G01.*

These two categories of instruction, both of which must be understood if students are to learn numerical control programming, normally are placed in two separate tables presented simultaneously or successively. Physical integration was achieved by providing a single manual instruction, immediately followed by the relevant NC instruction in parentheses:

To commence cutting, move along the carriage towards the head-stock for 16 mm. (A straight line cut is to be made: The NC command for a straight line cut is G01.)

In this fashion, a single set of instructions was created integrating both sources of information. In this experiment, one group of students were instructed using the integrated approach, and compared with a second group that received two separate sets of instructions presented successively. Results indicated that the integrated group required less time to study the information and obtained higher scores on subsequent test results. As was the case for diagrams and text, the result was attributed to a reduction in extraneous cognitive load due to a reduced need to search for correspondences and referents.

More Than Two Sources of Information

Chung (2007) investigated split-attention in the domain of learning Chinese as a second language using three different sources of information. Chung simultaneously presented three flash cards to learners consisting of a Chinese character, the English translation and the pinyin (a phonic transcription system) equivalent. Not only was the order of the three cards manipulated, but also the physical distance between them. It was found that superior learning and pronunciation was obtained when the English or pinyin card was presented close to the Chinese character, rather than spatially apart, indicating a split-attention effect.

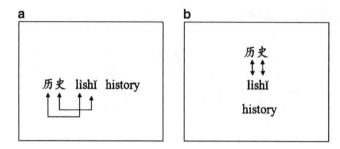

Fig. 9.4 Diagrams demonstrating (**a**) split-attention in a horizontal presentation format (**b**) vertical presentation format reducing split-attention

Lee and Kalyuga (2011b) also investigated the effectiveness of pinyin in learning Chinese as a second language from the perspective of cognitive load theory. They suggested that when learning vocabulary, the commonly used horizontal layout format for presenting pinyin could impose high levels of cognitive load and hinder learning of characters due to split-attention caused by learners searching and matching corresponding characters and pinyin. In an alternative vertical format, pinyin is placed exactly under the corresponding characters, thus reducing potential split-attention. Figure 9.4 depicts the two formats. In an experiment involving high school students learning Chinese as a second language, the learning effects of the vertical and horizontal layouts of characters, pinyin and English translations were compared. Results indicated a significant advantage of the vertical format that was attributed to the elimination of split-attention.

Split-Attention While Learning to Use a Computer

One of the most common examples of split-attention occurs when instructing learners how to use hardware. An example is learning how to use a computer by following instructions either from a computer manual or more commonly these days, from a computer screen. Learners are required to read the information and learn how to manipulate various parts of the computer, such as the mouse, or type in specific commands to run a particular application. Almost invariably, learners' attention will be split between the hardware and the text in a classical split-attention scenario.

Sweller and Chandler (1994) and Chandler and Sweller (1996) demonstrated this phenomenon with learners required to learn about a CAD/CAM (computer aided design/computer aided manufacture) package either using a conventional split-source procedure (computer and manual in this particular case) or an integrated strategy that used only a modified manual. In the integrated strategy, text and diagrams were presented in physically integrated form in the manual, but learners were not permitted access to a computer, as all commands concerning the keyboard and computer screen were depicted in the manual. In contrast, learners in the split-source condition could try out various procedures on a computer while reading the manual. On subsequent tests of knowledge and tests of ability to use the applications that had been taught, the integrated method produced superior results indicating a split-attention effect. Surprisingly, students in the integrated group who had not used a computer during learning were able to demonstrate superior competence in using a computer to solve the primary tasks than students who had practised with the actual physical equipment.

These studies showed that instructions on how to use computer programs could be learned quite effectively by presenting all instructions in a single, integrated module without, in the first instance, presenting learners with a computer on which to practice. A follow-up study by Cerpa, Chandler, and Sweller (1996) showed that it made no difference whether the instructions were presented on a screen or in a paper-based manual. Using spreadsheets as the learning domain, students were required to learn how to create some elementary mathematical formulae within cells. An integrated format was achieved by inserting all instructions into the spreadsheets at the most spatially relevant points, within the cells themselves. This strategy was compared with a split-source format in which the screen-based instructions were not integrated with the spreadsheet. Again, the physically integrated instructions were superior demonstrating the split-attention effect.

A notable finding of Sweller and Chandler (1994), Chandler and Sweller (1996) and Cerpa et al. (1996) was that the split-attention effect only occurred using materials high in element interactivity. For example, in learning about spreadsheets, tasks such as locating a cell or simply typing in a value are low in elementary interactivity, as they can be processed sequentially with very few interacting elements. In contrast, tasks such as devising quite complicated mathematical formulae are high in elementary interactivity. Not only do students need to know what the formula is, but also which symbols on the keyboard represent the mathematical symbols, how these are put together in the correct cell, and what cell markers are used in the formula. The split-attention effect was only obtained with such high element interactivity materials. The impact of element interactivity is discussed in more detail in Chapter 15.

The results in this section indicate that instructions in how to use machinery need to be carefully considered. We all know that frequently, we would much prefer to try to use machinery without even reading the instructions. That may, in fact, be an effective strategy under many circumstances. Split-attention, both within the instructions and in the present context, between the instructions and the machinery generate such a heavy working memory load that learners feel the need to dispense with either the instructions or the machine. Since the instructions tend to be unintelligible without the machine, we jettison the instructions. We now know how to present instructions in a manner that does not inflict an extraneous cognitive load. Properly structured instructions that can be fully understood, without reference to the machinery, can be much more intelligible than instructions that split attention between the instructional material and the machinery.

Split-Attention and Other Cognitive Load Theory Effects

Several studies have considered relations between the split-attention effect and other effects. When investigating the use of self-explanations with worked examples, Mwangi and Sweller (1998) included instruction presented in split-source or integrated formats. They studied very young students solving mathematics problems. A notable finding was that an integrated format led to more inference making while self-explaining than a split-source format. In addition, while self-explaining, the integrated group made more solution-oriented re-reads of the materials compared to the split-attention group.

These results can be explained in terms of an increase in working memory load associated with split-attention instructions. Inferencing is likely to impose a heavy working memory burden. Instructions presented in split-source format may leave insufficient working memory resources to allow inferences to be made. The reduction in load imposed by integrated instructions may permit inferencing. Similarly, the reduction in extraneous load associated with integrated instructions may permit solution-oriented re-reading of material that might be difficult under split-attention conditions. If learners are using working memory resources to integrate disparate sources of information, they may have few resources available to consider the solution.

Yeung, Jin, and Sweller (1998) investigated the use of explanatory notes in reading comprehension and demonstrated how sensitive the split-attention effect is to the prior knowledge of the learner. In this study, integration was achieved by placing the explanatory notes above the relevant sections in the text, whereas in the split-source format, the notes were placed together at the end of the text. In a series of experiments it was found that the integrated format enhanced comprehension, on a difficult, high element interactivity task, for primary students and low-ability learners of English as a second language, but did not enhance vocabulary acquisition, on a relatively easy, low element interactivity task. For vocabulary, the explanatory notes were redundant and could be more easily ignored when placed at the end of the text. Reducing split-attention mattered for complex, high element interactivity tasks but not for simpler, low element interactivity tasks. However, these results reversed for more experienced, adult learners providing an example of the expertise reversal effect. Kalyuga, Chandler, and Sweller (1998) obtained similar findings in the technical domain of learning about electrical circuits. These studies demonstrated the relation of the split-attention effect to both the redundancy and expertise reversal effects, discussed more fully in Chapters 11 and 12, respectively.

Temporal Split-Attention

To this point, we have discussed spatial split-attention in which learners must handle information that is spatially separated, and so needs to be mentally integrated in order to be understood. Improved learning following physical integration results in the split-attention effect. Spatial split-attention is not the only form of split-attention. The effect can be temporal as well as spatial. If multiple sources of information that need to be integrated are presented at separate times rather than separate locations, we might expect a split-attention effect identical to the one obtained using spatial split-attention.

Work on the temporal split-attention effect can be closely related to work on spatial split-attention. With temporal separation (displacement in time), learners must find referents between the separated sources of information. Finding referents involves search, in the same way that spatially separated information must be searched for referents. In addition, learners must integrate the different sources of information after searching before they can be understood. Consequently, extraneous cognitive load is generated in much the same way as in physically separated materials. In summary, temporally separated learning materials can generate significant extraneous load. To alleviate this load, the verbal and visual sources of information should be presented simultaneously in *temporally* integrated form (for an overview see Mayer, 2009)

There is considerable empirical support for Mayer's temporal split-attention principle. Initial evidence came from the research of Baggett (1984), who conducted an experiment in which students were shown different versions of an instructional film. Either the narrative was presented before the corresponding visual information (7, 14 or 21 s before) or after it (7, 14 or 21 s after). Another version that can be considered analogous to physical integration presented the visual and auditory information simultaneously. On recall tests, the simultaneous presentation and the version in which the visual information was presented 7 s before the narrative outperformed the other groups, demonstrating the temporal split-attention effect.

Mayer and Anderson (1991, 1992) collected further evidence of the temporal split-attention through two studies presenting information via narrated animations on how a bicycle pump worked. The first study compared a group presented with the complete narrative before the animation with an integrated group in which the narrative and animation were presented concurrently. Test results using problem-solving tasks indicated that the integrated group performed significantly better than the split-attention group. In the second study, Mayer and Anderson (1992) increased the number of presentations by using repetitions of narrative and visual animations. Animations were presented before as well as after narration. Groups that received temporally displaced sequences were compared with a group that received integrated sequences. Results indicated that the integrated group was superior to the split-attention formats on problem-solving tasks.

Mayer and Anderson made some interesting additional observations. Firstly, the results were achieved with novices in the domain and may not have been achieved with students who had higher levels of prior knowledge. Secondly, the content focused on mechanical systems that show how something works, and the results may not transfer to more descriptive passages relying on the recall of facts. Thirdly, the effect was only found on problem-solving transfer tasks and not on retention tasks. The hypotheses that flow from these observations are plausible but have not yet been tested. Mayer, Moreno, Boire, and Vagge (1999), Mayer and Sims (1994) and Moreno and Mayer (1999) confirmed the temporal split-attention effect. Mayer et al. (1999) investigated the influence of the length of the narrations and animations. If narrations and animations were significantly reduced in length (called small bites), no difference was found between integrated and separated formats. However, if the sizes of the animations and narrations were much larger (large bites) then an integrated format was superior. Mayer et al. explained this effect in terms of working memory load. Holding large sections of narrative in working memory at any time can easily overload it and so it may be important to reduce cognitive load by eliminating temporal split-attention. Maintaining much smaller bites should be more manageable and so it may not be as important to reduce cognitive load by eliminating split-attention.

Owens and Sweller (2008) extended the findings on temporal split-attention to include music education. In two experiments, the effect was demonstrated in both spatial (visual musical notation positioned above written explanations) and temporal displacements (visual musical notation shown after verbal explanations).

Alternative Methods to Overcome Split-Attention

The studies reported so far have all used an integration strategy to compensate for the problems associated with split-source presentations of information. A number of alternative methods have also been investigated.

Directing Attention and the Split-Attention Effect

Kalyuga, Chandler, and Sweller (1999) developed an alternative strategy to physical integration based on helping the learner by directing attention to appropriate sources of information. In an experiment that required apprentices to learn about electrical circuits, a colour coding system was used to connect the text directly with the relevant parts of the diagram. Attention was directed appropriately by the learner clicking on the particular paragraph of text being studied that triggered the corresponding parts of the electrical circuit to change to a unique, identifiable colour, thus reducing the amount of visual search required. This strategy when compared with a split-source format, where the text was written below the diagram, showed superior learning outcomes and efficiency. Reducing visual search by cuing was also found to be an effective strategy by Tabbers, Martens, and van Merriënboer (2000). In this study, visual cueing was achieved by colouring red those parts of the diagram to which the text, either spoken or written, referred. However, Tabbers et al. (2000) only found an effect for tests of recall and not transfer.

Florax and Ploetzner (2010) also provided more explicit links to the different sources of information by combining segmentation and signalling techniques.

It was found that if substantial explanatory text was divided into smaller segments and each segment labelled with a number corresponding to an equivalent number on the accompanying diagram, then no difference in learning was found when compared with a fully integrated group, where the text segments were inserted into the corresponding diagrams. In contrast, both strategies were superior to a format that had unsegmented text displaced from the relevant diagram. A further finding from this study was that segmentation had a stronger effect than labelling. This study can be explained from a cognitive load theory perspective in that smaller chunks of information are easier to hold in working memory, facilitating mental integration from the two sources. In addition, labelling the segments and points on the diagram reduces search processes and so further reduces cognitive load. This combination may reduce cognitive load sufficiently to overcome the negative impact of split-attention. The findings in this study provide some support for previous studies by Mayer and colleagues (Mayer et al., 1999; Moreno & Mayer, 1999), who found that smaller segments alone could eliminate the split-attention effect.

The Pop-Up Alternative to Text Integration

As indicated above, the most common form of text–picture integration is to place the text into the diagram closest to the relevant referents. Some researchers have used a text hyper-linking procedure as an alternative, giving more control to the learner. Bétrancourt and Bisseret (1998) noted that presentations could become very cluttered if large amounts of text are inserted into a picture. To avoid such over-crowding, they designed an alternative presentation format where the text was inserted into the diagram at the relevant position but hidden from sight unless activated by the learner by clicking on the mouse. This 'pop-up' procedure was compared with a split-source format (text to the right of the diagram) and traditional integration (text embedded into the diagram). Results indicated that both forms of integrated material generally led to superior learning outcomes compared with a split-source presentation. Although not statistically significant, the pop-up display led to quicker solution times and reduced error rates than the traditional integrated format. It should also be pointed out that user-control adds a further dimension to the study (the pop-up procedure gave more control to the users than an integration procedure), which may interact with the split-attention effect.

Further evidence supporting the effectiveness of a pop-up method was found by Erhel and Jamet (2006). In a similar design to Bétrancourt and Bisseret (1998), a pop-up procedure was compared with integrated and separated formats. On a number of learning measures the pop-up and integrated procedures were found to be superior to the separated format, demonstrating a split-attention effect. However, on tasks that measured inferences and matching text with illustrated materials, the pop-up procedure was superior to the integrated format.

Crooks, White, Srinivasan, and Wang (2008) also used the pop-up design in a study, which used modified definitions of the split-attention principle with respect to interactive geography maps. It was argued that in a situation where a learner selects features on a map, and supporting text appears almost immediately, the time difference is so slight that no temporal separation is realistically experienced. Using a pop-up strategy, Crooks et al. (2008) showed that the text could be positioned away from the map and still remain effective. It was shown that the text, having been activated by the mouse click on a specific map label, could appear on a separate screen, and still facilitate more learning than a presentation format that relied on two screens with constant split-attention. Even though the pop-up format created split-attention in the same way as conventional spatially split designs, the linking between the map label and explanatory text counteracted this negativity. The authors argued that spatial split-attention does not impact on learning over and above temporal split-attention. However, this conclusion must be treated with some caution, as the linking of labels on the diagram with explanations may be considered as a form of cuing strategy, as well as reflect the impact of user interactivity.

Procedural Information and the Split-Attention Effect

Kester, Kirschner, and van Merriënboer (2005) investigated the specific use of procedural information in a computer-simulated environment where high school students were required to solve electrical circuit problems. An integrated and split-source format was compared using a combination of supportive and procedural information. Using a *just-in-time* strategy (see Kester, Kirschner, van Merriënboer, & Bäumer, 2001), vital supportive information in the form of explanations about electrical circuits was provided to students before solving problems. In addition, essential procedural information was also provided during practice, enabling students to learn about components in the circuits and what actions they need to carry out. In the split-source format, the procedural information was separated from the diagram of the circuit, whereas in the integrated format, the procedural information was embedded within the diagram. Results indicated that the integrated group spent less time than the split-source group studying supportive information and scored higher on transfer tasks.

Learner Integration of Split-Source Materials

Bodemer, Ploetzner, Feuerlein, and Spada (2004) investigated the consequences of learners rather than instructors eliminating split-attention. Using materials that described how a bicycle pump works, a split-source format was designed by presenting the written text above the diagrams, whereas for the integrated condition, the text was embedded within the diagrams, as is normally found in two-group, split-attention experiments. However, a further two groups were formed by adding another condition to the split-source and integrated formats. Learners were required to physically build the materials themselves by placing the various explanatory notes onto an integrated or split-format diagram using interactive commands on the computer. The materials were presented in a split-attention format initially so in the case of the split-source format diagram, learners had to move the written components from one split-source location to another split-source location. In the case of the integrated diagram, they had to move components from the original split-source location to an integrated location. Thus, instead of just mentally integrating sources of information (either in integrated or split-source format) as learners did under the normal conditions, this design required learners to both physically and mentally integrate the two sources as well.

Results indicated that the integrated format was superior to the split-source format on understanding test tasks, and a trend suggested that a combination of mental and physical integration was superior to just mental integration alone. A second experiment, within a more complex domain, demonstrated that a joint physical and mental integration approach led to better learning outcomes than strategies that required mental integration only (both split and integrated formats). This experiment showed that learner interactivity in constructing the integrated diagram rather than just being presented one had a positive effect. Nevertheless, in this experiment, unlike the first experiment, no regular split-attention effect was found for groups that did not physically integrate the materials.

A Meta-Analysis of the Split-Attention Effect

Ginns (2006) completed a meta-analysis of the split-attention effect. Fifty studies were included, of which 37 involved spatial split-attention and 13 temporal. The overall effect size had a Cohen's d value of 0.85, which is a large effect (Cohen, 1988). No significant difference was found between spatial split-attention ($d = 0.72$) and temporal split-attention ($d = 0.78$). As would be expected, the effect was weak for low element interactivity materials ($d = 0.28$) and significantly greater for materials with higher levels of element interactivity ($d = 0.78$). Consistently high effect sizes were found across mathematics, science and technical learning domains, similar and transfer tests, various age groups, as well as static and dynamic presentations. This meta-analysis demonstrated that the split-attention effect is robust and occurs across different learning domains and types of instructional designs. Learning from integrated materials has a large advantage over learning from split-source materials.

Conditions of Applicability

The split-attention effect occurs when a learning strategy that physically integrates different sources is shown to be more effective than a strategy that keeps the materials separate. An overriding condition for the effect to occur is that each source of information is essential and non-redundant. For example, if students are able to learn from one source alone, then there is no need to physically integrate information. The research reported above demonstrates that the split-attention effect can be based on both spatial and temporal factors. The effect occurs across many learning domains and under various combinations of text (both written and spoken), pictures, diagrams, graphs and machinery such as computers, but is more likely to occur with learning material that is high in intrinsic element interactivity (see Chapter 15).

Instructional Implications

Research on the split-attention effect provides a clear message for instructional designers: Different sources of information that must be considered simultaneously for understanding and learning to occur should be integrated as far as possible. As has been demonstrated in this chapter, requiring learners to mentally integrate different sources of information that are separated in space or time is detrimental to learning. If written text is used, it must be positioned next to its referents, or in the case of spoken text, it must be synchronised with the visual representation. Without such integrated alignments, learning is likely to be inhibited.

Conclusions

The split-attention effect is important for several reasons. First, it provides us with an important instructional design principle that is frequently ignored. Information that needs to be considered simultaneously, in order to be understood needs to be presented in a manner that eliminates spatial or temporal separation. Secondly, the split-attention effect indicates why the worked example effect sometimes fails. Simply presenting worked examples does not guarantee a reduction in extraneous cognitive load. Worked examples must be deliberately structured to ensure that they do not themselves impose a heavy extraneous cognitive load. Thirdly, the split-attention effect flows directly from cognitive load theory. Holding information in working memory, while searching for referents, imposes a heavy extraneous cognitive load that should be reduced.

For these reasons, the split-attention effect is one of the most important cognitive load effects. Indeed, its importance transcends these points because of its wider implications, especially its implications for other cognitive load effects. The modality effect, discussed in the next chapter, also relies on the split-attention effect.

Chapter 10
The Modality Effect

The modality effect is closely related to the split-attention effect (Chapter 9). According to cognitive load theory, the split-attention effect occurs when learners must process separate but related sources of information that cannot be understood without mental integration. The cognitive resources required to effect this integration are unavailable for learning and may exceed the available capacity of working memory. This chapter describes an alternative way of dealing with split-attention conditions by engaging both auditory and visual channels of information in working memory rather than just the visual channel. For example, rather than presenting a diagram and written text that rely entirely on the visual channel, a diagram and spoken text relying on both auditory and visual modalities are used.

We need to emphasise that as was the case with the split-attention effect, the modality effect only is obtainable when the two sources of information are unintelligible in isolation. Textual information presented in spoken form will not generate a modality effect if it merely re-describes a diagram or some other form of information. If a diagram and text are being used, both must contain information that requires learners to refer to the other source in order to enable comprehension. If for example, a diagram is intelligible in isolation and contains all of the required information, providing a spoken re-description of the diagram will no more generate a modality effect than providing a written description will generate a split-attention effect. The issue of text that re-describes a diagram is discussed in Chapter 11 on the redundancy effect.

The modality effect described in this chapter is associated with multimedia learning and instruction that use multiple forms of information input and representation. According to the available models of multimedia learning (Mayer, 2009; Schnotz, 2005), cognitive processing of related texts and pictures, including dynamic visualisations such as animations and simulations, involves the selection and organisation of the relevant elements of visual and auditory information resulting in a coherent unified representation. These processes occur in the learner's working memory.

The cognitive architecture described in the early chapters of this book applies similarly to both the split-attention and the modality effects with one additional, critical point. Whereas we have not evolved to handle written text that refers to a

J. Sweller et al., *Cognitive Load Theory*, Explorations in the Learning Sciences,
Instructional Systems and Performance Technologies 1,
DOI 10.1007/978-1-4419-8126-4_10, © Springer Science+Business Media, LLC 2011

visual information such as objects, pictures or diagrams and so may need to learn how to process such information, it is very likely that we have evolved to listen to speech while looking at objects. If so, presenting information in dual-modality form may tap into biologically primary knowledge resulting in an advantage over visual only, written text plus objects, pictures or diagrams. Such visual-only information may require us to acquire relevant biologically secondary information.

With respect to the general cognitive architecture of Part II, the presentation of information relies on the borrowing and reorganising principle to facilitate the transfer of information to the long-term memory information store, that information needs to be structured to take into account the limitations of working memory as indicated by the narrow limits of change principle, and once knowledge is stored in long-term memory, it can be used to govern activity as specified by the environmental organising and linking principle. If dual-modality presentation taps into a biologically primary ability, it will automatically reduce working memory load leading to an advantage.

The Effect of Replacing Written with Spoken Text

While working memory is often treated as if it is a unitary structure, in fact it includes multiple processors that correspond to the modality in which information to be processed is presented. Several well-established models of working memory assume its functions are distributed over partly independent components usually associated with processing auditory/verbal or visual/pictorial information (e.g. Bandura, 1986; Penney, 1989; Schneider & Detweiler, 1987). For example, the model suggested by Baddeley (1986) includes three subsystems: a phonological loop, a visuospatial sketchpad and a central executive. The phonological loop processes auditory information, while the visuospatial sketchpad processes pictorial or written visual information. In Penney's (1989) "separate streams" model of working memory, processing of verbal items presented in auditory and visual forms is carried out independently by auditory and visual processors.

Thus, according to the most common theories of working memory, we have two different, partially independent processors for dealing with visual and auditory information. We will assume that both of these processors have capacity and duration limitations. In some situations, effective working memory capacity may be increased by using both processors, and this possibility has important instructional implications associated with the presentation of information. The presentation formats should be designed in a way that can help learners to avoid an unnecessary cognitive overload by using both, rather than a single processor. In that way, the cognitive load can be spread over both processors, thus reducing the load on a single processor.

Imagine two related sources of information presented in a visual form, for example, a diagram with an accompanying, explanatory, written text. Initially, both sources of information must be processed in the visual channel of working memory.

Subsequently, the visual text may be partially or fully re-coded into the auditory form for further processing but when dealing with written text, auditory processing cannot occur until after the text has been dealt with by the visual processor and re-coded into auditory form. If high levels of element interactivity are involved in processing and integrating these two sources of information, the visual channel of working memory may become overloaded, especially when these sources are spatially separated through a split-source presentation.

However, when one of the sources of information such as the text, when dealing with a diagram and text, is presented in an auditory form, it can be processed immediately in the auditory channel of working memory without imposing a cognitive load on the visual channel, while visual information such as diagrams continues to be processed in the visual channel. The use of both channels increases the capacity of working memory, although it does not consist of a simple addition of the capacity of both channels because they are only partially independent. Nevertheless, the amount of information that can be processed using both auditory and visual channels should exceed the processing capacity of a single channel. In addition, dual-modality presentations eliminate possible visual split-attention that may occur when only visual sources of information are present.

Thus, limited working memory can be effectively expanded by using more than one presentation modality. The modality effect occurs when dual-modality presentations are superior to single-modality-only presentations of the same information. Instructional materials involving dual-modality presentations of related sources of information can eliminate cognitive overload in situations where equivalent single-modality formats might fail. The resulting effect on learning is similar to the effect of physically integrating separate sources of information to eliminate split-attention.

A number of experiments have demonstrated that replacing written or on-screen text with orally narrated text improved student learning using several different indicators of learning: higher post-test scores combined with lower cognitive load during instruction (e.g. Kalyuga, Chandler, & Sweller, 1999, 2000; Tindall-Ford, Chandler, & Sweller, 1997); less time required for subsequent problem solving (Jeung, Chandler, & Sweller, 1997; Mousavi, Low, & Sweller, 1995); and higher retention, transfer and matching tests scores (Mayer & Moreno, 1998; Moreno & Mayer, 1999; see Mayer, 2009 for an overview).

Mousavi et al. (1995), using geometry materials, first demonstrated the instructional modality effect. They hypothesised that if working memory has partially independent processors for handling visual and auditory material, effective working memory may be increased by presenting material in a mixed rather than a unitary mode. Therefore, the negative consequences of split-attention in geometry might be avoided by presenting geometry statements in auditory, rather than visual, form. The results of a sequence of experiments supported this hypothesis. They demonstrated that a visually presented geometry diagram with statements presented in auditory form improved learning compared to visual-only presentations. Tindall-Ford et al. (1997) replicated the initial results of Mousavi et al. (1995) by comparing an audio text/visual diagram or table in elementary electrical engineering with purely visually presented instruction. In addition, they also provided evidence for a cognitive load interpretation of the results by comparing cognitive load indicators using subjective rating scales.

An alternative explanation of the modality effect has been provided by Tabbers, Martens, and van Merriënboer (2004). They argued that the effect was caused by the reduction of extraneous cognitive load due to the simultaneous presentation of pictorial and verbal information in a dual-modality format rather than due to the effective expansion of working memory capacity. We can simultaneously listen to spoken text while looking at a diagram, but it is difficult or impossible to simultaneously read text while looking at a diagram, especially under split-source conditions. This argument is plausible. Nevertheless, Mousavi et al. (1995) studied the role of temporal contiguity in the modality effect by comparing sequential and simultaneous presentations of geometry diagrams and associated textual explanations in both visual-only and dual-modality formats and found no evidence for the influence of temporal contiguity on the modality effect. The effect was obtained irrespective whether the textual information was provided simultaneously with the diagrams or before the diagrams were presented. This result renders a temporal contiguity explanation of the modality effect unlikely.

The cognitive theory of multimedia learning (Mayer, 2005, 2009; Mayer & Moreno, 2002, 2003) has been used to provide detailed theoretical arguments that effectively supported the modality effect along with a cognitive load explanation. The works of Mayer and his collaborators have applied the modality effect to dynamic visualisations such as instructional animations. According to the cognitive theory of multimedia learning, different mental representations are constructed from verbal and pictorial information, and meaningful learning occurs when the learner actively establishes connections between these representations.

Within a framework of the cognitive theory of multimedia learning, Mayer and Moreno (2003) considered the modality effect as a means of off-loading some of the processing demands from the visual channel to the auditory channel. Mayer and his collaborators (Mayer, 1997; Mayer & Anderson, 1991, 1992; Mayer & Moreno, 1998; Moreno & Mayer, 1999; Moreno, Mayer, Spires, & Lester, 2001; for overviews, see Clark & Mayer, 2003 Mayer, 2009) have conducted many experiments demonstrating the superiority of dual-modality instructions for meaningful learning. In most cases, they used narrated scientific explanations of animated visuals as experimental materials. One of their findings was that the modality effect is usually stronger for measures of transfer rather than retention. Dual-modality presentations offload information from the visual channel, reduce extraneous load, and thus may leave more resources for germane cognitive processing (Harskamp, Mayer, & Suhre, 2007).

The Modality Effect in Interactive Learning Environments

Many earlier studies of the modality effect used well-structured, system-controlled instructions explaining procedures. In contrast, interactive learning environments usually involve non-linear features that allow learners to determine the sequence of information access, select the content and its presentation format. Learners may choose different learning pathways depending on their interaction with the system, or they may just follow system suggestions. For example, electronic hypermedia learning environments include elements of information interconnected by hyperlinks and presented in various modalities. Such environments usually offer more learner control than traditional system-controlled, multimedia learning environments.

Most multimedia learning principles are believed to be applicable to hypermedia learning environments (Dillon & Jobst, 2005). However, Gerjets, Scheiter, Opfermann, Hesse, and Eysink (2009) failed to find evidence for a modality effect even though the hypermedia-based instruction in solving probability problems used in their study involved a relatively low level of learner control. While learners could choose to retrieve well-specified sources of information such as animations or audio text files with spoken explanations, to skip presented information, and to select the pacing of instruction, in all other respects, they had linear access to information. Gerjets et al. (2009) concluded that the modality effect may not be applicable when designing hypermedia learning environments that do not provide sufficient information indicating whether students should use spoken rather than written explanations of animated visuals. Students may need to be prompted to use appropriate external representations (Gerjets, Scheiter, & Schuh, 2008). In addition, learner control of the pacing may have reduced the cognitive load associated with split attention in the case of the visual-only representations, similar to the findings of Tabbers et al. (2004). Since there was sufficient time to read the written materials, written text resulted in similar, or even better, performance compared to transitory spoken text. While these studies indicate that learner control may be a relevant variable when considering the modality effect, length and complexity of auditory information is a far more likely explanation of the findings (see Chapter 17 on the transient information effect).

An example of the effective use of dual-modality presentations for reducing cognitive load in interactive, collaborative learning was provided by a study of After-Action Review (AAR) procedures in a computer-based collaborative problem-solving environment (O'Neil & Chuang, 2007). Some of the verbal feedback was presented to learners in the auditory modality so that visual and auditory channels were both engaged in a complementary manner. The results indicated that this complementary audio/visual textual feedback significantly improved student content understanding and communication scores in comparison with visual-only text.

Animated pedagogical agents are visual characters enabled with speech, gestures, movements and other human-like behaviour. They have recently become very popular in interactive multimedia learning environments. Such agents increase the possibility of combining verbal and non-verbal forms of information (Atkinson, 2002; Atkinson, Mayer, & Merrill, 2005) and according to social agency theory (Atkinson et al., 2005; Mayer, Sobko, & Mautone, 2003; Moreno et al., 2001), may also enhance learner engagement by simulating natural human-to-human interactions.

Atkinson (2002) and Moreno et al. (2001) experimentally demonstrated modality effects with pedagogical agents. Mayer, Dow, and Mayer (2003) replicated the effect in an interactive agent-based environment. Students learned about electric motors by asking questions and receiving answers from an on-screen pedagogical agent who stood next to an on-screen diagram of the electric motor. Results of post-test transfer tasks indicated that students performed better when the agent's explanations were delivered as narration rather than on-screen text.

There are negative results using animated, interactive, pedagogical agents. Using instruction concerning the human cardiovascular system with college students, Dunsworth and Atkinson (2007) failed to demonstrate a modality effect with pedagogical agents comparing an agent with narration vs. an agent with on-screen text. They did, however, find a large and significant agent effect where an animated agent delivering aural instructions was more effective than on-screen text only. They also found an image effect in which an agent with aurally delivered instructions was superior to aural instructions only. It should be noted that the learning materials used by Dunsworth and Atkinson (2007) introduced many new scientific terms that had to be related with relevant visual information. We might expect very high levels of cognitive load associated with the transient, auditory information for students with little or no prior knowledge of the human circulatory system, explaining the failure to obtain a modality effect (Chapter 17).

Factors Moderating the Modality Effect

Most of the early studies of the instructional modality effect were conducted in strictly controlled, laboratory settings with relatively short instruction times and used materials from well-defined technical domains like mathematics (Jeung et al., 1997; Mousavi et al., 1995), science (Mayer & Moreno, 1998, 1999), and engineering (Kalyuga et al., 1999, 2000; Tindall-Ford et al., 1997). These materials addressed explanations of technical or scientific processes and procedures with limited levels of learner control allowed. The studies were conducted mostly with senior high school students, higher education students and technical trainees. The applicability of the effect in domains and learning environments with different characteristics had to be further investigated.

For example, De Westelinck, Valcke, De Craene, and Kirschner (2005) investigated several multimedia design principles including dual-modality presentations using social sciences materials. The study failed to replicate multimedia, split-attention (see Chapter 9) and modality effects and in some cases, found statistically significant differences opposite to those expected. Several other studies also reported failures to replicate a modality effect under some conditions (e.g. Brünken, Plass, & Leutner, 2004; Dutke & Rinck, 2006; Goolkasian, 2000; Lowe, 1999; Moreno & Durán, 2004; Schnotz & Bannert, 2003). Therefore, establishing the boundaries and conditions of the applicability of the modality effect is an important research issue.

Ginns (2005b) conducted a meta-analysis of modality effect studies based on 43 experiments involving a broad range of instructional materials, age groups and outcome measures. The meta-analysis generally supported the positive effects of dual-modality presentations as well as the effect of two major moderators, the level of element interactivity and pacing of presentation.

We indicated above that the modality effect only can be expected to be obtained if multiple sources of information must be processed together in order for the information to be understood. There are several other conditions required for the modality effect.

Levels of Element Interactivity

Tindall-Ford et al. (1997) found strong effects in favour of dual-modality formats only for materials with high levels of element interactivity. There were no differences between alternative formats for low element interactivity instructions. A sufficiently high level of element interactivity for the learning material is an essential moderating factor for the modality effect. According to the element interactivity effect (see Chapter 15), instructional materials with very low levels of element interactivity, or intrinsic cognitive load, are unlikely to demonstrate any benefits of dual-modality presentations or, indeed, any other cognitive load effects.

If learning materials are characterised by high levels of element interactivity, they may initially overload the visual channel. That overload may be escalated by split attention between visually presented sources of information that refer to each other. Using a dual-modality format in this situation may effectively reduce this load and expand cognitive resources available for learning, thus resulting in a modality effect. On the other hand, if learning materials have low levels of element interactivity, then even relatively high levels of extraneous cognitive load may still be within working memory limits and may not interfere with learning.

However, an excessively high level of element interactivity may also eliminate the advantages of dual-modality presentations. When dealing with complex, unfamiliar or abstract representations, learners may experience very high levels of intrinsic cognitive load, especially if they do not have sufficient prior knowledge relevant to the representations. Using complex, transitory, spoken information may itself overburden working memory, resulting in a failure to demonstrate a modality effect (see Chapter 17).

Pacing of Presentations

The meta-analysis by Ginns (2005b) indicated that strong effects of dual-modality presentations were observed only under system-paced conditions. Most experiments that initially established the modality effect used system-controlled pacing, and the fixed instruction time was determined by the pace of the narration in the dual-modality condition. Tabbers et al. (2004) noted difficulties with observing a modality effect under learner-controlled pacing of presentation. They investigated the modality effect in a realistic classroom setting with second-year university students studying a web-based multimedia lesson on instructional design for a relatively prolonged time (over an hour). The instruction was learner-paced (e.g. in the audio conditions, students had the opportunity to listen to narrated text repeatedly). The results indicated that students in the visual condition performed better than students in the audio condition on both retention and transfer tests. Students in the visual condition also spent significantly less time on the instructions, although slow downloading of the audio may have negatively influenced students' attention and learning in the audio condition. It was suggested that the main reason for this "reverse modality effect" was the learner-paced environment in contrast to system-paced instructions used in earlier research.

In system-paced conditions, learners presented with visual text need to spend part of the fixed instruction time on visual search while constantly switching their attention back and forth between verbal and pictorial elements and mentally integrating them while faced with a time constraint imposed by the system. These processes may result in a high extraneous cognitive load. In learner-paced presentations, students may have extra time to manage this load by reviewing the material at their own pace. In this case, the benefits of dual-modality formats could be reduced or eliminated. More available time for processing and relating the text to the pictures presumably may compensate for extraneous cognitive load. For example, learners can read segments of printed text repeatedly without the risk of missing important elements of transitory, narrated information. In realistic settings though, students do not usually have an unlimited amount of time to learn specific materials, and self-pacing is not always possible.

Thus, even though the modality effect was established mostly in laboratory-based system-paced conditions, these conditions are not too distant from the reality of educational practice.

Harskamp et al. (2007) demonstrated the modality effect with a self-paced, web-based multimedia science lesson in a regular school setting. Another experiment in their study showed that the effect occurred only with students who required less time to learn and not with students who took more time to learn. Thus, the differences in learning time between students may need to be taken into account when analysing conditions of applicability for the modality effect.

An Alternative Explanation for the Reverse Modality Effect

While the use of self-paced presentations can plausibly explain the elimination of the modality effect, it is difficult to see how it can explain a reverse modality effect where visual-only material is superior to audio-visual material. Leahy and Sweller (in press) provided an alternative explanation along with accompanying data. The theory and data will be discussed in more detail in Chapter 17 when discussing the transient information effect, but for the sake of completeness, we will provide a brief introduction here.

Successful demonstrations of the modality effect may require relatively brief, relatively simple, textual information. If the textual information is lengthy and complex, presenting it in spoken form may have negative consequences due to cognitive load factors. We know working memory for novel information is severely limited in duration and we also know that spoken information is transitory. A lengthy, complex, high element interactivity segment of spoken text may exceed working memory limits. The same text presented in written form may be much easier to process because more time can be spent on complex sections while easier sections can be skimmed rapidly. We suggest that the reverse modality effect has been obtained exclusively using lengthy, complex, auditory textual material. Lengthy auditory material may overwhelm working memory and override any possible benefit due to an audio-visual presentation. The result is likely to be superiority of a visual-only presentation resulting in a reverse modality effect.

Leahy and Sweller (in press) tested this hypothesis in two experiments. One experiment, using lengthy text, obtained a reverse modality effect with visual-only information proving superior to an audio-visual presentation. Another experiment used the same material but broke it down into much smaller segments and yielded a conventional modality effect with an audio-visual presentation being superior to a visual-only presentation.

In spite of the results of Tabbers et al. (2004), there is now considerable evidence that the use of either self-paced or system-paced conditions has no effect on the modality effect (e.g. Harskamp et al., 2007; Schmidt-Weigand, Kohnert, & Glowalla, 2009; Wouters, Paas, & van Merriënboer, 2009). Nor is there any theoretical reason to suppose that pacing should result in a reverse modality effect. In contrast, based on cognitive load theory considerations, the length of textual material should affect the modality effect. Some studies that fail to find an effect and all studies that have found a reverse modality effect seem to use much longer, more complex auditory segments than studies that succeeded in obtaining a modality effect. The suggestion that lengthy auditory segments may overwhelm working memory accords closely with cognitive load theory. The data provided by Leahy and Sweller (under editorial consideration) support this hypothesis.

Reducing Visual Search

When a diagram is accompanied by a spoken explanation, learners usually still have to search through the diagram to locate the sections being referred to in the auditory text. Dual-mode presentations often show superiority over alternative single-modality formats only when techniques for attracting student attention to the relevant sections of the diagram are used. A cueing or signalling effect provides an example (Jeung, Chandler, & Sweller, 1997; Mayer & Moreno, 2002, 2003). Jeung et al. (1997) compared three conditions: visual only, audio-visual and audio-visual with flashing in which the relevant sections of the diagram flashed whenever they were referred to by the audio statements. Two types of geometry tasks were used that differed in the degree of complexity of the required visual search. A modality effect was observed only when a flashing technique was used as a cue and only in the case of complex visual search. The results showed that the audio–visual with flashing format was superior to the other two conditions that did not differ between themselves.

It was suggested that learners have to hold auditory information while searching for the relevant visual information on the screen. If this search is too complex and extensive to be accomplished simultaneously with the spoken explanation, an advantage of a dual-modality format may not be obtained unless appropriate visual signals are used to coordinate visual and auditory information and thus assist the learner in locating and processing the relevant information. In contrast, if the material is simple and so does not require assistance in locating relevant sections, element interactivity may be too low to generate a modality effect. Dual-modality presentations may only enhance learning when appropriate visual cues are added to relate corresponding elements in spoken text and complex, visual representations.

Mayer and Johnson (2008) demonstrated that a short on-screen version of narrated text that highlighted its key points and was placed next to the corresponding portions of a graphic could provide an appropriate visual signal. In two experiments using a series of narrated static slides explaining lightning formation and how a car's braking system works, each slide appeared for 8–10 s and contained a diagram with a brief (1–2 sentences) narration. In one format, each slide also contained 2–3 printed words placed next to the corresponding part of the diagram that were identical to the words in the narration and conveyed the main event described in the narration. Results demonstrated that the format with embedded short phrases (labels) resulted in better post-test retention scores than the format without the phrases, with no difference on the transfer test. It was suggested that the embedded on-screen words guided the learners' attention in locating the relevant graphical information.

Lee and Kalyuga (2011) have recently provided additional evidence to support this assumption. They demonstrated that a conventional method of presenting Chinese characters and verbal pronunciation instructions concurrently resulted in better learning of pronunciation when written pronunciation information was provided next to new key characters in the sentences to draw learners' attention. Again, the placement of written information guided attention to appropriate parts of a visual display (see Chapter 9 on the split-attention effect).

Summary of Conditions of Applicability

Under appropriate conditions as defined by cognitive load theory, the modality effect is stable and robust. Nevertheless, like all extraneous cognitive load effects, the critical issue is always whether an extraneous cognitive load is imposed, not whether a particular category of instruction is used. Simply using audio-visual instructions can never guarantee improved learning if those audio-visual instructions do not reduce extraneous cognitive load. We have identified several conditions required to obtain the modality effect:

(a) As is the case for the split-attention effect, diagrammatic and textual information must refer to each other and be unintelligible unless they are processed together.
(b) Element interactivity must be high. If element interactivity is low, neither the modality effect nor any other cognitive load effect can be obtained.
(c) Auditory text must be limited. Lengthy, complex text should be presented in written, not spoken form. Lengthy text that cannot be held and processed in working memory will prevent a modality effect and can generate a reverse modality effect.
(d) If diagrams are very complex, cuing or signalling may be required so that learners can focus on those parts of the visual display being referred to by the auditory information.

There is one other known condition that affects the modality effect that will not be discussed in detail in this chapter. Levels of learner expertise may also influence the effect. Even though most of the research studies investigating the modality effect have been conducted with novice learners, there is evidence that the effect may be eliminated or reversed with relatively more experienced learners (e.g. Kalyuga et al., 2000). The expertise reversal effect that explains the reasons why cognitive load effects are not obtainable with more knowledgeable learners will be considered in detail in Chapter 12.

Instructional Implications

The major instructional implication that flows from the modality effect is that under certain, well-defined circumstances, there can be considerable benefits to presenting information in a dual-mode, audio-visual form rather than in a visual-only form. Care must be taken to ensure that the conditions for the superiority of audio-visual instructions apply. The most important conditions, all of which flow directly from cognitive load theory, are that the audio and visual sources of information must rely on each other for intelligibility, element interactivity needs to be high and the audio component needs to be sufficiently short to be readily processed in working memory.

There are many curriculum areas where these conditions can be readily met. Many areas of mathematics and science provide examples. Statements such as "Angle ABC equals Angle XBZ (vertically opposite angles are equal)" in association with a geometric diagram may be far better presented in spoken rather than written form. Audio-visual presentation is likely to be beneficial because the diagram and the text must be processed in conjunction with each other, element interactivity in geometry is usually very high, and the statement can readily be held and processed in working memory. By using auditory rather than visual text, visual working memory resources can be devoted entirely to the diagram while auditory memory resources are used to process the text. By sharing the cognitive load between the auditory and visual processors, the visual processor is less likely to be overloaded and so learning should be facilitated.

Equally, there are many curriculum areas where the use of dual-mode presentation is quite inappropriate. Lengthy text that does not have to be processed in conjunction with a diagram, or anything else, will not lead to the modality effect. Simply presenting information in an audio-visual format does not guarantee the advantages that accrue from the modality effect. The ultimate criterion is not whether an audio-visual format is used but rather, whether extraneous cognitive load is reduced. If it is not reduced, an audio-visual format will not assist and may even interfere with learning.

Conclusion

When textual information accompanying pictures, animations or simulations is presented in an auditory rather than visual form, working memory capacity may be effectively increased by using the combined resources of the visual and auditory channels of working memory rather than loading all information on the visual channel. Dual-modality presentations can be used to reduce the extraneous cognitive load caused by visual split-attention. Within a cognitive load framework, the modality effect is explained by a more efficient use of the available cognitive resource. By engaging two channels of working memory and by reducing visual search and associated split-attention situations when verbal information is presented in the auditory modality, learning can be facilitated.

It is frequently suggested that presenting the same verbal information in both an auditory and a visual modality could enhance learning. A shallow interpretation of the modality effect can readily lead to this conclusion. However, the available evidence obtained within a cognitive load framework indicates that presenting the same information simultaneously in spoken and written forms is not advantageous. The following chapter will discuss this evidence within the context of the redundancy effect.

Chapter 11
The Redundancy Effect

The redundancy effect may appear on the surface to be related to the split-attention effect but in fact is quite unrelated. There are similarities because both effects deal with multiple sources of information such as visuals and text. As is the case for the split-attention effect, any combination of diagrams, pictures, animations and spoken or written verbal information can lead to the generation of extraneous cognitive load. Nevertheless, despite their surface similarities, the redundancy effect has very different characteristics to the split-attention effect. The two effects differ because the logical relations between the multiple sources of information required as essential pre-requisites to produce each effect differ; that difference is critical and should never be ignored.

As was discussed in Chapter 9, the split-attention effect occurs when learners must integrate in working memory multiple sources of related information presented independently but unintelligible in isolation. A set of geometry statements such as Angle ABC equals Angle XYZ cannot be fully comprehended without reference to a diagram. Both sources of information, the diagram and the statements, must be present and if presented in physically separate form, must be mentally integrated because they refer to each other. The working memory resources used to accomplish this integration become unavailable for learning and may exceed the available capacity of working memory.

This chapter describes a different logical relation between the multiple sources of information. The redundancy effect may occur when the multiple sources of information can be understood separately without the need for mental integration. Written or spoken text that simply re-describes a diagram that can be fully understood without the text provides an example. In this situation, the physical integration of, for example, the written text with the diagram is unlikely to be beneficial. There is no reason to suppose that learning will be enhanced by physically integrating within a diagram text superfluous to comprehension. Indeed, such conditions may be detrimental to learning by imposing an extraneous cognitive load. Accordingly, redundant information should be omitted to preclude an increase in extraneous cognitive load caused when learners inevitably focus attention on unnecessary information and physically integrate it with essential information.

J. Sweller et al., *Cognitive Load Theory*, Explorations in the Learning Sciences, Instructional Systems and Performance Technologies 1, DOI 10.1007/978-1-4419-8126-4_11, © Springer Science+Business Media, LLC 2011

Using the example of a diagram and redundant text, rather than presenting a self-explanatory diagram and a verbal explanation that just re-describes the diagram (either as visual text, spoken text or both), it should be beneficial to present the diagram alone without any explanatory text.

The most common form of redundancy occurs when the same information is presented in different modalities. A diagram with text that re-describes the diagram, or text presented in both spoken and written form provide examples. Nevertheless, it needs to be noted that in cognitive load theory, any additional information not required for learning is classified as redundant. A cartoon associated with text does not re-describe the text but is still redundant if it is not required to understand the text, as is an explanation of sections of a procedure that learners already understand. Any information presented to learners that they may unnecessarily process is redundant. Cognitive load theory does not distinguish between types of redundant information because it is assumed that they have the same negative cognitive consequences that can be eliminated by the same instructional procedures, i.e. the omission of such redundant information.

The redundancy effect occurs when information that includes redundant material results in less learning than the same information minus the redundant material. The effect provides a clear example of extraneous, interacting elements. If essential information is provided along with unnecessary information, the elements associated with the unnecessary information are likely to be processed resulting in an extraneous working memory load. That extraneous working memory load violates the narrow limits of change principle that requires working memory load to be minimised. Less information will be transferred to the long-term memory information store resulting in less effective use of the environmental organising and linking principle, the critical principle used to generate action. It follows that only essential information should be presented to learners in order to maximise use of the borrowing and reorganising principle when acquiring information.

Some Empirical Evidence for the Redundancy Effect

Chandler and Sweller (1991) first demonstrated the redundancy effect within a cognitive load framework using learning materials consisting of text and diagrams that did not have to be mentally integrated in order to be understood. In several experiments with electrical engineering materials, learners who were not explicitly requested to integrate text and diagrams needed less time to learn but performed better than learners who were explicitly instructed to integrate text and diagrams. Furthermore, a single self-explanatory diagram was found to be superior to the text-and-diagram instructions in either a conventional or an integrated form.

These results were replicated in experiments with biology materials using a self-contained diagram of blood flow through the human body. The diagram indicated, for example, that blood flowed from the left ventricle of the heart into the aorta. The corresponding statement said, 'Blood is also forced from the left ventricle into the aorta'. The relation of this statement to the diagram should be carefully noted. It is very different to the relation of a statement such as, 'Angle ABC = Angle XYZ' associated with a geometry diagram. The diagram of the blood flow in the heart, lungs and body can be readily understood in isolation. The statements merely repeat information that is clear from the diagram. They do not say something that is essential to understand the solution to a problem as occurs in the case of a geometry problem solution. In the blood flow example, the additional, explanatory textual segments were redundant and interfered with learning.

Furthermore, an integrated format in which the statements were integrated with the diagram was even less effective than conventional instruction with separated diagrams and text. The diagram-only format resulted in the best learning outcomes. It was assumed that processing redundant text would impose an extraneous cognitive load and require additional working memory resources. In a conventional split-source format, learners can partially reduce this load by ignoring the text (Chandler & Sweller, 1991). It is more difficult to ignore the text when it is physically integrated with the diagram. Bobis, Sweller, and Cooper (1993) also replicated the redundancy effect using a paper-folding learning task with primary school students. In this study, diagrams were redundant and a text-only instructional format resulted in the best learning outcomes.

The redundancy effect is pervasive. It can be found in a wide variety of instructional contexts unrelated to diagrams and text. For example, traditional forms of instruction found in manuals or presented as on-screen instruction provided with software packages or technical equipment usually require using the actual hardware or equipment when following the instructions. As indicated in Chapter 9 on the split-attention effect, if such instructions are essential, they may cause learners to split their attention between the manuals, computer screen and keyboard, or the equipment, and so result in a heavy extraneous cognitive load. If the instructions replicate information obtained more readily in other forms, the redundancy effect may need to be considered. For example, presenting learners with diagrams of hardware as well as the hardware itself may lead to redundancy. There may be learning benefits in eliminating the computer hardware or equipment during the initial stages of instruction and using diagrams of the computer screen and keyboard or technical equipment with embedded textual instructions instead. Including both the hardware and the diagrams may lead to redundancy and a heavy extraneous cognitive load that interferes with learning.

In a series of experiments, such integrated diagram and text instructions placed in a manual without the hardware being available to learners were compared to manuals with hardware (Sweller & Chandler, 1994; Chandler & Sweller, 1996). Beneficial effects of the integrated manual only instructions without the presence of actual hardware were demonstrated in both written and practical skill tests despite reduced learning times and the absence of any practical experience using the hardware prior to the tests. The results suggested that the hardware was redundant and the manual only instructions were self-explanatory for the learners.

These results should not be interpreted as indicating that it is necessarily better to learn, for example, how to use software without access to functioning software. The results should be interpreted as indicating that it is better to learn either with access to the software (or hardware) or with diagrams and integrated text representing the software and hardware, but not both. Cerpa, Chandler, and Sweller (1996) found that presenting instructions on a screen alone was superior to presenting them on both a screen and in a manual. In combination with the results indicating that it is better to learn from a manual alone than a manual plus equipment, we can conclude that it does not matter whether instructions are presented on a screen or in a manual. The important point is that they should not be presented simultaneously in both forms. The extraneous cognitive load associated with redundancy will interfere with learning if students must process similar material on a screen and in a manual. Learning is enhanced if the material is presented in one or the other, but not both.

Pociask and Morrison (2008) demonstrated the effectiveness of eliminating redundant information in instructional materials used for teaching complex, orthopaedic, physiotherapy cognitive and psychomotor skills to first-year physiotherapy students in a realistic classroom setting. The performance measures that included written and psychomotor tests, ratings of cognitive load and task completion times indicated significantly increased learning outcomes and reduced levels of cognitive load for the modified, instructional format group.

The Effect of Simultaneously Presented Written and Spoken Text

As indicated in the previous section, the split-attention and redundancy effects appear to be related because they both feature multiple sources of information. For similar reasons, the modality effect described in the previous chapter and the multimedia redundancy effect described in this section appear to be related but are not. The relation between the sources of information determines whether a modality effect or a redundancy effect will be obtained. Whether material should be presented in audio-visual form or in visual form alone is determined by the relation between the multiple sources of information. If two or more sources of information refer to each other and can only be understood in conjunction, they should be presented in audio-visual form, if possible. In contrast, if the two sources of information can be understood in isolation, only one source, either the audio or the visual source should be used. If both are used, one source will be redundant and having to process both will lead to an extraneous cognitive load.

Thus, deciding whether both sources or only one source should be used depends on the relation between the two sources. Geometry statements that cannot be understood without reference to a diagram should be presented in spoken form, or physically integrated if they must be presented in written form. In contrast, descriptions of blood flow that merely re-describe a highly intelligible diagram should not be presented in spoken or indeed, written form. They should be eliminated. The logical relation between a diagram and text is important, not the existence of a diagram and text.

Many multimedia instructional materials use narrated explanations simultaneously with written text. From a cognitive load perspective, such duplications of essentially the same information in two different modalities may overload working memory and have negative rather than positive learning effects. When spoken explanations are used concurrently with the same written text, learners may also be required to relate and coordinate the corresponding elements of written and spoken information. This extraneous to learning processing may consume additional working memory resources. Therefore, eliminating a redundant source of information might be beneficial for learning.

Kalyuga, Chandler, and Sweller (1999) used computer-based instructions in mechanical engineering to compare three different forms of textual explanations presented together with an animated diagram: written text, spoken text and written plus spoken text. The results demonstrated a multimedia redundancy effect. The spoken text group outperformed the written text plus spoken text group with a higher posttest score, a lower number of re-attempts at interactive exercises and a lower subjective rating of cognitive load. Subjective ratings of cognitive load indicated that presenting on-screen textual explanations of the diagram together with the same auditory explanations actually resulted in additional cognitive load.

Using scientific explanations of animated visuals with instructions explaining the formation of lighting storms, Mayer, Heiser, and Lonn (2001) demonstrated in two experiments with university students that learners who studied narrations with concurrent animations performed better on retention and transfer posttests than learners who studied animations with concurrent narration and on-screen text that either summarised or duplicated the narration. Craig, Gholson, and Driscoll (2002) demonstrated a similar effect with animated pedagogical agents in which visual characters were enabled with speech, gestures, movements and other human-like behaviours.

This effect of superior learning following spoken rather than spoken and written text was clearly demonstrated by Kalyuga, Chandler, and Sweller (2004). Both in instructional and other contexts, identical or similar verbal information frequently is provided in simultaneous spoken and written form. This tendency has increased first with the advent of overhead projectors and then with the introduction of PowerPoint because both of these technologies facilitated the simultaneous presentation of spoken and written text. Based on the redundancy effect, we might expect learning to be inhibited by the concurrent presentation of the same information in both modalities. Using technical, text-based instructions without diagrams (Experiment 3), Kalyuga et al. (2004) obtained precisely this effect. Learning was facilitated when instructions were presented in spoken form alone rather than both spoken and written forms concurrently.

Jamet and Le Bohec (2007) tested the effect of presenting learners with information on the development of memory models. One group were presented diagrams along with spoken information. The other two groups were presented exactly the same diagrammatic and spoken information along with the equivalent written sentences presented either sequentially, sentence by sentence, or as a full-text group in which the sentences were displayed as a block next to the diagram. In a variety of subsequent tests, the spoken text alone group demonstrated superior learning to either of the spoken plus written text groups, demonstrating that the written text was redundant.

Gerjets, Scheiter, Opfermann, Hess, and Eysink (2009) obtained a multimedia redundancy effect in hypermedia learning. Hypermedia consists of multimedia learning environments with elements of information interconnected by a network of hyperlinks to increase levels of learner interactivity. Gerjets et al. (2009) demonstrated that arithmetical information supplemented with spoken and written explanations resulted in less efficient instruction than providing written only text. Also, in this study, spoken only explanations did not result in better learning than the dual-modality redundant format. These results may indicate that lengthy spoken text is unlikely to improve learning in any combination – with diagrams, written text, or both – as lengthy, complex, spoken information may generate a heavy working memory load in its own right (see Chapter 17 on the transient information effect). The role of the length of instructional segments is discussed below in the section on conditions of applicability of the redundancy effect.

The Redundancy Effect in Second/Foreign Language Learning

The negative effects on learning of presenting the same information in spoken and written form can be expected to have particular relevance when learning a second language. The redundancy effect has been mostly investigated in technical domains (e.g. mathematics, science, or engineering) with relatively well-structured problems. It was important to replicate these results and investigate the conditions of applicability of the effect in relatively poorly specified task areas that are typical of the social sciences and humanities. Foreign or second language acquisition is an important domain for the extension of cognitive load research. There have been a number of recent studies of cognitive load theory implications for instructional design in this area. For example, Moussa, Ayres and Sweller (in preparation) reported a redundancy effect in learning English as a foreign language. They established that a simultaneous presentation of oral and written material could inhibit learning and, paradoxically, students could learn to listen more efficiently by reading alone rather than by reading and listening at the same time. This result is only likely to be obtainable using learners with some degree of proficiency in listening. Plass, Chun, Mayer, and Leutner (2003) found that pictorial annotations were redundant for second language learners' reading comprehension.

Using first-year tertiary students as participants, Diao, Chandler, and Sweller (2007) and Diao and Sweller (2007) investigated whether the redundancy effect would apply to reading comprehension in learning English as a foreign language by comparing written presentations only and written presentations concurrent with verbatim spoken presentations. They suggested that for learners who had not achieved a sufficiently high level of foreign language proficiency, the listening rate could lag far behind the reading rate (Hirai, 1999) resulting in poor audio-visual correspondence. When the same text is presented in different modalities, learners must process these two sources of information simultaneously and build referential relations between them. Because decoding text presented even in a single modality may impose a heavy working memory load for beginner foreign language learners, they may have no available working memory capacity to read and listen at the same time, resulting in a redundancy effect.

Results demonstrated that the presence of a concurrent spoken presentation rendered reading comprehension less effective compared with written only instructions. At the lexical level, the concurrent presentation group gained less lexical knowledge than the read only group. At the level of text comprehension, the concurrent presentation group reported a higher cognitive load and demonstrated a lower level of main/general idea understanding and recall. Also, as can be expected from the element interactivity effect (Chapter 15), the interference of a concurrent spoken presentation was more evident for a textual passage with more complex syntax and text structures and, accordingly, a higher level of intrinsic cognitive load.

These results contradict the common practice of teachers to read out a text while students follow their words in a textbook. It needs to be noted that there is extensive evidence in the literature on second/foreign language comprehension suggesting a positive effect of presentations consisting of concurrent written and spoken text (e.g. Borrás & Lafayette, 1994; Garza, 1991; Markham, 1999). Almost without exception, these results are due to a common, specific flaw in the experimental designs used. There is a difference between comprehension and learning. If learners are presented text and then given a comprehension test, they will almost always score more highly on that test if the information is presented in dual-modality rather than single-modality form because they can choose to concentrate on reading or listening, whichever they feel will most increase comprehension. Nevertheless, in instructional contexts, an increase in comprehension is less important than an increase in what has been learned and an increase in comprehension does not mean more has been learned. To determine whether more has been learned, learners must be presented with new material following the phase in which dual- or single-modality material has been presented. They should be tested for their comprehension on that new material rather than the original material. If they have learned more following a single- or dual-modality presentation of the original material, then comprehension of the new material should be improved and a comprehension test of the new (not the old) material should demonstrate the extent to which learning has occurred during the original presentation of the old material under single- or dual-modality conditions. Using this experimental design, the common result suggests that single-modality presentations result in more learning than dual-modality presentations (Diao & Sweller, 2007; Diao, Chandler, & Sweller, 2007; Moussa, Ayres, & Sweller, in preparation).

Thus, cognitive load theory suggests that when teaching novice second/foreign language learners to read or to listen, the common procedure of presenting both written and spoken text simultaneously may not be appropriate. If the aim of instruction is to teach novice learners to read, involving them in listening together with reading instruction could interfere with rather than facilitate learning. Furthermore, beyond the novice level, learning to listen is facilitated more by reading than by listening and reading.

Evidence for the Redundancy Effect in Pre-Cognitive Load Theory Research

Several examples of phenomena that can readily be related to the redundancy effect were demonstrated before cognitive load theory was developed and applied to redundancy. These examples are notable in that in a very wide variety of disciplines and procedures, they provide evidence of the redundancy effect but have no consistency in their theoretical explanations. None were explained in terms of a working memory load.

Reder and Anderson (1980, 1982), in a particularly interesting example of redundancy, found that students could learn more from summaries of textbooks than from the full chapters. Most textbook writers take the traditional view that providing learners with additional information is at worst neutral in its effects and could be beneficial. Not only is information frequently presented at considerable length, redundant material such as cartoons and other irrelevant pictorial information is often included. All require scarce working memory resources to process. From a cognitive load theory perspective, it is not surprising that more can be learned from a summary than a full textbook chapter, consistent with the result obtained by Reder and Anderson.

Schooler and Engstler-Schooler (1990) found that the requirement to verbalise a visual stimulus could impair its subsequent recognition. Verbalising visual information can be difficult and may place a considerable load on working memory. Furthermore, that load may add little to the ability to subsequently recognise the visual material, explaining the Schooler and Engstler-Schooler results in terms of redundancy and cognitive load.

Lesh, Behr, and Post (1987) found that mathematical word problems could become more difficult to solve if additional concrete information is included in the problem statements. Many mathematics educators have suggested that the difficulty students have in learning to solve word problems could be ameliorated by the inclusion of concrete, physical representations of the problems. Some of these suggestions can be sourced to a Piagetian view of the distinction between concrete and formal operational thought. Piagetian stage theory suggests that we learn to manipulate concrete objects prior to learning to manipulate more abstract, formal entities. In fact, whether or not we know how to manipulate concrete objects, we still need to be able to process the abstract representations of objects incorporated in many word problems. If working memory resources are devoted to manipulating the concrete objects, we may have insufficient resources left to learn how to deal with their abstract equivalents. Seeing the objects is merely likely to interfere with learning how to manipulate the abstract representations, leading to redundancy.

Using a flow diagram of the nitrogen, water, oxygen and carbon dioxide cycles, Holliday (1976) demonstrated that high school students who studied a diagram only achieved better comprehension than two groups that studied the diagrams alongside a text that presented the same material, or the text alone. Students who were presented with text and diagrams performed no better than those who studied the text only.

The diagram alone was all that was needed to learn the material. Adding text to the diagram was redundant while text alone either did not include sufficient information or else provided the information in a form that was difficult to process.

Miller (1937) demonstrated that presenting children with a word associated with a picture was less effective than the word alone in teaching children to read. In order to learn to read, working memory resources must be devoted to the graphics that constitute text. Based on cognitive load theory and the redundancy effect, nothing is gained by devoting working memory resources to pictures as well as the text. Most beginning readers know what a cat looks like and do not need to see a picture of a cat. Their working memory resources need to be concentrated on the graphics that constitute the written word 'cat'. Miller's results were replicated by Saunders and Solman (1984) who demonstrated that adding pictures to words interfered with learning.

It might be noted that this picture-word effect equally applies to learning to read whole sentences as well as individual words. Torcasio and Sweller (2010) extended this work to learning to read phrases and sentences. They found that the picture books commonly used to teach young children to read and consisting of sentences on one page and corresponding pictures on the opposite page resulted in less learning than the same sentences without the pictures. For young children, learning to read requires them to attend to a sentence such as 'Mrs. Smith lived in the house on the hill'. If they see a picture of Mrs. Smith and the house on the hill, working memory resources are likely to be devoted to the picture rather than the text resulting in less textual learning compared to learners who only see the text, a classic redundancy effect.

It can be seen that there is a wealth of data demonstrating the redundancy effect. Until the advent of cognitive load theory, most of these results had little influence because they were treated as individual, unrelated findings. Hopefully, the advent of cognitive load theory and knowledge of the redundancy effect will result in a reconsideration of these important findings.

Factors Moderating the Redundancy Effect

Investigating specific boundaries for the redundancy effect is an important research issue. Some established conditions required for the redundancy effect are described below.

Independence of Information Sources

We have emphasised above and in previous chapters that the split-attention and modality effects are obtainable only when the related sources of information are unintelligible in isolation. In contrast, this chapter is concerned with conditions under which sources of information are intelligible in isolation. An example is textual information presented in written and/or spoken form that merely re-describes a diagram, a table or another section of text. If a diagram, table or text is intelligible in isolation and contains all of the required information, its spoken and/or written re-description should be eliminated rather than included. We have emphasised these points because they frequently are ignored in the literature.

For the redundancy effect to occur, either source of information must be intelligible separately. If a source of information (textual or graphical) is fully intelligible on its own, then any additional redundant sources of information should be removed from the instructional materials rather than integrated into them.

Levels of Element Interactivity

As with other cognitive load effects, sufficiently high levels of element interactivity for the learning material are an essential moderating factor if the redundancy effect is to be observed. According to the element interactivity effect (see Chapter 15), instructional materials with low levels of element interactivity and consequently, a low intrinsic cognitive load, are unlikely to demonstrate noticeable benefits from eliminating redundant elements of information. Even relatively high levels of extraneous cognitive load may still be within working memory limits and not interfere with learning. In contrast, if learning materials are characterised by high levels of element interactivity and therefore generate a heavy intrinsic cognitive load, an additional extraneous cognitive load caused by processing redundant information can be harmful to learning.

For example, a modified, self-contained manual without a requirement to refer to actual hardware can be beneficial compared to the manual plus the hardware, but only for tasks characterised by high levels of element interactivity (Chandler & Sweller, 1996). No redundancy effect was demonstrated by Chandler and Sweller (1996) for low element interactivity material. Measures of cognitive load confirmed the importance of element interactivity to the redundancy effect. Significantly better test results associated with a lower cognitive load favoured an integrated, modified manual only group compared to the manual and hardware group in areas of high element interactivity. No effects were found in areas of low element interactivity.

At the other end of this spectrum, when dealing with excessively complex materials for which learners do not have sufficient prior knowledge, very high levels of intrinsic cognitive load may be experienced. Even eliminating redundant sources of information for such materials may not alleviate the experienced cognitive overload, resulting in a failure to demonstrate a redundancy effect.

Pacing of Presentations

In most audio-visual learning experiments that have demonstrated multimedia redundancy effects, system-controlled pacing was used, and the fixed instruction time was determined by the pace of the narration. In such conditions, learners presented with visual text in addition to its auditory form need to engage in visual search by switching their attention back and forth between on-screen text and pictorial elements while under strict time constraints imposed by the system. These processes may result in a high extraneous cognitive load. In learner-paced presentations, students may review the material at their own pace with extra time available for managing potential overload, thus reducing the benefits of non-redundant presentations. Of course, when narration is used, learner-paced presentations, while feasible, can be difficult to implement and difficult for students to use.

In two experiments with technical apprentices, Kalyuga, Chandler, and Sweller (2004) compared simultaneously presented written and auditory forms of the same information with an instructional format in which these sources of information were temporally separated with the redundant written text presented only after the narration ended. The experiments demonstrated that the sequential presentation of auditory and visual explanations of a diagram resulted in superior posttest scores and lower ratings of cognitive load than the concurrent presentation of the same explanations. However, this effect was obtained only when instruction time was constrained in a system-controlled condition (Experiment 2). There were no differences in a learner-controlled condition (Experiment 1). The unrestricted instruction time might have partially compensated for the unavailable processing resources that were used to deal with the increased extraneous load during concurrent presentation compared with sequential presentation. In contrast, in the restricted condition, simultaneous presentations may have overloaded working memory with neither visual nor auditory text processed adequately. The delayed presentation of the visual text could have effectively served as a repetition of the presentation, thus enhancing the positive effects of the earlier auditory text.

The Length of Instructional Segments

As was the case for the modality effect, the length of textual segments may also be a factor influencing the redundancy effect. When simultaneously processing uninterrupted, long textual descriptions presented in visual and auditory modalities, learners may have to relate and reconcile too many elements of information within a limited time frame. Segmenting the text may eliminate negative effects of verbal redundancy.

Experiment 3 of Kalyuga et al. (2004) used lengthy, technical textual materials without diagrams and demonstrated a redundancy effect through concurrent presentation of auditory and visual material compared with the auditory-only text. Possible influences of visual split attention were excluded in this experiment as no diagrams were involved. However, Moreno and Mayer (2002) demonstrated that when no visual diagrams were involved, concurrent presentations of the same auditory and visual text produced better results than auditory-only text, indicating a reverse redundancy effect. This difference in results could be due to the length of textual segments that were processed continuously. In the Kalyuga et al. (2004) study, the text was presented to participants continuously as a single large chunk of around 350 words without breaks. In contrast, Moreno and Mayer (2002) presented the text in several consecutive small segments with appropriate breaks between them. Such breaks may have allowed the learners to consolidate their partial mental models constructed from each segment of the text before moving to the next one.

Thus, if text is partitioned into logically complete and easily managed sequential segments with time breaks between them, a narration with concurrent, visual text may not only eliminate negative effects of verbal redundancy, but actually improve learning. For example, such formats could be effective for learners for whom the language of instruction is a second language and who may have problems with understanding auditory text without a written back-up. On the other hand, continuously presenting long textual descriptions may contribute to the intrinsic complexity of instructional materials by forcing learners to relate and reconcile many elements of auditory and visual information within a limited time frame.

Thus, while demonstrating a modality effect may require relatively brief and simple textual information, the multimedia redundancy effect usually occurs if the textual information is lengthy and complex. Presenting this information in spoken form, especially concurrently with the same information in visual form, may cause a cognitive overload and have negative learning consequences similar to the reverse modality effect (Chapters 10 and 17). Lengthy sections of spoken text that is transitory in nature may exceed working memory capacity limits. Similar to the modality effect, the length of textual segments may override pacing of the presentation as a factor influencing the conditions of applicability of the multimedia redundancy effect.

Summary of Conditions of Applicability

Several conditions that are essential for occurrence of the redundancy effect have been identified:

(a) Different sources of information must be intelligible independently with no requirement for mental integration and simultaneous processing.
(b) Element interactivity of learning materials must be high.
(c) For the multimedia redundancy effect, the text must be presented concurrently in written and spoken forms and be sufficiently lengthy and complex to cause high levels of working memory load.

It is also plausible that levels of learner expertise could influence the effect as the notion of redundancy may be affected by learner levels of expertise. Information that is essential and non-redundant for novices may become redundant for experts. The expertise reversal effect observed in such situations depends on the redundancy effect and will be considered in detail in the next chapter.

Instructional Implications

The major instructional implication that flows from the redundancy effect is that in many instructional situations, there may be more costs than benefits in concurrently presenting essentially the same information in different forms such as different modalities, or presenting any unnecessary information. The most important conditions for the redundancy effect to occur, all of which flow directly from cognitive load theory, are that the sources of information must not rely on each other for intelligibility, element interactivity should be high, and where different verbal modalities are involved, the audio component needs to be sufficiently complex to impose high processing demands on working memory.

There are many instructional situations that meet these conditions. For example, the effect may often occur during PowerPoint presentations when large amounts of textual information are presented on the screen and simultaneously narrated by the presenters. In this situation, the audience needs to relate the on-screen text with the presenter's oral explanations, often also needing to pay attention to additional graphical information presented on the screen. These processes may require excessive working memory resources that become unavailable for comprehending and learning essential information. Reducing the on-screen text to a short list of the most important points and explaining them in detail orally may provide a better presentation technique.

Repeatedly occurring examples of redundancy can be found in maps, street directories, pie-charts and other diagrams complemented with textual explanations. When a diagram is self-contained, any additional verbal explanations can unnecessarily distract learner attention and generate an extraneous cognitive load irrespective of whether they are presented in an integrated visual form, auditory form or both.

Many traditional manuals instructing people how to use various software applications or technical devices require learners to simultaneously pay attention to explanations in the manual, in many cases, illustrated by screenshots or pictures, to the actual computer screen or equipment, and also enter data or commands using the computer keyboard. In addition to the common occurrence of split-attention, these types of instruction may also contain redundant sources of information, most notably, the computer or device itself. These sources of redundancy may contribute to high levels of extraneous cognitive load. As was noted above, temporarily eliminating computers or redundant hardware at the initial stages of learning should facilitate learning. Such self-contained manuals, dealing with highly interactive components of instruction, have proved to be effective for novice computer users (Sweller & Chandler, 1994; Chandler & Sweller, 1996). Eliminating the manual and placing all information on the screen also may be effective from a cognitive load perspective. In this case, the only role of the computer during the initial stages of learning would be to turn on-screen pages. After learners acquire some knowledge of the application or hardware, they will be able to handle higher levels of cognitive load because the effective capacity of working memory increases significantly when dealing with familiar information (see Chapter 4). Therefore, in the following stages of learning, the computer may be used for more interactive modes of learning. However, in areas where motor components and spatial-motor coordination are essential (e.g. typing), extensive practice with real equipment from initial learning is likely to remain essential.

Conclusions

For many of us, a common sense perspective often suggests that by presenting the same information in multiple forms such as presenting verbal information in both auditory and visual modalities will enhance student learning. Counter to this intuition, the available experimental evidence obtained within a cognitive load framework indicates that this perspective may contain a basic fallacy and instructional presentations involving redundant information more often inhibit rather than enhance learning. This chapter reviewed the theory and empirical evidence, outlining the conditions under which the redundancy effect might occur.

Within a cognitive load framework, the redundancy effect is explained by the increases in extraneous cognitive load generated by the need to process redundant information. Learners who are presented with several sources of essentially the same information simultaneously such as written and spoken text may need to attempt to coordinate them. Randomly searching for connections between elements from different sources of information that are not related to the learning goal can produce heavy demands on working memory and thus be detrimental to learning. Even when additional sources of information are unrelated to the major source such as background music, talk or movement, they are likely to capture attention and so divert working memory resources away from the task at hand, resulting in a reduction in learning due to redundancy. Irrelevant, unnecessary information can easily capture working memory resources and reduce learning. It should be eliminated.

The notion of redundancy may depend on levels of learner expertise. Information that is essential and non-redundant for novices may become redundant for experts. Therefore, as learners acquire more expertise in a domain, the information that has been previously essential and non-redundant may become redundant and cause increased levels of extraneous cognitive load for these learners. The associated expertise reversal effect will be considered in detail in the following chapter.

Chapter 12
The Expertise Reversal Effect

The expertise reversal effect was initially predicted by cognitive load theory as a form of the redundancy effect (see Chapter 11) that occurs when information beneficial to novice learners becomes redundant to those more knowledgeable. It is one of several cognitive load effects that rely on an interaction between a basic cognitive load effect, in this case the redundancy effect, and other factors, in this case levels of expertise. As an example of the expertise reversal effect, detailed textual explanations, especially if they are embedded into diagrams thus reducing the possibility of ignoring them, may be essential for novices but redundant for experts.

When discussing the redundancy effect, we dealt with material and learners for whom additional information was redundant. In the case of the expertise reversal effect, we are concerned with a combination of material and learners for whom, in the case of novices, the additional material is essential for understanding but for experts, the same additional material is redundant. Novices, because of their levels of knowledge when dealing with these materials, may be unable to process information contained in diagrams unless additional textual material is included. Neither textual explanations nor diagrams are redundant for novices in this situation, as these sources of information are not intelligible independently for these learners. In contrast, presenting the same textual information and diagrams to experts may require them to process material superfluous to their understanding, consuming unnecessarily additional cognitive resources compared with instruction which excludes this material. A series of empirical studies, as described below, confirmed this prediction.

The expertise reversal effect flows as a logical consequence of some fundamental features of human cognitive architecture. The critical role of learner knowledge in long-term memory is central to human cognition. As was indicated in Part II, long-term memory provides an information store and information in that store can drive appropriate action via the environmental organising and linking principle. It is therefore reasonable to expect that levels of learner knowledge (or levels of learner expertise) should influence the occurrence of all cognitive load effects. If learners already have acquired information, requiring them to process that information again via the borrowing and reorganising principle may result in an extraneous cognitive load due to the narrow limits of change principle. Learners who already have acquired information will be unnecessarily processing excess interacting elements. In contrast, learners who do not have the required information will need to process those elements. Instructional procedures need to reflect these differing cognitive states. Instructional techniques and procedures that are optimal for novice learners may become suboptimal when learners acquire more expertise in the domain.

Most of the studies reviewed in the previous chapters were conducted with novice learners who did not possess substantial amounts of relevant, domain-specific knowledge. While novices are more in need of instruction than more expert learners, as expertise increases, there still is a need for instruction and that instruction may differ substantially from that required by novices. As learners acquire more expertise in a specific area of knowledge, the information or activities that previously were essential may become redundant, causing increased levels of extraneous cognitive load. As a consequence, instructional techniques effective for novices may become ineffective for more expert learners due to redundancy. Conversely, techniques ineffective for novices may become effective for more expert learners. These changes in the relative effectiveness of instructional procedures according to levels of expertise underlie the expertise reversal effect. This chapter describes empirical findings associated with the expertise reversal effect, their interpretation within a cognitive load theory framework, their relation to some associated studies undertaken prior to the development of cognitive load theory, the conditions of applicability of the effect and finally its instructional implications.

Some Empirical Evidence for the Expertise Reversal Effect

Within the cognitive architecture described in Part II of this book, knowledge structures in long-term memory perform an executive role in complex cognitive processes by appropriately directing learner attention and governing performance (see Chapter 4). To handle a task in the absence of suitable knowledge, learners need to perform mostly random and cognitively inefficient search processes followed by tests of their effectiveness with an inevitable and frequently considerable expenditure of working memory resources, resulting in cognitive overload. When knowledge is absent, direct, explicit instruction may provide an effective substitute for the missing knowledge-based executive function. For novice learners, externally provided instruction may be the only available source of executive function. For more knowledgeable learners, on the other hand, much of the required knowledge may be available in long-term memory. At intermediate levels of expertise, these two sources may complement each other, with an executive function ideally based on long-term memory knowledge when dealing with familiar elements of information, and on direct instruction when dealing with unfamiliar elements of information.

When direct instructional guidance is not provided to novices for dealing with new units of information, for example, during unguided discovery learning, an extraneous cognitive load may be generated that reduces resources available for learning. On the other hand, an extraneous load may also be generated if direct instructional guidance is provided to learners who already have a knowledge base sufficient for dealing with the information presented. These learners are likely to need to reconcile the information available in long-term memory knowledge with the externally provided guidance. That need to reconcile two different sources of essentially identical information requires working memory resources leading to an extraneous cognitive load. Thus, as levels of learner knowledge in a domain increase, the provision of the same information during instruction may become redundant and so an instructional technique that was relatively effective for novices may become relatively ineffective for more knowledgeable learners. Instruction that is optimal for novices may hinder the performance of more experienced learners by distracting them from fluently executing already learned procedures and taking full advantage of their available knowledge base. There are several categories of the expertise reversal effect that have been investigated empirically. These are discussed in the following sub-sections.

Longitudinal Studies

Initial investigations of the effect were conducted in a series of longitudinal studies. Groups of technical apprentices were intensively trained from novice to more expert states of knowledge in engineering areas (Kalyuga, Chandler, & Sweller, 1998, 2000, 2001; see Kalyuga, Ayres, Chandler, & Sweller, 2003; Kalyuga, 2007 for overviews). Levels of learner performance and cognitive load were measured at different points to observe changes in the relative effectiveness of different instructional methods.

The first experiments observed the consequences of changes in expertise on the split-attention effect (Chapter 9) using instructional materials that included textual on-screen explanations of electrical wiring diagrams. It was demonstrated that physically integrated formats with sections of text embedded into diagrams that were effective for novices compared to a split-source format became ineffective as learners acquired more knowledge in the domain (Kalyuga et al., 1998). After extensive training in the domain, the effectiveness of the integrated diagram and text format decreased while the effectiveness of a diagram-alone condition increased. Subjective ratings of cognitive load also indicated that diagrams alone were easier to process for more knowledgeable learners while an integrated diagram and text format was easier to process for less knowledgeable learners. Thus, for novices, the text was essential to understand the diagram and so needed to be presented in an integrated format. A diagram alone was ineffective because novices needed the text. With increasing expertise, the text gradually became redundant and needed to be eliminated rather than integrated. The reversal in status of the integrated diagram and text format from most to least effective, and the concomitant inverse status reversal in the diagram-alone condition with increasing expertise (i.e. least to most effective) provides an example of the expertise reversal effect.

In subsequent studies (Kalyuga et al., 2000, 2001; Kalyuga, Chandler, Tuovinen, & Sweller, 2001), more evidence for similar interactions was obtained. For example, detailed narrated explanations of how to use specific types of diagrams in mechanical engineering that were presented concurrently with animated diagrams were effective for novice learners in comparison to written explanations, thus demonstrating the modality effect (Chapter 10). However, after a series of intensive training sessions, when the same learners achieved higher levels of expertise, presenting a version of the diagrams with detailed narrated explanations inhibited learning compared to instruction including diagrams only Kalyuga et al. (2000). As knowledge levels increased, the advantage of the narrated diagrams over a diagram-alone condition gradually disappeared, and eventually reversed in comparison with results obtained for novice learners. For more expert learners, diagrams alone were better than the same diagrams along with narration. Subjective ratings of cognitive load supported a cognitive load explanation of the phenomenon.

Kalyuga, Chandler, Tuovinen, et al. (2001) showed that the advantages of worked examples on how to program industrial equipment over learning by problem solving (the worked example effect, see Chapter 8) disappeared as trainees acquired more knowledge in the task domain. In an additional experiment, worked examples and problem-solving instruction were compared for students learning to write Boolean switching equations for relay circuits. Comparisons were made initially using less experienced learners and then after two consecutive training sessions. By varying the number of elements in the circuits, it was possible to gradually increase the level of task difficulty throughout the experiment and observe continuous development of learner expertise in the domain. Because the learners were sufficiently knowledgeable at the beginning of the experiment, worked examples were of no advantage in comparison with the problem-solving procedure. With additional training, worked examples became redundant, resulting in a negative effect compared with problem-solving practice. Thus, this experiment demonstrated that with increasing expertise, an initial result indicating no difference between worked examples and problem solving changed to an advantage for problem solving.

A full switch from the worked example effect to a reverse worked example effect was obtained by Kalyuga, Chandler, and Sweller (2001). They compared worked examples with exploratory-based instructions on writing switching equations for relay circuits. Although the worked examples group initially outperformed the exploratory group, as the level of learner expertise increased after a series of training sessions, the exploratory group eventually outperformed the worked examples group. It should be noted that these experiments demonstrating the decreasing and eventually reversing advantages of worked examples compared to problem solving as expertise increases are critical to the guidance fading effect, discussed in the next chapter.

Nückles, Hübner, Dümer, and Renkl (2010) provided evidence of the expertise reversal effect in learning journal writing skills. Journal writing provides an example of cognitive and metacognitive strategies and is an effective follow-up after a lecture or seminar session in which students are asked to reflect on the previously studied material. Two studies investigated long-term effects of instructional support for writing learning journals provided in the form of prompts for applying appropriate cognitive and metacognitive strategies. Students wrote a journal entry about each weekly seminar session over a whole term. One group received prompts, while another group received no prompts. In the first half of the term, while students were still novices, the prompt group applied more strategies in their learning journals and showed higher learning success rates than the no-prompt group. Towards the end of the term, with increases in expertise, the amount of cognitive and metacognitive strategies elicited by the prompt group decreased while the number of cognitive strategies applied by the no-prompt group increased. Accordingly, when learning success was measured again at the end of the term, the prompt group performed worse than the no-prompt group. In order to avoid these negative long-term effects of prompts, a gradual and adaptive fading-out of the prompts was subsequently introduced. (See the following chapter for details of the fading effect.)

Brunstein, Betts, and Anderson (2009) investigated the effects of minimal guidance during instruction on learning (Kirschner, Sweller, & Clark, 2006) using algebra tuition. They found that with sufficient practice, minimal guidance was superior to explicit instruction but with less practice, minimal guidance was inferior to explicit instruction. These results are in accord with the expertise reversal effect. Once students have learned enough during practice, they no longer require guidance and indeed, redundant guidance has negative effects. Guidance via explicit instruction is required when learners have had limited practice and so limited experience. This result also is in accord with the guidance fading effect discussed in the next chapter.

Cross-Sectional Studies Using Worked Examples and Other Forms of Guidance

We discussed the expertise reversal effect and worked examples in longitudinal studies above (Kalyuga, Chandler, & Sweller, 2001, Kalyuga, Chandler, Tuovinen, et al., 2001). In those studies, learners were given sufficient training to increase their levels of expertise. Cross-sectional studies achieve the same aim by using learners who currently differ in levels of expertise.

Based on the expertise reversal effect as exemplified in the longitudinal studies, it might be expected that novice learners would benefit from well-guided instruction that reduces their need for random search for suitable solution steps. For more experienced learners, on the other hand, studying detailed instructional guidance and integrating it with available knowledge that provides essentially the same information might generate an unnecessary extraneous cognitive load. A number of studies have indicated that while less knowledgeable students benefited more from worked examples that provide considerable guidance than from problem solving with less guidance, for more knowledgeable learners, the benefits of minimally guided instruction were apparent. For example, Tuovinen and Sweller (1999) compared worked examples with minimally guided exploratory-based instruction on how to use a database program. Worked examples were better than exploration for low-knowledge learners, but the difference disappeared for higher knowledge learners.

Kalyuga and Sweller (2004) obtained a similar pattern of results using coordinate geometry with high school students divided into two groups of relatively more and less knowledgeable learners based on pretest scores. Results of the posttest indicated a significant interaction between knowledge levels and instructional formats. Less knowledgeable students benefited more from worked examples providing guidance. For more knowledgeable learners, there was a clear indication of problem-solving benefits.

Reisslein, Atkinson, Seeling, and Reisslein (2006) compared the effectiveness of different approaches to sequencing instructional guidance for university engineering students with different levels of expertise in the domain. While novices benefited more from worked examples, more experienced learners benefited more from various versions of problem solving.

Kyun, Kalyuga and Sweller (in preparation) demonstrated an expertise reversal effect in learning English literature. In three experiments, Korean university students for whom English was a foreign language answered essay questions. The experimental design was based on the design used to demonstrate a traditional worked example effect (Chapter 8). During the learning phase, half of the students i.e. those in the problem-solving condition, were presented conventional essay questions that they were asked to answer. The other half of the students, i.e. those in the worked example condition, were presented the same questions along with model answers that they were asked to study, followed by similar questions that they had to answer themselves. All students then were asked to answer retention, near and far transfer tests. Experiment 1 and 2 used more knowledgeable students, while Experiment 3 used students with minimal knowledge of the subject. For the retention, near and far transfer tests, there were no significant effects for the students of Experiment 1, while for Experiment 2, the worked example group performed significantly better on the retention test. In Experiment 3, the worked example group was significantly better on the retention test and marginally significantly better on near transfer tests. Furthermore, using efficiency measures (see Chapter 6), the less knowledgeable students of Experiment 3 revealed a worked example superiority on all measures while the more knowledgeable students of Experiments 1 and 2 revealed a superiority on none of the test measures except for the retention test in the case of Experiment 2. In summary, more knowledgeable learners did not need the assistance of worked examples while less knowledgeable students did need worked examples in these language-based studies, similar to the results of Kalyuga, Chandler, Tuovinen, and Sweller (2001) and Kalyuga, Chandler, and Sweller (2001) in technical training areas.

Seufert (2003) compared a no-help condition with two kinds of assistance in studying scientific text and pictures. The first type of assistance consisted of directive support in which students were given specific guidance while the second type of assistance consisted of non-directive support using questions to students with non-specific hints. The results indicated that for learners with a lower level of prior knowledge, both directive and non-directive assistance conditions were significantly better than the no-help condition, with the direct help better than the non-direct help condition. On the other hand, for learners with a higher level of prior knowledge, there were no differences between these conditions.

In one of the earliest demonstrations of the expertise reversal effect, Yeung, Chandler, and Sweller (1998) compared a traditional technique of placing a glossary of unfamiliar words at the end of the whole text with integrating the glossary definitions into the text directly above the defined word. As was expected, with novice learners (primary school students) separate glossaries caused a split-attention effect, and better comprehension was achieved using the integrated definition format. However, more experienced learners (university students) demonstrated better comprehension with the separate glossary format. The same reversed pattern of results was obtained using 8th grade students at different levels of English as a second language experience. Low-knowledge students benefited from the integrated instruction, while more experienced learners benefited from the separate glossary format (Yeung et al.). Novice learners needed the glossary and could use it more effectively if split-attention was eliminated. Experienced learners did not need the glossary but could ignore it when it was placed at the end of the text. If it was integrated into the text, the redundant information was harder to ignore and interfered with text processing.

Oksa, Kalyuga, and Chandler (2010) investigated the effects of explanatory notes on comprehension of Shakespearean text. Such texts are usually replete with classical references communicated through a language that is markedly different from Modern English. High levels of extraneous cognitive load may be imposed by traditional formats of such texts due to split attention as students search through endnotes or refer to footnotes. The design of instructional materials that was expected to assist learners in comprehending Shakespearean plays was based on interpretations of play extracts in Modern English that were physically integrated line by line with Shakespeare's original Old English text. In two experiments, extracts from different plays (*Othello* and *Romeo and Juliet*) were used with novice groups of high school students who had no prior knowledge of the texts. As expected, the results demonstrated that the integrated explanatory condition group reported a lower cognitive load and performed better in a comprehension test than the traditional format group that had the explanations in footnotes rather than integrated with the text. In another experiment, the same material was presented to a group of professional Shakespearean actors who were experts in interpreting the text. A reverse effect occurred, with the traditional format group outperforming the integrated explanatory condition group. The test performance data along with verbal protocols indicated that the explanations were redundant for these high-knowledge readers. Those explanations could be ignored when placed as an endnote but interfered with processing when integrated with the text. Thus, an expertise reversal effect was demonstrated in the literary comprehension area.

Using high school biology instructional texts, McNamara, Kintsch, Songer, and Kintsch (1996) found that a highly coherent text explaining all details benefited low-knowledge readers while high-knowledge readers benefited from a minimally coherent format. From a cognitive load perspective, the high-knowledge learners may have found the minimally coherent text intelligible without additional explanatory information that could increase working memory load. This text was coherent for these learners because of their available knowledge base while the text with full details was redundant. However, for less knowledgeable learners, the additional explanatory information was required while the reduced text contained insufficient information for these learners to adequately process. The interaction between levels of expertise and textual detail provides an example of the expertise reversal effect.

Pawley, Ayres, Cooper, and Sweller (2005) found an expertise reversal effect when investigating the augmentation of worked examples with a checking strategy. Learning how to generate and solve simple algebraic equations, students were also shown how to check the accuracy of their answers. This additional help was shown to benefit students with low levels of general mathematical ability, but not students with higher levels of mathematics, who scored lower in tests if they were also taught checking methods. Clearly, more able students found instruction to check their answers redundant.

Lee and Kalyuga (2011) investigated cognitive load aspects of learning Chinese language using a phonic transcription system called pinyin. Because traditional Chinese characters provide pictorial rather than phonetic information, it is conventionally taken for granted that the phonetic nature of pinyin is always useful in providing pronunciation information for Chinese characters. It is also a common practice to present characters with both pinyin and verbal pronunciation instructions concurrently. The results demonstrated that such concurrent presentations resulted in better learning of pronunciation only for learners beyond the beginner level. For less experienced learners, no differences were found between pinyin and no-pinyin transcription conditions. For these learners, concurrent presentation of pinyin and verbal pronunciation instructions represented excessive information, overwhelming working memory. Additional information, while potentially useful, in practice could not be used until sufficient knowledge had been acquired. The more experienced learners had sufficient knowledge to be able to use the additional information without cognitive overload. For these learners, a pinyin condition outperformed the no-pinyin format.

Expertise Reversal and the Isolated Elements Effect

According to the isolated elements effect (see Chapter 16), presenting complex material as a set of isolated elements of information that ignore relations between the elements during the initial stages of learning may reduce an excessive intrinsic cognitive load. While students do not learn the necessary interactions between elements, that learning can be left to later. Learning isolated elements allows students to build partial schemas that can be converted to full schemas with additional instruction that emphasises the interactions between elements (Pollock, Chandler, & Sweller, 2002). Such isolated elements learning tasks followed by fully interacting elements instruction benefited low-knowledge learners. However, this method did not provide an advantage for learners with higher levels of prior knowledge in the domain, thus demonstrating an expertise reversal effect. High knowledge learners were able to process the interacting elements and so did not need to have the information presented in isolated form.

Blayney, Kalyuga, and Sweller (2010) investigated an expertise reversal effect in the area of accountancy training with undergraduate university students. Blayney et al. compared two instructional formats that differed in their levels of generated intrinsic cognitive load: An isolated-interactive elements instructional format and a fully interactive elements format. The results provided support for the predicted expertise reversal effect. Learner levels of expertise interacted with instructional formats using isolated or interactive elements of information. As expected, novice learners benefited from studying isolated elements first. In contrast, more experienced learners benefited primarily from the fully interacting elements instruction that allowed these learners to take advantage of their knowledge base. When more experienced learners were presented the isolated elements instruction, these learners had to integrate and cross-reference the simplified and for them, redundant information with their available knowledge. That process may have unnecessarily consumed additional cognitive resources. The Blayney et al. (2010) study replicated the findings of Ayres (2006b) who found that students with little mathematical knowledge benefited from worked examples in an isolated elements format in learning elementary algebra tasks, whereas student with more mathematical knowledge benefited more from worked examples demonstrating the interactive elements more fully.

Expertise Reversal and the Variability Effect

The variability effect occurs when students learn more by studying highly variable worked examples rather than worked examples with more similar features (Chapter 16). Scheiter and Gerjets (2007) looked at two types of variability. They presented learners with algebra word problems that were grouped either according to their surface features or according to their structural features. Grouping according to surface features resulted, for example, in all motion problems or all finance problems being grouped together. Grouping according to structural features placed together all problems requiring the same type of algebraic equation for solution.

In their first experiment, Scheiter and Gerjets found that surface feature grouping enhanced performance more than structure grouping performance. Placing together structurally different problems that look the same teaches learners how to distinguish the important structural features of problems and ignore irrelevant surface features. Scheiter and Gerjets second experiment was similar except that they divided learners into those with less knowledge of the problem categories according to structure and those with more knowledge. The results indicated that for learners with less knowledge, the results were similar to those obtained in the first experiment. Grouping according to surface features was better because these students needed to learn the defining, structural features. Those structural features differed from problem to problem with surface feature grouping. Reverse results were obtained for the learners with more knowledge of structural features, providing an example of the expertise reversal effect. These more expert learners performed better when the problems were grouped according to structural rather than surface features.

Learners who already can distinguish between problem structures, do not need to be taught how to make this distinction. It is a redundant activity. They merely need to practice the procedures needed to solve the various categories. Placing problems with the same solution together allows learners to devote their working memory resources to learning how to solve each category of problem without interference by different categories of problems.

If this interpretation of Scheiter and Gerjets results is valid, it suggests that learners who have not learned to distinguish between problem categories need to be taught the relevant distinctions. The manner in which problems are grouped may assist in acquiring this knowledge. How one should group problems depends on levels of expertise. While these results are promising, they still await replication.

Pre-Training and the Expertise Reversal Effect

Both the initial use of worked examples and of isolated elements constitute a form of pre-training. There are other examples of pre-training and the expertise reversal effect that do not explicitly rely on worked examples or isolated elements.

Clarke, Ayres, and Sweller (2005) investigated the use of spreadsheets to learn mathematics. Before learning mathematics using spreadsheets, learners must know how to use spreadsheets. They may be taught mathematics and how to use spreadsheets simultaneously or they may be taught how to use spreadsheets first and then taught mathematics using spreadsheets. Clarke et al. investigated interactions between the timing of learning spreadsheet skills and levels of learner expertise. In the sequential condition, instructions on how to use spreadsheets were provided prior to applying this knowledge in learning mathematics. In the concurrent condition, instructions on using spreadsheet and mathematical concepts were presented concurrently in an integrated form so that necessary new spreadsheet skills were acquired during the learning of mathematical concepts. The results indicated that students with low-level knowledge of spreadsheets learned mathematics more effectively in the sequential formats. On the other hand, students who were more experienced in using spreadsheets benefited more from an integrated format. Measures of cognitive load (using subjective ratings) supported a cognitive load interpretation of the effect. Concurrently presented information on spreadsheet applications and mathematics could overload novice learners, thus inhibiting learning compared to a sequential presentation. In contrast, for more experienced learners who already had acquired basic spreadsheet skills, such information may be redundant. Thus, when learners are technologically inexperienced, the technology should be learned prior to learning a specific subject area. More experienced learners may learn relatively new technological skills concurrently with learning a specific subject discipline (Clarke et al., 2005).

Van Gog, Paas, and van Merriënboer (2008) compared the relative effectiveness of product-oriented worked examples and process-oriented worked examples with learners at different levels of prior knowledge. Traditional, product-oriented worked examples demonstrate only the procedure for obtaining the final product by providing a step-by-step solution without explanations supporting each step. In contrast, process-oriented worked examples include statements explaining why each step is taken (Van Gog, Paas, & van Merriënboer, 2004). Students were exposed to product–product, product–process, process–product or process–process sequences. Although a transfer test administered after the first phase demonstrated no significant differences between conditions, when combined with measures of cognitive load, it resulted in better efficiency indicators for learners who studied process-oriented examples than for learners who studied product-oriented examples. After two practice sessions, the process–product group outperformed the process–process group and demonstrated higher efficiency. Van Gog et al. (2008) concluded that process-oriented worked examples could be more efficient than product-oriented worked examples, but only during the initial stages of learning. As the learners acquired more experience during the learning phase, the process-related information could become redundant causing an expertise reversal effect.

Expertise Reversal for Multimedia and Hypermedia Representations

Early studies of cognitive aspects of multimedia learning demonstrated that using graphics with text usually enhanced learning outcomes for students with low prior knowledge levels, but not for those with higher knowledge levels (e.g. Mayer & Gallini, 1990; Mayer, Steinhoff, Bower, & Mars, 1995; see Mayer, 2009 for an overview). Recent studies in this area have provided more evidence for the expertise reversal effect.

Using sophisticated, dynamic visual representations of gas law simulations in middle-school chemistry, Lee, Plass, and Homer (2006) obtained an expertise reversal effect with two different modes of representations. A format using words such as 'temperature', 'pressure' and 'volume' along with corresponding numerical values was compared with an identical format with added visual scaffolds such as depictions of burners for temperature and weights for pressure. While low prior knowledge students benefited more from the added iconic scaffolds, high prior knowledge learners benefited more from symbolic only representations. The visual scaffolds are likely to have been redundant for these learners.

Homer and Plass (2010) used similar formats that compared purely symbolic versus added iconic representations in web-based simulations of the Kinetic Theory of Gases. They examined the effect of individual learner characteristics by measuring learner spatial abilities in addition to levels of prior knowledge, hypothesising that icons were more likely to help learners with lower rather than higher levels of spatial ability. This result was obtained. Adding iconic representations to the simulation significantly facilitated learning for low prior knowledge students only.

Schnotz and Rasch (2005) compared the effects of animated and static pictures concerned with the relation of time to the Earth's rotation. Low-experience students learned more from static pictures than from animated pictures, while there were no differences for high-experience students. In a follow-up experiment, two different forms of animations were compared: simple visual simulations and more complex, interactive animations allowing manipulations of parameters. High-experience students learned more from interactive animations than from simple simulations, while low-experience learners benefitted more from simple simulations than from interactive animations.

These results can be explained by assuming that for novice learners, continuous animations may be too cognitively demanding due to high levels of transience (see Chapter 17 for cognitive load aspects of learning from animations and the transience effect that occurs when information that is presented disappears as instruction continues). These learners may benefit more from studying equivalent static pictures. More knowledgeable learners may be able to handle the transience of animations. This assumption was supported by a study by Kalyuga (2008a) that investigated the interaction between levels of learner expertise and effectiveness of animated and static examples. University students learned how to construct graphs of linear and quadratic equations. The study demonstrated that less knowledgeable students learned better from static diagrams that showed major transformation stages on one screen. Students with higher levels of prior knowledge learned better from animated instructions.

Similar considerations may apply to hypertext and hypermedia learning. High prior knowledge learners may be able to process random instructional segments without overloading working memory using their existing knowledge, and changing the levels of structure in the presented materials may make little difference to performance. Low prior knowledge learners may experience cognitive overload when dealing with unstructured materials by devoting most of their cognitive resources to search processes resulting in these resources being unavailable for constructing relevant schemas. These learners may therefore benefit from more structured and restricted hypertext environments (Shapiro, 1999; Shin, Schallert, & Savenye, 1994). The most important factor may not be the specific form of learning materials (linear or hypertextual), but rather how well the material is structured. Well structured hypertext may be better suited for novice learners than poorly structured traditional linear text.

Amadieu, van Gog, Paas, Tricot, and Mariné (2009) explored the effects of prior knowledge on cognitive load when learning from non-linear hypertext concept maps in the area of biology. Structured maps demonstrated explicitly the hierarchy in relations between concepts, while unstructured maps showed only the network of relations without an explicit hierarchy. The results showed that low prior knowledge learners gained more conceptual knowledge from the structured format. These learners also indicated less cognitive load in the posttest performance after learning from the structured format. On the other hand, there was no difference for high prior knowledge learners on conceptual knowledge gains from both formats. Both types of learners indicated less cognitive load involved in processing the structured concept maps. Amadieu, Tricot, and Mariné (2009) demonstrated that for low prior knowledge learners, the hierarchical structure better supported their free recall of the material, while high prior knowledge learners performed better after studying the unstructured format. Low prior knowledge learners needed the information provided by the hierarchical structure. The same information was redundant for high prior knowledge learners and so processing that information imposed an extraneous cognitive load that interfered with further learning, providing a classic expertise reversal effect.

Using multimedia materials in chemistry, Seufert, Schütze, and Brünken (2009) found the modality effect for measures of comprehension and transfer with learners who were less skilled in using memory strategies. The modality effect was not obtained with highly skilled learners indicating an expertise reversal effect.

The Expertise Reversal Effect and Aptitude-Treatment Interactions

The expertise reversal effect can be related to a long history of studies in aptitude-treatment interactions (ATIs) that occur when different treatments result in differential learning rates and outcomes depending on student aptitudes (e.g. Cronbach, 1967; Cronbach & Snow, 1977; Lohman, 1986; Mayer, Stiehl, & Greeno1975; Shute & Gluck, 1996; Snow, 1989, 1994; Snow & Lohman, 1984). In those studies, the concept of aptitude was broadly used as any learner characteristics such as knowledge, skills, learning styles or personality characteristic that influence learning processes.

Interactions between prior knowledge or achievement in a domain and instructional treatments have been considered to be a form of an ATI. Stable interactions have been found for several forms of instructional support in programmed learning. A consistent pattern of results indicated that higher levels of learner prior achievement or familiarity with a domain required lower levels of instructional support and structure and vice versa (Tobias, 1976, 1987, 1988, 1989), a result in line with the expertise reversal effect. However, in ATI research, instructional support was considered in a narrow sense, mostly as assistance in eliciting responses and providing feedback. In the ATI approach in general, cognitive processes were little considered when either measuring aptitudes using traditional psychometric test batteries or selecting instructional procedures (Federico, 1980).

Conditions of Applicability of the Expertise Reversal Effect

Most of the initial studies of the expertise reversal effect within a cognitive load framework were conducted as longitudinal studies with novice learners gradually trained to eventually become more expert in specific task domains, in controlled laboratory settings with materials from technical domains (Kalyuga et al., 1998, 2000, Kalyuga, Chandler, & Sweller, 2001). Subsequently, interactions between different instructional methods and levels of learner expertise have been found in a wide variety of instructional contexts including a large range of instructional materials in mathematics, science, engineering, programming, accountancy, ESL, literature, management and social psychology. Participants ranged from primary school to university, in experiments that were designed as either longitudinal or cross-sectional studies. Expert-novice differences were established using a range of techniques from extended objective pre-tests of knowledge to rough estimates based on years of schooling. The effect seems to be very robust.

Despite the robustness of the effect, there is one condition of applicability common to all extraneous cognitive load effects. For all cognitive load effects associated with extraneous cognitive load, sufficiently high levels of element interactivity (or intrinsic cognitive load) in learning material is an essential condition of applicability of the expertise reversal effect. According to the element interactivity effect (see Chapter 15), instructional materials with low levels of element interactivity and consequently, low intrinsic cognitive load, are unlikely to demonstrate any significant expert–novice differences in the effectiveness of different instructional methods. The important issue is whether some of the methods or materials impose excessive levels of extraneous load beyond the cognitive capacity of learners, either novices or experts. Without a high intrinsic cognitive load, extraneous cognitive load effects will not be obtained. Results from the following two studies illustrate this issue well.

Kalyuga, Chandler, and Sweller (2001) compared worked examples-based instruction on how to construct switching equations for relay circuits with an exploratory learning environment. When the knowledge level of trainees was raised as a consequence of specifically designed training sessions, the exploratory group demonstrated better results than the worked examples group. Subjective measures of mental effort supported the cognitive load interpretation of the effect. However, these results were obtained only for relatively complex tasks with high levels of element interactivity. In that study, two levels of tasks were involved: simple tasks with few input elements and a very limited number of possible options to explore, and complex tasks with numerous options to explore. There were no differences between the instructional methods for the simple tasks.

At the other end of the complexity spectrum, excessively high levels of element interactivity also may prevent the occurrence of the expertise reversal effect. When dealing with very complex materials, even knowledgeable learners may experience excessively high levels of intrinsic cognitive load. For example, Lee et al. (2006) demonstrated an expertise reversal effect (see above) but only with interactive simulations that had manageable levels of intrinsic cognitive load, at least for some learners. For higher complexity materials, no expertise reversal effect was demonstrated.

Instructional Implications

The main instructional implication of the expertise reversal effect is the need to tailor instructional methods to levels of learner expertise as it changes during learning. In order to minimise extraneous cognitive load in learning, detailed, direct instructional support should be provided to novice learners, preferably, in integrated or dual-modality formats. At intermediate levels of expertise, a mix of direct instruction and problem-solving practice with reduced support may be optimal for learning. For advanced learners at higher levels of expertise, minimally guided problem-solving tasks should provide cognitively optimal instructional methods. Changes in the learner knowledge base need to be dynamically monitored and specific instructional techniques and procedures tailored accordingly.

A simple approach to such tailoring, suggested by researchers within the ATIs framework, was to assign students to specific treatments and levels of instructional support based on measures of their prior achievement taken before the learning session (Tennyson, 1975; Tobias, 1976). A more advanced approach needs to be based on continuously monitoring learning behaviour and appropriately refining instructional procedures. This approach may be combined with prior achievement measures for the initial selection of optimal instructional methods (Federico (1999). Such an adaptation strategy combining prior achievement measures and continuous monitoring has been realised within the cognitive load theory framework based on the expertise reversal effect (Kalyuga, 2006a; Kalyuga & Sweller, 2004, 2005; Salden, Paas, Broers, & van Merriënboer, 2004; Salden, Paas, & van Merriënboer, 2006b; van Merriënboer, Kirschner, & Kester, 2003; van Merriënboer & Sweller, 2005; see the following chapter for adaptive fading procedures).

This adaptation strategy has been primarily implemented in system-controlled environments that dynamically select an instructional method that is most appropriate for the current level of learner expertise. Even though a learner-controlled approach has been long considered as an alternative to system-controlled tailoring of instruction (e.g. Merrill, 1975), empirical findings have been more negative rather than positive (Chung & Reigeluth, 1992; Niemiec, Sikorski, & Walberg, 1996; Steinberg, 1977, 1989). According to cognitive load theory, since the effectiveness of learner control depends on students' ability to select appropriate learning strategies on their own, learners should have control over instructional methods only when they have sufficient knowledge in the domain to understand the consequences of their choice. Less experienced learners may be easily overloaded both by the need to select a task and by the consequences of an inappropriate selection. Novices require appropriate instructional support. The cognitive load effects indicate the nature of that support.

Conclusions

Frequently, we automatically assume that if instructional techniques and procedures work well for novice learners, they should also work for more experienced learners or, at least, not have negative consequences. Counter to this expectation, the theoretical considerations and the available experimental evidence provided by cognitive load theory indicates that instructional methods effective for novices may indeed inhibit learning for more experienced learners (Kalyuga, 2007; Kalyuga & Renkl, 2010).

Within the cognitive load framework, the expertise reversal effect is explained by the need to provide novices with information that is essential for their under- standing and in the case of experts, to unnecessarily process that same information that is redundant for more knowledgeable learners. The need for experts to establish connections between elements of presented information and their existing knowl- edge base can interfere with learning. Where learner knowledge is unavailable as may occur for novices, instruction should compensate for the deficiency. Where learner knowledge is available as may occur for more expert learners, the elimina- tion of redundant information allows learners to take advantage of their knowledge base in the most efficient way.

This chapter described empirical findings associated with the expertise reversal effect providing general implications for the design of instructional systems tailored to pre-existing learner knowledge. Adaptive learning environments that dynamically tailor instructional methods to changing levels of learner expertise have the best potential for optimising cognitive load based on the expertise reversal effect. A general strategy of gradually decreasing the degree of instructional guidance as the level of learner expertise increases may be implemented by using a completion strategy (van Merriënboer, 1990; van Merriënboer & Paas, 1990; see Chapter 8 for more details) or faded worked examples (Renkl, 1997; Renkl & Atkinson, 2003; Renkl, Atkinson, Maier, & Staley, 2002; see Chapter 13). Recent studies of rapid diagnostic assessment techniques (Kalyuga, 2006c, 2008b; Kalyuga & Sweller, 2004, 2005) may also offer suitable real-time measures of expertise with sufficient diagnostic power to tailor instructional procedures to learner knowledge levels. Some recent experimental attempts at implementing these techniques in adaptive learning environments using faded worked examples will be considered in the fol- lowing chapter.

Chapter 13
The Guidance Fading Effect

According to the expertise reversal effect described in Chapter 12, instructional designs and techniques that are relatively effective for novice learners can lose their effectiveness and even have negative consequences with increasing levels of expertise. As a result, instructional methods including the amount of instructional guidance provided to learners should be dynamically tailored to changing levels of learner expertise in a particular area or domain.

While levels of expertise interact with a wide range of cognitive load effects to generate the expertise reversal effect, as discussed in Chapter 12, expertise is particularly important to the worked example effect given its significance as an instructional tool for novice learners. Multiple research studies have demonstrated that for novice learners, especially during the initial stages of skill acquisition, worked examples represent a very efficient form of instruction (see Chapter 8 for a discussion of the worked example effect). They minimise use of the randomness as genesis principle, maximise use of the borrowing and reorganising principle and so reduce the extraneous interacting elements associated with problem solving resulting in a reduced working memory load as required by the narrow limits of change principle. As a consequence, information can be readily transferred to the long-term memory store and used by the environmental organising and linking principle to solve subsequent problems.

However, for more experienced learners, practice at problem solving without the assistance of worked examples is likely to be superior during later phases of skill acquisition. Worked examples are likely to be less effective for more knowledgeable learners because integrating the detailed instructional guidance of the sort provided by worked examples with knowledge structures already available in a learner's long-term memory may require additional cognitive resources and thus impose an unnecessary cognitive load. Instructional formats that provide reduced guidance or minimal support, such as problem-solving practice or exploratory learning environments, may be more cognitively efficient for relatively advanced learners. Worked examples and other forms of guidance, important for novices, may become redundant and so increase extraneous cognitive load as levels of expertise increase. If worked examples are redundant for more knowledgeable learners, the cognitive procedures associated with redundancy can be expected to come into play. Processing redundant elements may increase working memory load as indicated by the narrow limits of change principle. It is unlikely to result in

J. Sweller et al., *Cognitive Load Theory*, Explorations in the Learning Sciences, Instructional Systems and Performance Technologies 1, DOI 10.1007/978-1-4419-8126-4_13, © Springer Science+Business Media, LLC 2011

additional information transferring to the long-term memory store via the borrowing and reorganising principle because the information store already contains the relevant information. It follows that procedures designed to effectively structure the transition from worked example-based instruction during the early stages of learning to problem-solving practice as learners acquire more expertise in the task domain becomes an important research and practical question.

One possible means of a smooth transition from worked examples to problem-solving practice is the use of completion tasks (van Merriënboer, 1990; van Merriënboer, Kirschner, & Kester, 2003; see Chapter 8 for an overview of the technique). A completion task provides a problem statement, a partially worked-out solution procedure, with learners required to complete the solution. Completion problems effectively combine a worked example with problem solving within one task. Faded worked examples use completion problems as a solution to the issue of transition from less to more expert learners. The instructional strategy is based on gradually decreasing the levels of instructional guidance as levels of learner expertise increase (Atkinson, Derry, Renkl, & Wortham, 2000 ; Renkl, 1997; Renkl, Atkinson, & Maier, 2000). With this instructional method, worked examples are gradually faded as learner knowledge increases. Worked-out steps provided by the instructor are progressively replaced with problem-solving steps for learners to complete. Faded worked examples thus, in effect, represent a coordinated series of completion problems in which early problems are presented as full worked examples with successive problems requiring learners to complete an increasing number of steps until eventually, full problems with no steps completed by the instructor are presented.

The fading effect is predicated on the assumption that by gradually decreasing problem-solving guidance and increasing problem-solving demands with increases in expertise, learners will retain sufficient working memory capacity to deal with the increasing demands. As learner expertise increases, knowledge held in long-term memory can be used to decrease the demands on working memory. The freed working memory resources instead can be used to engage in problem solving.

The guidance fading procedure can be contrasted with traditional example–problem pairs (see Chapter 8). While the use of such pairs is highly effective and relatively simple to implement, example–problem pairs ignore the consequences of changes in levels of expertise as exemplified by the expertise reversal effect. Based on the expertise reversal effect, it can be hypothesised that continuing to provide worked examples after levels of expertise have increased can result in redundancy and an increased extraneous cognitive load compared to a fading procedure.

Empirical Evidence for the Guidance Fading Effect

The guidance fading effect is demonstrated by enhanced learning due to the use of gradually faded worked examples instead of a consistent use of worked examples, problems or worked example–problem pairs. This section reviews empirical evidence for the effect and its instructional implications.

Effects of Fading Worked-Out Solution Steps

As intrinsic load gradually decreases when learners acquire more experience in a task domain, a gradual increase in the proportion of time allocated to problem-solving practice is possible without an excessive load. An introduction of problem-solving steps can be accomplished in a graduated manner. Initially, after a complete example is presented, an example can be provided in which a single solution step is omitted with learners required to provide that step themselves. For subsequent stages, the number of steps learners must complete by themselves without explicit guidance can be increased until only a problem statement is left (Renkl & Atkinson, 2003) with learners required to complete all steps. Compared to traditional example–problem pairs, fading can be expected to reduce cognitive load and, as a result, enhance learning. For instance, after seeing a full worked example, the learner only is required to complete a single step on the next problem rather than search for a solution to the whole problem.

Two types of fading procedures have been proposed. In backward fading, the first learning task is presented as a completely worked-out example, the second task is presented with the solution to the last step omitted, the third task with the solutions to the last two steps omitted, etc. For instance, the previously used (Chapter 8) example of a completion strategy for a simple two-step problem can be used to represent an example of the second task in a backward-fading procedure, as follows:

Make a the subject of the equation $(a + b)/c = d$.

Solution

$$(a+b)/c = d$$
$$a+b = dc$$
$$a = ?$$

In contrast to this backward-fading procedure, in a forward-fading procedure, the first learning task is also presented as a completely worked-out example, followed by the second task with the solution to the first step omitted, the third task with the solutions to the first two steps omitted, etc. Using the above algebra example, the second task in a forward-fading procedure requires learners to provide a solution to the first step with the last step provided by the instructor, as follows:

Make a the subject of the equation $(a + b)/c = d$.

Solution

$$(a+b)/c = d$$
$$a+b = ?$$
$$a = dc - b$$

Renkl, Atkinson, Maier, and Staley (2002) compared a fading procedure with example–problem pairs in realistic, secondary school physics lessons on electricity.

A backward-fading procedure was used with the first task as a completely worked-out example, the second task with the last solution step omitted, the third task with the last two steps omitted, etc. In a delayed post-test conducted 2 days after tuition, the fading group outperformed the example–problem pairs group in near transfer performance. The results were replicated with fading again proving superior to example–problem pairs in a follow-up laboratory-based experiment with psychology university students learning probability calculation procedures. This follow-up experiment used a *forward-fading procedure* that omitted guidance for the first solution step initially, then omitted the first two steps, etc. The third experiment, again laboratory-based using university educational psychology students, compared traditional example–problem pairs with two alternative conditions, one backward fading and the other forward fading. The results indicated a positive effect of fading on a near transfer post-test for both backward and forward fading. In addition, the backward-fading condition also was superior on a far transfer post-test. The backward-fading condition was generally more efficient than forward fading, as learners presented backward fading also required less time to study the examples. From a cognitive load perspective, the backward-fading condition whereby the learner supplies the final problem-solving step may impose a lower cognitive load than the forward-fading condition where the learner supplies the first problem-solving step, a step often a critical step in the overall solution (see Ayres & Sweller, 1990).

However, Renkl, Atkinson, and Große (2004) demonstrated that the position of the faded steps did not actually influence how much was learned about each step. Students learned most about those problem-solving steps that were faded irrespective of whether backward or forward fading was used. A follow-up experiment using think-aloud protocols generated by the learners demonstrated that fading was associated with fewer unproductive learning events, thus explaining better learning outcomes. Accordingly, there may not be a universal recommendation for sequencing the fading procedure. The selection of an appropriate fading procedure and a decision about which type of solution step should be faded first may depend largely on specific structures and content of the material to be learned.

In additional work, Renkl and Atkinson (2001) investigated the efficiency of self-explanation prompts at the faded steps (see Chapter 8 for details about the self-explanation technique). At each worked-out step, the university students learning the probability calculation procedures were asked to identify which probability rule had been applied. Two backward-fading groups with and without self-explanation prompts were compared, and the results indicated strong advantages associated with self-explanation prompts on both near and far transfer post-tests.

Knowledge-Dependent Dynamic Provision of Guidance

Based on the expertise reversal effect, an appropriate sequencing of learning tasks with decreased guidance as expertise increases is important. Accordingly, tasks that provide optimal levels of instructional guidance for novice learners may not be optimal for more experienced learners. These learners have already acquired sufficient knowledge so additional support provided through instructional guidance may be redundant, counterproductive and inhibit rather than facilitate further learning.

Reisslein (2005) examined the pace of transitioning from worked examples to independent problem solving for university engineering students with different levels of prior knowledge. In the immediate transitioning condition, learners practised problems immediately after an introduction. In the fast fading condition, worked-out solution steps were faded at a rate of one step with each example. In the slow fading condition, the rate was one step for every second example. The results of the retention post-test indicated significant interactions between levels of learner prior knowledge and the pace of transitioning. More knowledgeable learners performed significantly better in the fast and immediate transitioning groups than in the slow transitioning group. Worked examples might have been redundant for these learners. On the other hand, learners with low levels of prior knowledge who required more detailed guidance benefited more from the slow transitioning condition than from the immediate or fast transitioning conditions.

As was mentioned in Chapter 12, Nückles, Hübner, Dümer, and Renkl (2010) demonstrated an expertise reversal effect based on instructional support for writing learning journals in which students reflected on the previously studied material. Support was provided in the form of prompts to apply appropriate learning strategies. At the beginning of the term, the group that received prompts applied more strategies in their learning journals and learned more than the no-prompts group. At the end of the term, the prompts group learned less than the no-prompts group. In order to avoid these negative long-term effects of prompts, a gradual and adaptive fading of the prompts was introduced in the second experiment. In the experimental group, each of the presented prompts was faded out as soon as a student applied the prompted strategy in a satisfactory manner. In the control group, the prompts were presented permanently. The results showed that, over the course of the term, the fading group applied increasingly more cognitive strategies, while the permanent prompts group applied increasingly fewer cognitive strategies. At the end of term, the permanent prompts group showed substantially lower learning outcomes than the fading group. At the beginning of the term, the prompts successfully facilitated the application of beneficial strategies. However, as the students became more skilled in journal writing, the external guidance by prompts became redundant and, thus, caused an extraneous load. Accordingly, a gradual fading-out of the prompts in line with the learner's growing level of expertise was effective in alleviating possible negative effects of instructional support.

Kester and Kirschner (2009) investigated whether fading conceptual and strategic support in a problem solving domain affected accuracy of hypertext navigation and problem performance in an e-learning environment. The research demonstrated that fading support during practice as a function of increasing levels of learner expertise helped learners to navigate more accurately during practice as compared to learners receiving full support or no support during practice.

Thus, in these studies, novice learners benefited most from well-guided, slow-paced instructional procedures that reduced extraneous cognitive load. For more experienced learners, studying redundant worked-out steps and integrating them with available knowledge that provided essentially the same guidance imposed an unnecessary extraneous cognitive load. These experienced learners were able to use their knowledge base to guide the learning process. They did not require external guidance and therefore benefited more from minimally guided instruction.

The Effect of a Gradual Change in Levels of Support Using Computer-Based Tutors

In intelligent tutoring systems (e.g. Anderson, Corbett, Koedinger, & Pelletier, 1995), learning by problem solving is usually supported by providing explicit sub-goals, immediate feedback, hints, dynamic evaluation of student progress and appropriate remedial problems. Because of this comprehensive instructional support that is embedded into most cognitive tutors, their reported instructional effectiveness could, in fact, be due to a version of the worked example effect. A worked example provides the ultimate example of guidance and support.

Renkl, Schwonke, Wittwer, Krieg, Aleven, and Salden (2007) conducted a study designed to compare a 'standard' problem-based tutor in circle geometry that also included self-explanation prompts, with an example-enriched tutor based on faded worked examples. The results of the first experiment indicated no differences in conceptual knowledge acquisition and transfer performance; however, lower instruction time and higher efficiency indicators were obtained for the example-enriched tutor. In a follow-up study that used a modified tutor with an improved introduction and individual learning sessions, higher post-test conceptual knowledge scores, lower instruction times and higher efficiency indicators for the faded example-enriched tutor were obtained. The participants in the faded example-enriched group made many errors at the beginning of the learning phase but exhibited a rapid catch-up. They also expressed more principle-based self-explanations. In comparison, the participants in the problem group uttered more superficial procedure-based self-explanations. Integrating intelligent cognitive tutors with faded example-based learning could be an effective instructional approach to developing learner expertise.

Salden, Aleven, Schwonke, and Renkl (2010) conducted an experimental study designed to investigate if learners' current skill levels determined by their self-explanation performance while studying examples and by their problem-solving performance could be used to determine an appropriate degree of guidance. A fading approach to structuring the transition from examples to problem solving that was adapted to the skill levels of individual learners was expected to be more effective than a predetermined fading approach. Such an individualised fading procedure (adaptive fading) was compared to a fixed procedure (fixed fading), and to a standard tutored problem-solving condition (problem solving) using high school students studying geometry lessons provided by the Cognitive Tutor. The results of the laboratory-based study showed that the adaptive fading procedure resulted in higher performance scores on the immediate post-test and a post-test delayed by a week. Another classroom-based study replicated these results on the delayed post-test with non-significant differences on the immediate post-test. Thus, these experiments provided evidence of better learning outcomes resulting from adaptive fading than from fixed fading or problem solving.

Applying Rapid Assessment Techniques to the Design of Adaptive Fading Procedures

There is considerable work that has been carried out using adaptive fading in contexts other than use of the cognitive tutor. That work is discussed next.

Rapid online evaluation of levels of expertise. The quality of adaptive fading procedures is likely to depend significantly on the accuracy of information about current levels of learner knowledge and skills. Knowing when to fade guidance depends on accurate information concerning learner knowledge levels. Traditional tests may not be sufficiently precise or timely to maximise the benefits of fading. Diagnosing levels of learner expertise rapidly and in real time is important for the development of dynamic, learner-tailored learning environments in general, and implementing fading procedures in particular. This section reviews a series of studies aimed at developing rapid diagnostic assessment methods that are directly based on characteristics of our cognitive architecture described in Part II of this book.

The knowledge base in long-term memory heavily determines what information working memory processes and how it is processed. Information in long-term memory transforms the characteristics of working memory and so long-term memory defines the effective processing capacity and the current content of working memory during knowledge-based cognitive processes. Accordingly, evaluating the content of long-term memory should provide a measure of levels of learner expertise. If such an evaluation can be conducted rapidly, it may be suitable as a formative evaluation technique that can be used to appropriately govern a fading procedure.

We know, based on the early work of De Groot (1965) and on subsequent work (see Chapter 2), that expertise in a domain is determined by the extent to which learners have acquired schemas held in long-term memory that allow them to recognise problem states and the best moves associated with each state. It would be beneficial to devise techniques that assess such learner knowledge directly. The techniques need to be sufficiently rapid to provide us with information allowing us to fade guidance at an appropriate time. De Groot's (1965) work has potential in this regard. Based on his work, we know that expert problem solvers can recognise problem states and the best moves associated with each state. It may be possible to devise a test intended to assess how learners approach briefly presented memory tasks similar to those used by De Groot. More expert-level learners should be able to retrieve appropriate higher-level schemas and immediately place a problem and its solution within their well-structured knowledge base. On the other hand, novices, not possessing such schemas may only identify random, lower-level components of the solution steps. In this manner, the presence or absence of an organised knowledge base in long-term memory may possibly be used as the main factor determining differences between more and less expert problem solvers.

Kalyuga and Sweller (2004) attempted to devise a rapid assessment procedure based on de Groot's findings. They suggested it may be possible to rapidly assess the contents of long-term memory using a 'first-step' diagnostic assessment procedure according to which learners are presented with selected problems for a limited time and asked to indicate their first step towards solution of each problem. Based on their schemas, more experienced learners are expected to rapidly indicate more advanced steps of the solution and skip some intermediate steps. Novices may only be able to indicate isolated, single, random steps. For example, if asked to indicate their first step towards the solution of the equation $4x = 5$, learners who are experienced in solving such equations (experts), might immediately produce the final answer ($x = 5/4$) as their first step. Less experienced but still knowledgeable students (intermediates) might provide the first step of the standard solution procedure that requires dividing both sides of the equation by 4 ($4x/4 = 5/4$), while students without any knowledge of the solution procedure (novices) may attempt a random step using a trial-and-error method. Different first steps may indicate different levels of expertise much more rapidly than conventional tests. This technique was validated in a series of studies using algebra, coordinate geometry, and arithmetic word problems by demonstrating high correlation levels between the results of the rapid tasks and traditional measures of knowledge that required students to provide the entire solution. Importantly, rapid tests could reduce testing times by up to a factor of 5 (Kalyuga, 2006a; Kalyuga & Sweller, 2004).

An alternative rapid assessment method is available that may be more suitable for online learning environments. Instead of generating the first steps themselves, learners can be presented with a series of potential, possible steps at various stages of the solution procedure and asked to rapidly verify the validity of these steps. This method may be useful in relatively poorly specified domains with many different possible solution paths. This rapid verification procedure was first used with sentence comprehension tasks (Kalyuga, 2006b) in which a sequence of sentences that gradually increased in complexity was displayed. For example, simple, composite and multiple-embedded sentences increase in complexity. Each sentence was displayed for a limited time, followed by a series of simple statements related to the content of the corresponding sentence. Students were asked to rapidly verify the correctness of each statement by clicking on the buttons 'Right', 'Wrong' or 'Don't know' underneath the statement on the computer screen. For example, after reading the sentence, 'The artist, who performed for the crowd that gathered to enjoy the show, left', students were briefly showed the following statements one at a time for rapid verification: 'the artist left'; 'the artist enjoyed the show'; 'the crowd gathered for the show'; 'the crowd left'.

Subsequently, the method was also used in the domains of kinematics and mathematics. In these domains, diagrammatic representations of selected potential solution steps were presented to students for rapid verification. Both correct and incorrect solution steps were used. These rapid tests demonstrated high levels of correlation with problem-solving scores obtained from the analyses of video records and concurrent verbal reports of students' problem-solving performance (Kalyuga, 2008b).

Expertise-based adaptive fading instruction. The above-mentioned studies suggest a sufficiently high degree of concurrent validity for the rapid assessment methods to warrant their implementation in adaptive fading procedures. The first-step assessment method was used to design a gradual transition from worked examples to unguided problem-solving practice. A computer-based tutor for secondary school students solving elementary algebra equations was used (Kalyuga & Sweller, 2004). This tutor and several subsequent tutors were designed to produce a series of faded worked examples. The initial allocation of learners to appropriate stages of fading was based on the outcomes of initial, rapid, first-step diagnostic pretests (see the example above). A learner progressing through the stages was monitored by rapid diagnostic probes, and instruction was tailored according to changing levels of expertise.

Learners who were classified as novices based on the initial pretest studied a series of fully worked-out examples, each followed by a similar problem-solving exercise. Depending on the outcome of a diagnostic test at the end of this phase, additional worked examples were provided if necessary before learners proceeded to the next stage after successfully completing the phase-exit rapid test. The second stage contained backward faded completion problems in which learners were asked to complete the last step themselves. At each of the following stages, reduced instructional guidance was provided to learners by eliminating solution explanations of progressively more procedural steps. The final stage contained only problem-solving exercises without any explanations provided. A flow chart of the procedure is represented in Fig. 13.1. This learner-adapted tutor resulted in significantly better knowledge gains as measured by differences between post-instruction and pre-instruction test scores than a non-adapted tutor in which students were required to study the whole set of worked examples and example–problem pairs available in the tutorial without fading.

In another study with similar materials (Kalyuga & Sweller, 2005), the rapid first-step measure of expertise was combined with measures of cognitive load using subjective ratings of task difficulty. It was assumed that expertise is associated not only with higher levels of performance but also with lower levels of cognitive load, as experts' available knowledge structures in long-term memory could significantly reduce working memory demands, as specified by the environmental organising and linking principle. Therefore, combining both measures could produce a good indicator of learner expertise in a domain. In contrast to the traditional 'deviation model' (Hoffman and Schraw, 2010) definition of instructional efficiency as the difference between standardised scores for performance and mental effort ratings (Paas & van Merriënboer, 1993; Paas, Tuovinen, Tabbers, & van

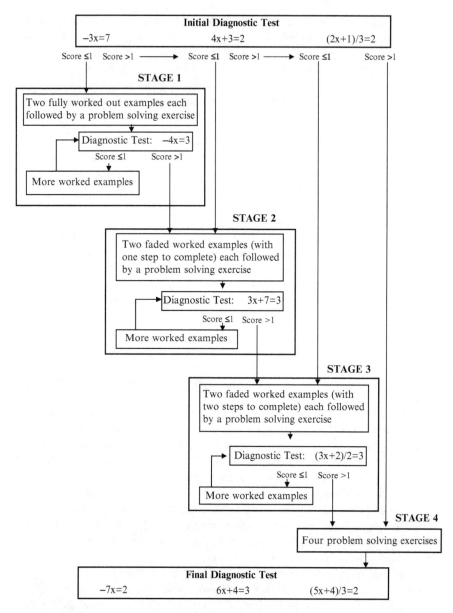

Fig. 13.1 Flow chart of the adaptive fading procedure using rapid first-step diagnostic assessment method. Reprinted from Kalyuga & Sweller (2004). Copyright © 2004 American Psychological Association

Gerven, 2003), efficiency was defined as a ratio of the current level of performance to the current level of cognitive load, called a 'likelihood model' by Hoffman and Schraw (see Chapter 6). This definition corresponds more closely to the common idea of efficiency as the relative cost of achieving a result. This indicator of cognitive efficiency was used for the initial selection of appropriate levels of instructional guidance, as well as for ongoing monitoring of learner progress and tailoring the fading procedure to changing levels of learner expertise. Results indicated that the learner-adapted instructional condition significantly outperformed the non-adapted group on both knowledge and efficiency gains.

Kalyuga (2006a) compared non-adapted instruction in the area of vector addition motion problems in kinematics for high school students with two learner-adapted instructional procedures, one of which was based on rapid verification performance tests as described above and another one that was based on efficiency indicators. Both adaptive conditions outperformed the non-adapted group on a number of dependent variables such as cognitive load ratings, instruction time and instructional efficiency. However, there were no significant differences between the two adaptation procedures on any of the dependent variables.

Similar results have been obtained in research on dynamic adaptation of learning task selection procedures in which the difficulty of learning tasks presented to students was determined by test results. Camp, Paas, Rikers, and van Merriënboer (2001) and Salden, Paas, Broers, and van Merriënboer (2004) investigated the use of test results to determine levels of learner expertise during air traffic control training. Unlike the previous studies that used rapid tests to determine levels of guidance, these studies were primarily concerned with gradual increases in task difficulty rather than with fading the levels of instructional support. Also, these studies used different performance assessment methods, definitions of instructional efficiency, and task selection algorithms to the ones described above. Nevertheless, learner-adapted conditions were superior to non-adapted formats in all of the studies. Salden, Paas, and van Merriënboer (2006a) also demonstrated that learner-adapted approaches to selecting learning tasks were superior to non-adapted formats.

Conditions of Applicability of the Fading Effect

Firstly, as is common for all cognitive load effects, high levels of intrinsic cognitive load are essential to the fading effect. It is unreasonable to expect any significant effect of fading for instructional materials that do not impose a sufficiently high level of intrinsic cognitive load, and therefore are relatively easy to learn even with abrupt transitions from examples to problem-solving exercises.

Secondly, although the fading effect is a direct consequence of the expertise reversal effect, levels of expertise are just as important to the fading effect as to most other cognitive load effects. Faded worked examples can be effective for learners at specific levels of prior knowledge and not optimal for other learners. For example, as was previously mentioned in this chapter, gradual transitioning procedures with slowly decreasing levels of guidance are likely to benefit most novice learners. Relatively more knowledgeable learners might benefit from more rapid transitioning procedures or from immediately beginning to practice problems after an introduction to a topic area, since detailed guidance during problem solving may be redundant for these learners (Reisslein, 2005).

Instructional Implications

As was mentioned in the previous chapter, a major instructional implication of the expertise reversal effect is the need to dynamically tailor instructional methods and levels of instructional guidance to changing levels of learner expertise during a learning session. According to the expertise reversal effect, appropriate instructional guidance needs to be presented at the right time, and removed in a timely fashion as learners gradually gain expertise. Detailed instructional support should be provided to novice learners as a substitute for missing knowledge structures. At higher levels of expertise, problem-solving practice using knowledge held in long-term memory should be the prevailing instructional method. At intermediate levels of expertise, an optimal mix of direct external guidance and problem-solving practice should be used. It can, of course, be a challenging task to establish the optimal mix and implement the corresponding transition procedures. Nevertheless, while challenging, the results of the experiments described in this chapter suggest it is worth the effort.

Conclusions

The instructional strategy of gradually decreasing the level of instructional guidance as levels of learner expertise increase is an implication of the expertise reversal effect. The most obvious instructional strategy that flows from the expertise reversal effect is the use of faded worked examples. This technique gradually fades worked-out steps to be replaced with problem solving sub-tasks as levels of learner expertise increase. The gradual reduction of instructional guidance as levels of learner expertise increase has proved to be a more effective instructional procedure than abrupt switches from worked examples to problems. The next step in this line of research has been the development of adaptive fading methods that dynamically tailor the rates of transition from worked examples to problems depending on current levels of learner expertise.

Research into adaptive fading methods is still in its early stages and the number of studies is limited. However, the available research has already demonstrated that adaptive fading procedures can improve learning outcomes with significant impacts on the acquisition of basic knowledge and skills for novice learners as well as more strategic knowledge and transfer capabilities for more advanced learners. Recent studies into rapid diagnostic assessment methods combined with advances in measures of cognitive load and instructional efficiency may offer appropriate, real-time diagnostic tools for the dynamic adaptation of fading techniques. This research area currently is very active.

Chapter 14
Facilitating Effective Mental Processes: The Imagination and Self-Explanation Effects

According to the expertise reversal effect (Chapter 12) during the initial phases of skill acquisition, worked examples (Chapter 8) represent an efficient form of instruction, while problem-solving practice is superior during later phases of skill acquisition. This reversal suggests that as levels of expertise increase, levels of instructional guidance should decrease. Completion tasks (Chapter 8) and faded worked examples (Chapter 13) were suggested as instructional procedures that can be used to gradually decrease the levels of guidance. Empirical evidence has indicated that these methods are a more effective and efficient means for a smooth transition from initial instruction based on worked examples to later problem-solving practice. This chapter reviews evidence supporting an alternative to studying worked examples or problem-solving practice for more knowledgeable learners. The method is based on imagining activities, procedures, or concepts, for example, imagining a problem solution provided in a recently studied worked example. Imagining is defined as the mental reproduction of a procedure or a concept.

In addition, we will discuss the self-explanation effect in this chapter. While the self-explanation effect, unlike the other effects discussed in this book, was neither initiated nor developed within a cognitive load theory framework, it is closely related to the imagination effect and can be explained using cognitive load theory concepts. Both effects differ from the other effects discussed in this book in that they do not rely on altering the instructional materials presented to learners. Instead, they rely on encouraging learners to engage in appropriate mental processes that may differ from the ones that they would normally use.

The Imagination Effect

Within a cognitive load theoretical framework, the imagination technique was first investigated by Cooper, Tindall-Ford, Chandler, and Sweller (2001) who asked students to imagine the computer-based instructional procedures on how to use a spreadsheet application instead of studying worked examples. The worked examples

J. Sweller et al., *Cognitive Load Theory*, Explorations in the Learning Sciences, Instructional Systems and Performance Technologies 1, DOI 10.1007/978-1-4419-8126-4_14, © Springer Science+Business Media, LLC 2011

184 14 Facilitating Effective Mental Processes

consisted of a set of diagrams with embedded textual explanations of sequential steps. After studying a worked example on the screen, students were instructed to turn away and try to imagine the steps involved in the procedure. The study demonstrated that instructing learners to imagine a previously studied worked-out solution path produced better learning outcomes than studying the same worked example again. However, the imagining technique was beneficial only for more knowledgeable learners. The results indicated that the imagining technique was not useful for low-knowledge students because of the heavy working memory load it generated for these learners.

In order to imagine a procedure or concept, learners must be able to process that procedure or concept in working memory. The act of processing in working memory should assist in transfer to the long-term memory store, but since working memory is limited in accordance with the narrow limits of change principle, for novices, imagining a procedure or concept may be difficult or impossible, rendering imagination instructions relatively ineffective. Therefore, conventional instructions to study the material are superior for novices because studying, in accord with the borrowing and reorganising principle, can facilitate schema construction. For novice learners in a domain, studying rather than imagining a worked example may provide more effective guidance. In order to imagine a procedure, the interacting elements that constitute that procedure must be processed in working memory. For a novice, the number of interacting elements may exceed working memory capacity, rendering an imagination procedure ineffective. The interacting elements may best be handled by studying a worked example rather than attempting to imagine it, resulting in a superiority of study over imagination instructions.

In contrast, more experienced learners may have already acquired sufficient task-relevant schematic knowledge held in the long-term store and available for use according to the environmental organising and linking principle. This principle allows large amounts of familiar information to be processed in working memory, and so imagining may be feasible for more expert learners while not feasible for novices. While novices need to study worked examples, continuing to do so may constitute a redundant activity for more experienced learners. They already have appropriate prerequisite schemas in long-term memory to incorporate the interacting elements. Imagining procedures provides additional practice that can lead to schema automation. From these results, it follows that with increasing levels of expertise, studying worked examples should be replaced by imagining those examples.

Switching from studying worked examples to imagining problem solutions may be as effective or even more effective as expertise increases than switching from studying worked examples to solving problems via faded worked examples. The imagination effect occurs when imagining a procedure or concept results in more learning than studying the same procedure or concept.

From a theoretical perspective, the imagination effect occurs because imagination instructions explicitly direct limited working memory resources to all of the interacting elements that constitute intrinsic cognitive load. Unnecessarily processing a worked example will result in processing elements that are extraneous to learning.

For example, reading that a particular geometry problem move was made because "opposite angles are equal" results in unnecessary processing for a learner who is fully aware of the relevant theorem. That learner does not need to study a worked example. Instead, imagining the theorem being used in a series of steps may more closely reflect the interacting elements that need to be processed and that constitute an intrinsic cognitive load.

The Imagination Effect Prior to Cognitive Load Theory Research

The effects of imagining the performance of a task or procedure have had a long research history under different names. In early research of the technique, Sackett (1934, 1935) suggested the term 'symbolic rehearsal', whereas Perry (1939) used the term 'imaginary practice'. Later, 'mental practice' (Clark, 1960), 'introspective rehearsal' (Egstrom, 1964), 'covert rehearsal' (Corbin, 1967) and 'mental rehearsal' (Dunbar, 2000; Rawlings & Rawlings, 1974) were used to describe the technique.

Mental rehearsal became an especially popular area of research in sports psychology and other motor skills-related areas (e.g. Etnier & Landers, 1996; Grouios, 1992; Kelsey, 1961; Mendoza & Wichman, 1978; Phipps & Morehouse, 1969; Romero & Silvestri, 1990; Shick, 1970; Surburg, 1968; Ungerleider & Golding, 1991), but it has also been applied to improving more cognitively oriented activities and components. For example, the technique was used in behavioural counselling (Hazler & Hipple, 1981) and clinical examinations (Rakestraw, Irby, & Vontver, 1983). Schirmer (2003) found it beneficial when used with special education students. Self-explanations of problem-solving steps (e.g. Chi, Bassok, Lewis, Reimann, & Glaser, 1989; Renkl, 1997) also include some components of imagination and, in this respect, can be related to the imagination effect.

Meta-analyses of mental practice were conducted by Driskell, Copper, and Moran (1994) and Ginns (2005a), and indicated generally positive effects. It was found that the greater the cognitive demands of a task, the more beneficial mental practice was in increasing learner performance. Recently, Van Meer and Theunissen (2009) conducted a comprehensive meta-review of educational applications of mental rehearsal as a technique for improving student performance based on about 630 studies published between 1806 and 2006. The analysis indicated that the effectiveness of this technique is influenced by the type of practiced skill, personal factors, time per trial, amount of trials, and instructional procedures. According to this meta-review, most of the available publications focused on using mental practice to learn motor skills, especially sports-related skills. Cognitive tasks were investigated only occasionally and included mostly simple tasks such as solving puzzles or tasks involving verbal practice. However, these tasks produced larger effects than motor tasks. The review concluded that the higher the level of involvement of cognitive elements in a task, the greater the improvement in performance due to mental practice. Van Meer and Theunissen's (2009) meta-review also concluded that mental practice associated with higher expertise levels seemed to enhance performance for both cognitive and motor skills. It was noted that in addition to expertise in a specific skill area, experience with the mental practice technique itself might also influence the effect.

Empirical Evidence for the Imagination Effect Within a Cognitive Load Theory Context

The fact that most work on imagination techniques was carried out using motor tasks rather than cognitive tasks but that larger effects were obtained when dealing with cognitive tasks than motor tasks suggested that the effect should be considered from a cognitive viewpoint. As indicated above, cognitive load theory may be used to explain the effect, leading to the Cooper et al. (2001) experiments demonstrating that imagining procedures and concepts produced better instructional outcomes than simply studying worked examples, but only for more expert students with an appropriate knowledge base. The imagining procedure produced a negative effect for low-knowledge students, thus reversing the effect and providing another example of the expertise reversal effect.

Following the Cooper et al. (2001) work, a range of studies on the imagination effect within a cognitive load theory framework was carried out. Leahy and Sweller (2004; Experiment 1) investigated the imagination effect with adults (primary school teachers) as participants studying or imagining contour maps. Imagination instructions were superior to study instructions on subsequent test questions.

Ginns, Chandler, and Sweller (2003) investigated the effects of the imagination technique by varying the complexity of learning materials relative to levels of learner expertise. The first experiment involved university students learning HTML code. This material was complex for these learners with low levels of prior knowledge in the domain. In accordance with the worked example effect (Chapter 8), these participants benefited from repeatedly studying worked examples rather than from imagining the examples. In the second experiment, secondary school students studied geometry materials in an area in which they had high levels of prior knowledge that rendered these materials relatively less complex for these learners. Results indicated that higher levels of post-test performance were reached by the students who imagined solution steps after studying worked examples rather than those who only studied the examples.

These results were extended by Leahy and Sweller (2005) in experiments with primary school students learning to read a bus timetable and temperature graphs. In the experiments, the same students were considered initially as novices, and 2 weeks later – following more practice with the materials – as relative experts in the domain. The results indicated that as learners' levels of expertise increased, the advantage switched from studying to imagining examples, in accord with the previously obtained findings. Furthermore, as intrinsic cognitive load increased, the interaction effect between instructional category and levels of expertise also increased. In other words, both the imagination and the reverse imagination effects were larger with higher element interactivity information than with lower element interactivity information (see Chapter 15 on the element interactivity effect).

In an experiment with Grade 10 students reading a science text on the dipole character of water molecules, Leutner, Leopold, and Sumfleth (2009) compared instructional techniques of drawing pictures of text content on paper against mentally imagining text content while reading. The results indicated that while drawing pictures increased cognitive load and decreased text comprehension, mental imagery decreased cognitive load and increased comprehension, however only when students did not have to draw pictures simultaneously while imagining text. Imagining text content may have fostered deeper processing of the material. Drawing pictures of text content on paper includes externalising the pictorial information, which may require additional cognitive resources, thus imposing an extraneous cognitive load. That cognitive load, at least in part, may be due to split attention between the corresponding elements of the text and the external pictorial representation drawn by the students.

Thus, the Leutner et al. (2009) study indicates that using mental imagery may enhance comprehension without imposing excessive levels of cognitive load. However, mental imagery enhances learning only when it is focused directly on the text content while reading rather than on other activities or aspects such as an external pictorial representation drawn from the text. An instructional implication of this study is that the process of imagining should not be accompanied by other activities such as learners drawing representations of the imagined elements of information. Students who attempt to draw pictures spontaneously should be discouraged from doing so if imagination instructions are used. A combination of imagination and drawing may overwhelm working memory.

The Self-Explanation Effect

The imagination effect can be related to the self-explanation effect (Bielaczyk, Pirolli, & Brown, 1995; Chi, Bassok, Lewis, Reimann, & Glaser, 1989; Chi, de Leeuw, Chiu, & LaVancher, 1994; Mwangi & Sweller, 1998; Renkl, 1997; Renkl, Stark, Gruber, & Mandl, 1998; Roy & Chi, 2005; VanLehn, Jones, & Chi, 1992; see Renkl, 1999 for a comprehensive review) according to which instructing learners to engage in self-explaining connections between interacting units of information can improve performance. Initially, work on self-explanations was not conducted within a cognitive load theory framework, other than emphasising the use of worked examples. Nevertheless, the self-explanation effect can be related to the imagination effect because self-explanations usually involve imagining a procedure or process while trying to relate the procedure or process to known principles of the domain.

Clark, Nguye, and Sweller (2006) defined a self-explanation as '...a mental dialogue that learners have when studying a worked example that helps them understand the example and build a schema from it' (p. 226). Within a cognitive load theoretical context, self-explanations require students to establish the interactions that relate various elements of a worked example both to each other and to previous knowledge. While not specified in the self-explanation literature, to process these interacting elements requires sufficient working memory resources, as indicated by the narrow limits of change principle. Whether the resources are likely to be available will depend heavily on the information store principle. If insufficient knowledge is held in long-term memory, as may be the case for novices, the environmental organising and linking principle cannot function, and so working memory resources may not be available to deal with the large number of interacting elements associated with self-explanations. In addition, for novices, self-explanation may require the randomness as genesis principle to a greater extent than for more expert learners who can use knowledge from long-term memory to generate appropriate self-explanations via the environmental organising and linking principle. More knowledgeable learners who can more readily self-explain may benefit considerably from the process.

In a seminal paper, Chi, Bassok, Lewis, Reimann, and Glaser (1989) demonstrated that learners who process an example more deeply by explaining and providing justifications for the example moves, called self-explanations, learn more than students who process only the surface structures. Chi et al. showed, using physics worked examples, that the most successful learners used a process of self-explanation. They also found that good learners monitored their comprehension more accurately than poor learners, referred to the worked examples less frequently, and targeted specific references, rather than the whole example. To explain why self-explanations are effective, it was argued that learners generate a number of inference rules from the principles and definitions provided in the worked example. These rules enable learners to link appropriate actions with specific conditions, which later become procedural skills. Subsequently, Chi (2000) extended this argument to generating inferences and repairing the learner's mental model (see Atkinson, Renkl, & Merrill, 2003).

Chi, De Leeuw, Chiu, and Lavancher (1994) using a randomised controlled study, demonstrated that self-explaining enhanced knowledge acquisition, although they did not control for time on task. In their study, one group of Grade 8 students were asked to self-explain after reading each line of a passage on the human circulatory system. Students in the control group read the same text twice and were not prompted to self-explain. The self-explanation group demonstrated a greater knowledge gain. Also, students in this group who generated large numbers of self-explanations (high explainers) learned better than low explainers.

Building on the earlier work by Chi and her collaborators, Renkl (1997) sought to investigate individual differences in the quality of self-explanations when learning from worked examples. College education students were given probability problems and were asked to engage in an anticipating, self-explanation technique that was similar to the imagination technique. In learning how to solve these problems, learners were shown a number of worked examples and were required to verbalise their thoughts concurrently. In this correlational study, it was found that learners showed fairly stable self-explanations over different problems. Successful learners had qualitative differences in their self-explanations compared with less successful learners. In particular, successful learners tended to provide principle-based explanations and to anticipate computation of future probabilities. Anticipating solution steps of a worked example, which constitutes effectively solving part of the problem, can be an effective learning technique. Importantly, similar to Cooper et al. (2001), Renkl found that this method improved learning only for relatively more advanced learners. This finding led Renkl to characterise successful learners as either principle-based learners or anticipative learners.

Although in the Renkl (1997) study, self-explanations were linked to effective learning, it was also shown that very few students provided good self-explanations. In a follow-up study, Renkl, Stark, Gruber, and Mandl (1998) predicted that most learners needed support in learning from worked examples and investigated what factors could influence the quality of self-explanations. In a randomised experiment, a sample of bank apprentices were required to learn about mathematical procedures in finance. Self-explanations were either spontaneous or elicited. In the spontaneous condition, learners were simply required to verbalise their thoughts, but in the elicited condition, learners received training in self-explanations. Results showed that the elicitation of self-explanations fostered both near- and far-transfer. In addition, measures of prior knowledge indicated that on near-transfer problems, learners with low prior knowledge benefited more from elicitation than learners with higher prior knowledge.

Research into worked examples and self-explanations was later extended to computer-based learning environments. Although previous research into computer environments had been rather mixed, Atkinson, Renkl, and Merrill (2003) found positive results using a prompting strategy. In learning about probability theorems, students in the prompting conditions were required to self-explain each solution step they completed and then identify the probability principle used from a list that had been previously covered in an introductory learning phase. Results indicated that on both near- and far-transfer test problems, students who received self-explanation prompts performed significantly better than students who did not receive prompting. The evidence suggested that self-explanations could be combined successfully with the use of worked examples. Other research has extended these findings by including a large variety of areas such as classroom teaching skills and argumentation skills (see Atkinson & Renkl, 2007; Berthold, Eysink, & Renkl, 2009; Hilbert & Renkl, 2009; Hilbert, Renkl, Kessler, & Reiss, 2008; Schworm & Renkl, 2006, 2007, for some of the areas covered). Nevertheless, self-explanation studies have not always been successful. Mwangi and Sweller (1999) failed to find an advantage on two-step arithmetic word problems, arguing that self-explanations may not always be suitable during learning as working memory load is likely to be increased when translating procedures into verbal form. As is the case for the imagination effect, self-explanations only may be effective once a sufficient level of expertise has been attained to allow the environmental organising and linking principle to function.

Conditions of Applicability

Imagination instructions are effective for learners with relatively higher levels of prior knowledge and unsuitable for novice learners. Higher levels of expertise increase the effectiveness of the imagination technique because more experienced learners have available knowledge structures accessible in long-term memory to process information in working memory while imagining. If already available, an existing schema can be transferred from long-term to working memory and processed in working memory while imagining, but studying is required to construct and store that schema in the first instance. As indicated above, Cooper et al. (2001), Ginns et al. (2003) and Leahy and Sweller (2005) provided evidence for this interaction.

Levels of element interactivity also influence the imagination effect (see Chapter 15 for the element interactivity effect). Leahy and Sweller (2008) experimentally manipulated the levels of element interactivity in instructional materials and post-test questions in order to test the hypothesis that higher levels of element interactivity would increase the likelihood of obtaining an imagination effect. A significant interaction between the imagination and element interactivity effects was obtained. Imagining materials that were low in element interactivity resulted in no significant benefits, whereas for high element interactivity materials, learners who were asked to imagine materials outperformed learners who were asked only to study the same materials. Imagining high element interactivity materials allowed learners to combine the multiple interacting elements of information into a single schematic element that could be more readily processed in working memory. The results also indicated that greater differences between the two instructional groups were obtained on post-test questions tapping high rather than low element interactivity knowledge.

Leahy and Sweller (2005) also demonstrated the interaction between levels of element interactivity and the imagination effect by demonstrating that the effect increased with increases in element interactivity, an interaction common to most, possibly all cognitive load effects (see Chapter 15). In addition, as indicated above, they also demonstrated the commonly obtained interaction between levels of expertise and the imagination effect.

There are other interactions between the imagination effect and other cognitive load effects. In order for the imagination effect to be obtained, learners must have sufficient working memory resources to allow them to imagine. Therefore, the imagination effect might be expected to be facilitated by techniques that reduce working memory load or otherwise enhance working memory functioning.

With Grade 4 students as participants, Leahy and Sweller (2004) compared studying and imagining temperature–time graphs that depicted temperature variations presented in either split-source or integrated formats. Whereas the split-source format used spatially separated diagrams and text, with text located on a separate page, in the integrated format, the text was spatially embedded into the diagram (see Chapter 9). Post-test results indicated that imagining was beneficial to student learning compared to studying the material, but the effect was only obtained with the integrated rather than the split-source instructional format. It was assumed from these results that the imagining procedure could only succeed if there were sufficient working memory resources to permit imagining. A split-source presentation might have imposed an excessive cognitive load making the use of the imagination technique difficult or impossible and resulting in a relative failure of this instructional procedure. It was easier and more effective to imagine integrated rather than split-source materials. Integrated instructions facilitated schema acquisition, and schema acquisition in turn facilitated the imagination effect.

According to the modality effect, working memory capacity can be effectively increased, and learning improved by using a dual mode presentation, involving for example visual diagrams and auditory rather than written text (see Chapter 10). Accordingly, Tindall-Ford and Sweller (2006) demonstrated that the imagination effect could be facilitated when accompanied by audio-visual instructions compared to visual only instructions. One of their experiments used instructions on how to construct a frequency table, how to sum frequencies and how to calculate the mean, mode and range using the table with Grade 8 secondary school students. Four instructional formats were compared: (1) audio-visual instructions followed by an imagination component; (2) audio-visual instructions followed by a conventional study-based strategy; (3) visual only instructions followed by an imagination component; and (4) visual only instructions followed by a conventional study-based strategy.

The results indicated that the imagination effect was only obtained under audio-visual, but not under visual only conditions. The audio-visual technique facilitated schema construction, and then the follow-up imagination procedure allowed for schema automation. Thus, students' ability to imagine the information was enhanced when audio-visual instructions were used prior to imagining the mathematical procedure. Verbal protocols used in a follow-up experiment (Tindall-Ford & Sweller, 2006, Experiment 2) provided evidence that learners processed the material differently when asked to study or imagine it, and that the imagination process was assisted by the use of audio-visual instruction. Learners who studied tended to engage in search, while learners who imagined focused on essential entities and relations in the materials.

In summary, under suitable conditions, the imagination effect is stable and robust. Imagining procedures or concepts reduces an extraneous cognitive load that is imposed on relatively more experienced learners when they study material that is redundant for these learners. The major conditions required for the effect are that element interactivity due to intrinsic cognitive load must be high, a condition required for all cognitive load effects, and that despite the requirement for a high intrinsic cognitive load, learners must have sufficient cognitive resources to enable them to imagine the procedures or concepts. Sufficient cognitive resources can be ensured either by using learners with some level of expertise in the domain or by associating imagination instructions with other cognitive load reducing procedures.

We might speculate that the conditions of applicability that are relevant to the imagination effect are equally relevant to the self-explanation effect. To this point, the relevant studies have not been carried out.

Instructional Implications

The imagination effect can be used in most education and training contexts. Based on the results reported in this chapter, once a sufficient level of knowledge has been attained for learners to be able to imagine complex concepts and procedures, they should be encouraged to do so. Neither learners nor instructors should assume a concept or procedure is 'known' once it is understood. Beyond understanding, most concepts or procedures need to be used flexibly in a variety of circumstances. That flexibility is likely to be enhanced by the use of the imagination technique. Knowledge also is likely to be needed in order to advance further in a field. By imagining procedures or concepts, students are likely to be better equipped when continuing to learn in a discipline area.

Similarly, we know that self-explanations can facilitate knowledge acquisition and understanding. Encouraging learners to engage in self-explanations can be expected to increase the effectiveness of instruction, especially instruction that uses worked examples.

The imagination and self-explanation effects may be related to deliberate practice in the acquisition of expertise. Deliberate practice is used intentionally to enhance performance on a specific skill (Ericsson & Charness, 1994; Ericsson, Krampe, & Tesch-Romer, 1993). Imagining or self-explaining a procedure can be regarded as a form of deliberate practice that requires intentional processing of information in working memory to strengthen schemas held in long-term memory.

Conclusions

Studying concepts and procedures is known to be an effective and efficient instructional method for novice learners in the initial stages of skill acquisition. For relatively more experienced learners, on the other hand, the use of techniques such as imagining is highly effective. The imagination effect provides evidence that encouraging learners to imagine can be advantageous providing they have acquired sufficient expertise in the domain to use the technique. We can predict that encouraging learners to self-explain should similarly be more effective for more knowledgeable than less knowledgeable students.

Chapter 15
The Element Interactivity Effect

As discussed in Chapter 5, total cognitive load, consisting of intrinsic and extraneous cognitive load, must not exceed working memory resources in order for learning to be effective. From this perspective, applying learning strategies aimed at reducing extraneous cognitive load is more important when intrinsic cognitive load is high. If intrinsic cognitive load is low, a high extraneous cognitive load may not inhibit learning because the total cognitive load may be well within the available working memory capacity. Thus, for instructional conditions with a low intrinsic cognitive load, optimising instructional design may not be as important as for situations with a high intrinsic cognitive load.

Intrinsic cognitive load is determined by the level of interactivity between essential elements of information. If this element interactivity is low, using an instructional design that causes a high extraneous load may not interfere with learning. On the other hand, if the level of interactivity between essential elements of information is high, adding more element interactivity associated with a high extraneous cognitive load due to a suboptimal instructional design (Chapter 5) may well result in a total load well in excess of working memory capacity. Under high intrinsic cognitive load conditions, optimising instructional designs may be critical. Therefore, most of the cognitive load effects discussed in the previous chapters dealt with instructional conditions under which both intrinsic and extraneous cognitive load were high.

As examples, when dealing with very few intrinsically interacting elements, it may not matter whether learners must use the randomness as genesis principle via a random generate and test process to solve a problem or to find relations between sources of information presented separately that result in split-attention. Learners may have sufficient working memory resources to deal with these situations whether they are using the randomness as genesis principle or the borrowing and reorganising principle if element interactivity due to intrinsic cognitive load is sufficiently low.

The fact that cognitive load effects tend to be obtainable only if intrinsic cognitive load is high is referred to as the element interactivity effect (Sweller, 2010; Sweller & Chandler, 1994). This effect depends on the total element

J. Sweller et al., *Cognitive Load Theory*, Explorations in the Learning Sciences,
Instructional Systems and Performance Technologies 1,
DOI 10.1007/978-1-4419-8126-4_15, © Springer Science+Business Media, LLC 2011

interactivity associated with both intrinsic and extraneous cognitive load. It is treated as a separate cognitive load effect because there is substantial empirical evidence that levels of element interactivity due to intrinsic cognitive load have profound effects on other cognitive load effects associated with extraneous cognitive load. This chapter consolidates this evidence by explaining in more detail some of the studies previously described in Part IV and how they specifically relate to element interactivity.

Empirical Evidence for the Element Interactivity Effect

From a theoretical perspective, element interactivity associated with intrinsic cognitive load should be a relevant factor for all cognitive load effects, especially effects relying on variations in extraneous cognitive load. The element interactivity effect has been demonstrated for a large range of extraneous cognitive load effects, but has not been tested for all. We will discuss element interactivity associated with intrinsic cognitive load for those extraneous cognitive load effects for which data are available.

Element Interactivity and the Split-Attention and Redundancy Effects

In a series of experiments, Sweller and Chandler (1994) and Chandler and Sweller (1996) tested for split-attention and redundancy effects associated with learning computer applications using manuals and computers. When both a computer and a manual are used during instruction, either split-attention or redundancy may occur (see Chapters 9 and 11). Alternative methods of presentation can be designed to reduce the extraneous load and facilitate learning in comparison with a traditional use of manuals together with hardware such as computers or other equipment. Sweller and Chandler suggested that if a properly designed manual was used that eliminated split-attention and redundancy, the hardware itself could be redundant. Eliminating the hardware during the initial instructional period and replacing it by corresponding diagrams with integrated textual explanations in the manual were hypothesised to reduce the extraneous cognitive load caused either by split-attention between the manual and the hardware or redundancy, where the hardware was redundant. For example, in the case of learning to use a computer, both the monitor and keyboard can be replaced by diagrams of the computer screen and keyboard with textual explanations physically integrated at their appropriate locations on the diagrams. By this procedure, split-attention or redundancy that is associated with the presence of the computer itself can be eliminated, thus reducing extraneous cognitive load.

The results of experiments using both computing-based materials as well as electrical engineering instructions demonstrated both the split-attention and redundancy effects with the modified instructional materials. A format consisting only of an integrated, self-contained manual outperformed a conventional manual that did not include integrated diagrams and text demonstrating a split-attention effect. A self-contained manual format in which learners did not have access to the hardware also outperformed the same self-contained manual along with the actual computer, thus rendering the hardware redundant and demonstrating the redundancy effect. Furthermore and critically for the current discussion, both the split-attention and redundancy effects were obtained only in areas where the instructional material involved a high level of element interactivity.

In the above studies, the degree of element interactivity was estimated a priori by counting the number of elements that must be considered simultaneously by learners with a specific level of expertise in order to learn a particular procedure. For example, when learning how to use a computer-aided design/computer-aided manufacture (CAD/CAM) package, the procedure for moving the cursor in 1 mm steps 'Press one of four arrow keys' represents a low element interactivity task that can be learned easily without reference to other elements such as the function of other keys. On the other hand, the procedure for moving between any two positions represents a high element interactivity task for a novice learner as it involves simultaneous processing of the following nine interacting elements (Chandler & Sweller, 1996, p. 170):

1. Read horizontal axis value for current position
2. Read vertical axis value for current position
3. Find position of the goal co-ordinate on the horizontal axis
4. Find position of the goal co-ordinate on the vertical axis
5. Find point of intersection for the goal horizontal and vertical positions
6. Calculate the difference between the current and goal positions on the horizontal axis
7. Press keys appropriate to value calculated in 6
8. Calculate the difference between the current and goal position on the vertical axis
9. Press keys appropriate to value calculated in 8

When the previously described instructional formats were tested with technical apprentices, Chandler and Sweller (1996) showed that for instructions that involved high element interactivity materials, the self-contained modified manual format demonstrated its superiority over the conventional manual plus computer format for both written and practical post-tests, demonstrating the split-attention effect. Similarly, the self-contained, modified manual also was superior to the modified manual plus computer presentation, thus demonstrating the redundancy effect. No differences were found between instructional formats when the learning materials were low in element interactivity.

Direct evidence that these findings were due to cognitive load rather than other factors came from measures of cognitive load based on a secondary task.

The secondary task was presented on a separate computer and involved a tone that was immediately followed by a letter appearing on the screen. Learners had to recall the previous letter seen on the screen, while encoding the new letter. When instructional materials involved low or no interaction between elements of information and, consequently, a low intrinsic cognitive load, the added extraneous load imposed by differing instructional formats did not substantially inhibit learner performance on the secondary task. In this case, a sufficient working memory capacity was still available to perform the secondary task at a high level irrespective of instructional format. Accordingly, all three groups had little difficulty on the secondary task when studying the low element interactivity segments of the instructional material and performed at similar levels. However, the secondary task performance of the conventional manual plus computer (split-attention) and the modified manual plus computer (redundancy) groups were reduced substantially when high element interactivity instructional segments were studied.

Element Interactivity and Understanding Instructions

The extent to which we understand instructions depends on levels of element interactivity. Increases in levels of element interactivity increase the difficulty of understanding as more elements must be processed simultaneously in working memory. If the number of elements exceeds the capacity of working memory, the material cannot be understood until some of the elements have been incorporated into schemas that can be treated as a single element. It is possible to present the same information in a form that alters element interactivity by altering the extent to which pre-existing schemas are used to process the required elements. If a schema can be used to incorporate interacting elements, working memory load can be reduced (Marcus, Cooper, & Sweller, 1996).

Marcus et al. (1996) presented primary school students with electrical resistor problems. Functionally identical instructions could be presented using either diagrams or text. Diagrams tended to be more familiar to learners with each incorporating several interacting elements. Because of familiarity, those interacting elements could be easily incorporated into a schema processed as a single element. The same interacting elements, presented in textual form, had to be processed as individual elements resulting in a large increase in element interactivity and cognitive load compared to diagrams. Cognitive load was measured using both subjective measures of load and secondary tasks. Results indicated that firstly, the greater the number of interacting elements the greater the cognitive load and the harder it was to understand the information, and secondly, the use of diagrams reduced cognitive load and enhanced understanding compared to the same information presented in textual form.

These experiments clearly established the relations between cognitive load, element interactivity and understanding. High levels of element interactivity are a major impediment to understanding.

Element Interactivity and the Modality Effect

A meta-analysis of modality effect studies by Ginns (2005b) supported element interactivity as a major moderator of the effect. Tindall-Ford, Chandler, and Sweller (1997) provided direct experimental evidence for the importance of element interactivity in obtaining the modality effect. They found strong effects in favour of dual-modality formats in which wiring diagrams or tables were provided with narrated textual explanations over single-modality formats in which diagrams or tables were provided with printed textual explanations. These effects were obtained only for materials with high levels of element interactivity. There were no differences between spoken and written text for low element interactivity instructions.

Experiment 1 of Tindall-Ford et al. (1997) used instructional material designed to demonstrate how to carry out electrical tests of an electrical appliance using a voltmeter. These materials involved a high degree of element interactivity for a novice learner. For example, to understand the test of insulation resistance, the learner must simultaneously consider the required setting for the voltmeter and where to place the earth lead and the other lead on the kettle, ensure the electric kettle switch is on, press the test button, know what the required result should be, and then change the earth lead from the active pin to the neutral pin and perform the test again. The results of this experiment demonstrated benefits of presenting instructional material in either an integrated or audio-visual format.

The instructions used in Experiment 2 constituted table-based information relating to electrical installation and current-carrying capacity used for selecting appropriate cables for electrical installations. The instructions required learners to relate different elements of information and were high in element interactivity. For instance, the purpose of cable size on the table is only made clear if it is related to other table entities such as type of cable, core of cable, maximum load of cable and installation techniques. A modality effect also was obtained in this experiment, and subjective ratings of cognitive load supported a cognitive load explanation of the results.

Experiment 3 used separate and independent low and high element interactivity instructional materials including electrical symbols and electrical circuits. Low element interactivity instruction consisted of 30 electrical symbols and their corresponding meanings that could be learned independently of each other. For instance, the electrical symbol for a fluorescent lamp could be learned independently of the symbol for a general switch. High element interactivity instructional materials included different electrical circuits and their associated explanations. To understand each circuit, many elements and their relationships needed to be assimilated simultaneously. The results from the test items, subjective rating scales and measures of instructional efficiency indicated strong modality effects for materials with high levels of interactivity. On the other hand, when learning electrical symbols, there were no differences between instructional presentation formats. Again, subjective ratings supported a cognitive load explanation of the results.

Thus, learning materials with high levels of element interactivity (e.g. complex wiring diagrams) may cause a cognitive overload of the visual channel that may be further worsened by the extraneous cognitive load due to split-attention between visually presented sources of information that refer to each other (e.g. diagrams and printed explanations). Using a dual-modality format may effectively reduce this load and expand cognitive resources available for learning by engaging both processing channels of working memory. On the other hand, if learning materials have low levels of element interactivity as occurs, for example, when learning the meaning of individual electrical symbols, then even relatively high levels of extraneous cognitive load may still be within working memory limits and not interfere with learning.

Element Interactivity and the Expertise Reversal Effect

We might expect element interactivity to interact with the expertise reversal effect. We know that levels of element interactivity are dependent on levels of expertise. As expertise increases, interacting elements become incorporated within schemas and can be treated as single elements. As a consequence, element interactivity becomes less of a problem with increasing expertise. This relation between element interactivity and levels of expertise gives rise to the interaction between the element interactivity effect and the expertise reversal effect.

Kalyuga, Chandler, and Sweller (2001) compared worked examples-based instruction on how to construct switching equations for relay circuits with an exploratory learning environment. When the knowledge level of trainees was increased through specifically designed training sessions, the exploratory group achieved better results than the worked examples group. Subjective measures of task difficulty supported the cognitive load interpretation of the effect.

In this study, two task levels were used: structurally simple tasks with few circuit elements and a very limited number of possible options to explore, and structurally complex tasks with more interactive circuit elements and numerous options to explore. These two task levels corresponded to low and high levels of element interactivity. Simple tasks included only three interacting input elements and allowed construction of nine different acceptable relay circuits with various possible connections. Complex tasks required learners to construct and write equations for various relay circuits containing five interacting input elements, three of which were already placed into the diagram at fixed locations. This complex task environment allowed construction of 89 acceptable relay circuits with various possible connections.

As expected, the expertise reversal effect was obtained only for relatively complex tasks with high levels of element interactivity. There were no differences between the instructional methods for the simple tasks. For the relatively simple circuits, cognitive load was much lower and within the limits of working memory for either instructional format.

Element Interactivity and the Imagination Effect

Leahy and Sweller (2005) demonstrated that as primary school students' experience in reading a bus timetable and temperature graphs increased, the advantage of studying worked examples declined in favour of imagining examples, in accord with the imagination and expertise reversal effects. In addition, the experiments also showed that as the intrinsic cognitive load imposed by the learning materials increased, the interaction between these instructional methods and levels of learner expertise also increased. Both the imagination and the worked example effects were larger for materials with higher levels of element interactivity than for materials with lower levels of element interactivity.

When investigating an imagination effect using bus timetable materials with primary school students, Leahy and Sweller (2008) experimentally manipulated the levels of element interactivity in the instructional materials and post-test questions by varying the complexity of tasks. For example, when students were requested to find the categories of route numbers for which buses did not stop at every street (odd numbered routes in the table), they had to simultaneously process many interacting elements in working memory, such as holding the meaning of buses not stopping at every street, holding the meaning of route numbers, searching for columns with blanks, looking up the route numbers, looking at odd numbers and checking that they were blank, etc. This task was high in element interactivity. On the other hand, answering a question such as: 'What does the letter "e" stand for?' required only three interacting element to be processed. These elements were: holding the letter in working memory, searching for 'e', and transforming the letter searched into its appropriate word to provide an answer.

As predicted, a significant interaction between the imagination effect and levels of element interactivity was obtained in this study. Imagining materials that were low in element interactivity resulted in no significant benefits, whereas for high element interactivity materials, learners who were asked to imagine materials outperformed learners who were asked only to study the same materials. Imagining high element interactivity materials allowed learners to combine the multiple interacting elements of information into a single schema that could be more readily processed in working memory. The results also indicated that greater differences between the two instructional groups were obtained on post-test questions tapping high rather than low element interactivity knowledge.

Conditions of Applicability

Similar to the expertise reversal effect (Chapter 12), the element interactivity effect relies on an interaction between other cognitive load effects and specific factors, in this case, levels of element interactivity associated with intrinsic cognitive load. There is also an obvious relation between these two effects as the levels of element interactivity that produce an intrinsic cognitive load are always relative to levels of learner expertise. The same material can reflect a high level of interactivity for a novice learner and at the same time a low level of interactivity for an expert because as expertise increases, interacting elements are incorporated into schemas, reducing working memory load in accord with the environmental organising and linking principle. Therefore, a complex task for a novice may be a relatively simple one for an expert. Learners' prior knowledge allows many interacting elements to be incorporated, or chunked, in a single schema acting as a single element in working memory. In contrast, learners with low prior knowledge are unable to chunk information into a single schema and must attempt to simultaneously process the interacting elements in working memory.

Accordingly, lower levels of element interactivity associated with intrinsic cognitive load are expected to have similar consequences to higher levels of learner expertise. As learners acquire more expertise in a specific task domain, the levels of element interactivity associated with particular instructional materials change. Categories of learning tasks that reflected relatively high levels of element interactivity become low in element interactivity as expertise increases. Lower levels of element interactivity associated with intrinsic cognitive load due to increased expertise allow higher levels of extraneous cognitive load to be handled without overloading working memory.

The element interactivity effect defines an essential condition of applicability for other cognitive load effects dealing with extraneous cognitive load. Another condition of applicability of this effect is that intrinsic cognitive load itself should not exceed the available working memory resources of learners. For example, when dealing with excessively complex materials for which learners do not have sufficient prior knowledge, very high levels of intrinsic cognitive load may be experienced. In this case, cognitive load effects aimed at reducing intrinsic cognitive load need to be applied (e.g. the isolated–interacting elements effect, Chapter 16).

Instructional Implications

If element interactivity associated with intrinsic cognitive load is low, adding more interacting elements associated with a high extraneous cognitive load may not inhibit learning provided working memory capacity is not exceeded. For example, if students learn a new foreign language vocabulary in which each new item can be learned independently from all other items, the manner in which the material is presented may not matter a great deal as the resulting, total working memory load will be within available working memory capacity. In this situation, redesigning instructional procedures or formats by applying cognitive load effects aimed at reducing extraneous load may have minimal (if any) effects on learning.

Alternatively, adding the interacting elements associated with a high extraneous cognitive load to the interacting elements associated with a high intrinsic cognitive load can exceed working memory capacity. In this situation, reducing the element interactivity associated with extraneous load by applying appropriate cognitive load techniques may be critical for learning. For example, if split-attention or redundancy is incorporated into learning materials with high levels of element interactivity associated with intrinsic cognitive load such as complex equations or wiring diagrams in electronics, the total number of interacting elements and corresponding total cognitive load may exceed working memory capacity. Reducing the number of interacting elements associated with extraneous cognitive load by integrating related sources of information or eliminating redundant information can reduce working memory load to manageable levels.

Conclusion

By definition, cognitive load theory is concerned with the instructional implications of an excessive working memory load. It is not surprising that those instructional implications are most likely to be manifest when dealing with materials that themselves impose a heavy cognitive load irrespective of how they are presented. If the element interactivity that leads to an intrinsic cognitive load is low, any additional element interactivity due to an extraneous cognitive load may be irrelevant if the total cognitive load is within working memory capacity limits. On the other hand, with a high level of element interactivity associated with intrinsic cognitive load, any additional element interactivity due to an extraneous cognitive load may be increasingly important. As a consequence, most cognitive load effects only manifest themselves under conditions of a high intrinsic cognitive load leading to the element interactivity effect.

The majority of cognitive load effects occur due to reductions in extraneous cognitive load. The element interactivity effect indicates that intrinsic cognitive load inevitably is equally important in determining total cognitive load and in determining the effectiveness of instructional manipulations carried out in order to reduce extraneous cognitive load. Fewer studies have been carried out in which intrinsic cognitive load has been directly manipulated. The fact that intrinsic cognitive load cannot be manipulated if the nature of the task and the expertise of the learners remain constant contribute to this dearth of studies. Nevertheless, element interactivity due to intrinsic cognitive load can be manipulated by changing the nature of a task. That issue is considered in the next chapter.

Chapter 16
Altering Element Interactivity and Intrinsic Cognitive load

As described in Chapter 15, the concept of element interactivity provides a theoretical construct underpinning understanding and learning. Instructional material that is low in element interactivity and consequently low in intrinsic cognitive load requires few working memory resources, because the constituent elements do not interact and can be understood and learned in isolation. Other material that is high in element interactivity and intrinsic cognitive load includes elements that interact and must be processed simultaneously as they cannot be understood and learned as single elements. High element interactivity information is a major category of information that is of interest to cognitive load theory. Processing such information requires working memory resources that may exceed its capacity. That information cannot be easily understood or learned and creates a significant challenge for teachers and instructional designers. How can students learn new, complex, high element interactivity information if the processing demand is greater than working memory capacity?

As previously discussed, we define complexity in terms of element interactivity and intrinsic cognitive load (Chapter 5). Such complexity requires particular instructional strategies. Whereas extraneous cognitive load can be manipulated by the instructional designer, and lowered accordingly, intrinsic cognitive load is fixed and cannot be changed without altering either what is being taught and learned or altering the knowledge of the learner. If learners have a high degree of domain-specific knowledge, they are able to process a number of interacting elements simultaneously without a heavy working memory load. Learners' prior knowledge allows many interacting elements to be incorporated in a single schema that can act as a single element in working memory. In contrast, learners with low prior knowledge are unable to chunk multiple, interacting elements of information into a single schema and must attempt to simultaneously process the individual elements in working memory, imposing a high intrinsic cognitive load.

In this chapter, we describe strategies that have proved to be effective in dealing with inappropriate levels of intrinsic cognitive load. As indicated above, intrinsic cognitive load only can be altered by either altering the knowledge of learners or altering the nature of the task. Several strategies focus on building domain-specific prior knowledge by an appropriate sequencing of learning tasks, but we also describe some studies that have focused on altering the nature of the task. Strategies

J. Sweller et al., *Cognitive Load Theory*, Explorations in the Learning Sciences, Instructional Systems and Performance Technologies 1, DOI 10.1007/978-1-4419-8126-4_16, © Springer Science+Business Media, LLC 2011

that sequence materials have taken many forms, but usually they involve progressing from simple to complex tasks. Whereas there has been much research into how topics should be sequenced over whole training programmes (see Reigeluth, 2007; Ritter, Nerb, Lehtinen, & O'Shea, 2007), we focus more on instructional sequencing within individual learning tasks.

Pre-training

One method of reducing intrinsic load is to develop specific prior knowledge before the key materials are presented. This method is often referred to as *pre-training*. From the perspective of human cognitive architecture, pre-training increases knowledge in long-term memory. Rather than searching for relations between elements using the randomness as genesis principle, those relations already are stored and can be used by the environmental organising and linking principle to process information and so reduce working memory load (narrow limits of change principle).

Mayer, Mathias, and Wetzell (2002) taught learners how brakes work from a narrated animation. When processing a narrated animation, both a component model (how the brake piston moves) and a causal model (relations between the piston movement and what happens to the brake fluid) need to be built simultaneously, which places very heavy demands on working memory. By pre-training on the component model as opposed to learning the component and causal models simultaneously, more attention can be paid later to causal effects. The results of Mayer, Mathias, et al. (2002) indicated that pre-training, limited to just names and behaviours of the component parts, led to significant improvements in problem solving. A further study by Mayer, Mautone, and Prothero (2002) using a game-based geology lesson demonstrated that students who received pre-training on illustrations of key geological features (e.g. a ridge) showed superior problem-solving performance than students who did not receive such training.

These results can be interpreted in terms of a reduction in element interactivity and intrinsic cognitive load due to pre-training. The component and causal models of Mayer, Mathias, et al. (2002) are closely related and so their elements interact. A causal model is unintelligible without the component model. Presenting both simultaneously best exemplifies the interactivity between the elements but at the cost of a very heavy intrinsic cognitive load that may prevent learning. By learning the component model first, many of the interacting elements can be embedded in schemas that can be treated as a single element when later considering the causal model. In this way, element interactivity remains relatively low throughout learning and so within working memory limits.

As indicated in Chapter 12 when discussing the expertise reversal effect, Clarke, Ayres, and Sweller (2005) conducted a study that focused on pre-training a secondary skill (spreadsheet knowledge) that was required for learning specific primary concepts (mathematical graphs). It is often recommended by educators that many mathematical concepts can be learned effectively with the aid of spreadsheets.

However, combining novel spreadsheets applications with novel mathematical concepts can result in a task that is very high in element interactivity. Clarke et al. (2005) found that students with initially low knowledge of spreadsheets benefited from pre-training on spreadsheets before using them to learn mathematical concepts compared with a concurrent strategy of simultaneously dealing with the spreadsheets and mathematical concepts. Simultaneously dealing with elements associated with both spreadsheets and mathematics overwhelmed working memory resources for these students. In contrast, students who had more knowledge of spreadsheets benefited from the concurrent approach. These more knowledgeable learners already had many of the elements associated with spreadsheets incorporated into schemas and so it was unnecessary to instruct them in using spreadsheets independently of the mathematics.

Focusing on Subgoals

Catrambone (1998) observed that learners have difficulty transferring knowledge gained through a set of examples to tasks that are conceptually similar but procedurally quite different. In a set of experiments in a statistical domain, Catrambone (1998) showed that if learners structured their solutions in terms of subgoals, transfer of knowledge was achieved. An important part of this process was a cueing strategy (borrowing and reorganizing principle), where labels were used to cue students into noticing that certain steps could be grouped. The underlying theoretical argument proposed that if the learners were cued that certain solution steps belonged together then they would try to self-explain (see Chi, Bassok, Lewis, Reimann, & Glaser, 1989) the purpose of the steps and why they belong together. The self-explanation effect occurs when learners who explain a concept or procedure to themselves learn more than learners who do not self-explain (see Chapter 14). It is notable that learners did not receive practice on predefined subgoals, as might be expected from a pre-training strategy, but were required to form them from the cues provided. Nevertheless, the strategy enabled learners to transfer their knowledge, suggesting that robust schemas were acquired.

Chi, de Leeuw, Chiu, and LaVancher (1994) commented that a learner is more likely to integrate new knowledge with old if tasks are completed in small sections. From a cognitive load perspective, this suggestion is consistent with a reduction in intrinsic cognitive load. By creating an instructional environment that focuses on subgoals, element interactivity is lowered because only the elements within a subgoal 'section' need to be considered at a given time rather than all of the elements in the task. If, for example, a solution to a problem requires eight steps, but it can be divided into two groupings of four steps each, then the added element interactivity of the two subgroups may be considerably lower than processing the eight steps together. Of course, it must be remembered that the reduction in element interactivity is caused by a change in the task. Learners no longer learn how elements in the two separate segments interact between the segments, only within the segments.

Presenting Declarative and Procedural Information Separately

Based on Anderson's (1996) ACT theory, Kester, Kirschner, and van Merriënboer (2006) distinguished between two types of information that must be managed during problem solving: declarative and procedural. In Kester et al.'s study, *declarative* information is defined as related to reasoning about the cause of the problem and finding a solution, whereas *procedural* information is related to manipulating the environment. Kester et al. argued that processing both types of information at the same time can lead to a cognitive overload. In particular, it was theorized that declarative knowledge has a higher degree of element interactivity than procedural information and therefore should not be presented during practice. Also, by avoiding procedures initially, more working memory can be devoted to elaboration of the new information, leading to schema acquisition. Kester et al. considered this process as a *just-in-time* strategy where intrinsic cognitive load is managed by initially not including the procedural aspects of the task.

In a four-group comparison using tasks that required troubleshooting in electrical circuits, it was found that a strategy that sequenced information in the order of declarative (pre-practice) followed by procedural (during practice) or vice versa was superior on transfer tasks than a strategy that presented both declarative and procedural knowledge before practice or during practice. These results indicated clearly that it was better to present some of the information before practice and some during practice in a piece-by-piece manner in order to reduce intrinsic cognitive load.

Reducing Intrinsic Load in Worked Examples

Gerjets, Scheiter, and Catrambone (2004) distinguished between *molar* and *modular* presentation of solutions in worked examples. According to theories of expertise and the relation of expertise to schema acquisition, successful problem solving is due to schematic knowledge and categorisation skills. Once a problem is identified as belonging to a certain category then a relevant schema (if available in long-term memory) is retrieved containing the required solution (Chi, Glaser, & Rees, 1982). Gerjets et al. pointed out that traditional textbooks, particularly in the sciences, emphasise the categorisation of problems as an important step in problem solving. Students learn categories of problems and their associated solutions. This strategy is referred to as 'recipe' or the molar way of learning. Gerjets et al. also argued that for novice learners, a focus on problem categories suitable for experts may create a high cognitive load and may not be an effective way to learn. They commented as follows:

> A category-based approach requires learners to keep in mind all category-defining structural features of a problem before they accurately decide on its problem category and the appropriate formula needed for its solution. Accordingly, studying molar examples requires that learners consider multiple structural task features at the same time in order to understand the problem's category membership. (p. 43)

Gerjets et al. (2004) suggested that a high degree of intrinsic cognitive load will prevent elaboration and comparisons between the different types of examples, thus leading to shallow learning. To prevent this situation, they advocated a decrease in intrinsic load through a modular approach that emphasised partly independent modules that could be used for the necessary calculation. Because each module could be considered meaningfully in isolation, element interactivity and intrinsic cognitive load was reduced.

In a series of experiments, Gerjets et al. directly compared a modular strategy with a molar strategy. Using problems from probability theory that required the use of permutations or combinations, they provided the example of working out the probability of correctly guessing the first three places in a 100-m race involving seven runners. For the molar solution, key features of the task were identified, explaining why it is a permutation-without replacement problem. This explanation was followed by a general formula that calculated the total number of permutations, $n!/(n - k)!$ Finally, the actual numbers relevant to the problem were inserted ($n = 7$, $k = 3$) and this number inverted for the final probability answer of 1/210. In contrast, the modular approach considered and calculated each event (1st, 2nd and 3rd) individually in separate, modular sections. Finally, the three probabilities (1/7, 1/6, and 1/5) were multiplied together for the final answer.

From a cognitive load perspective, considering a generalised formula (molar approach) involves a number of interacting elements that must be processed simultaneously including who comes first, second and third in the race. For the modular approach, by concentrating on one finishing position at a time, element interactivity is significantly decreased. By breaking down the formula into constituent parts, corresponding elements are isolated.

The results reported in this paper indicated that the modular approach was superior to the molar approach on similar and novel (transfer) problems, involving different types of problem categories and learners (both low and high prior knowledge), and took less study time. In a further study, Gerjets, Scheiter, and Catrambone (2006) investigated the impact of instructional explanations and self-explanations on modular and molar techniques in the same probability domain. Both instructional explanations and self-explanations made no difference to either molar or modular presentations. However, consistent with their previous studies, a significant difference was found in favour of the modular strategy on learning time, as well as problem solving on similar and novel problems.

Gerjets et al.'s (2004, 2006) work suggesting that the modular approach reduces element interactivity and intrinsic cognitive load compared to a molar approach is important and interesting. Nevertheless, the results do require replication because the experiments reported altered multiple variables simultaneously and so we cannot know the true cause of the modular superiority. For example, the molar approach used an equation while the modular approach placed its emphasis on the logical rationale of the procedure without reference to an equation. The difference between the two conditions may have been caused by this difference or any of the other differences in procedure between the molar and modular approach. Further experiments that alter only one critical variable will need to be carried out.

In the Gerjets, Scheiter, and Catrambone studies, the complexity of the tasks themselves were not reduced. Only the presented solutions were reduced in complexity. A study by Nadolski, Kirschner, and van Merriënboer (2005) adopted a similar strategy. In this study, law students were required to learn how to conduct a law plea. In a complex learning environment that included whole-task training, support tools and feedback, three groups of learners were compared who received identical conditions, apart from the number of solution steps provided in worked examples. It was found that students who received an intermediate number of steps outperformed students who received the maximum number or minimum number of steps. In the case of too many steps, Nadolski et al. argued that the learning task became less coherent. Reduced coherence may occur because of increased element interactivity. In the case of too few steps, the researchers did not offer a plausible reason for this effect, but presumably not enough information was provided for these learners to construct meaningful schemas.

Isolated Elements Effect

Reducing intrinsic cognitive load through a scaffolded progression from learning with simpler part tasks to more complex full tasks has proven effective. Some experiments have used a related procedure in which some of the interacting elements have been removed from the full task resulting in a sequence of isolated, non-interacting elements that needed to be processed and learned. This instructional strategy has been called the isolated/interacting-elements effect but in this book will be referred to by the simpler name, the isolated elements effect.

In the first study of this issue within a cognitive load theory framework, Pollock, Chandler, and Sweller (2002) used a strategy to directly reduce intrinsic cognitive load. In two experiments, apprentices were taught how to conduct electrical safety tests. To learn how to conduct these tests, students must understand the complex interactions that take place between the appliance to be tested (e.g. a kettle), voltmeter settings, insulation, electrical leads, set criteria for safety readings and the consequences of incorrect readings. To isolate elements in this domain, Pollock et al. initially focused instruction on explaining only basic procedural steps. For example, for the insulation resistance test, nine steps were demonstrated in a worked example outlining consecutive procedures, such as 'Set the metre to read 500 volts' (Pollock et al., p. 65). In contrast, the interacting-elements group received this instruction, as well as other relevant explanatory information to fully understand all aspects of the task: 'By setting the meter to read 500 volts, a larger than normal average voltage will be introduced into each circuit in order to test the appliance under a heavy load. Set the metre to read 500 volts' (p. 65). It was estimated that for novices in this domain (first year electrical trainees), seven elements would have to be simultaneously processed in the isolated-elements condition, but 16 in the interacting-elements condition.

In the second phase, the learning materials were repeated but both groups received the instructional materials with full interacting elements. Thus, the isolated-elements group experienced a progression from low to high element interactivity and intrinsic cognitive load, while the interacting-elements group experienced the high element interactivity and intrinsic cognitive load conditions twice. Results indicated that for high element interactivity test problems, the isolated-elements group significantly outperformed the interacting-elements group. For low element interactivity tasks, there was a similar but not statistically significant trend. Significant differences on self-rating measures of cognitive load using a difficulty rating scale indicated that cognitive load was lower for the isolated-elements group. However, these differences only were found for novices in the domain. For students with greater knowledge, no significant differences were found.

Pollock et al. recognised that the method they used to isolate elements had a high reliance on procedural knowledge, which may have influenced the overall results. Consequently, they designed two further experiments where more conceptual understanding was required. In these experiments, students were required to learn about an electrical circuit powering an industrial oven. Both groups received a circuit diagram with numbered text points. During the first phase of instruction, the isolated-elements group had less text associated with fewer interacting elements. The interacting-elements group had more text and a greater emphasis on cause and effect relations underpinning the whole system. Results from these two experiments were similar to the previous experiments. For students with high prior knowledge, no significant differences were found between the two strategies, with possible trends in favour of the interacting-elements group. In contrast, for learners with less prior knowledge, all measures favoured the isolated-elements group, with significant differences found on high element interactivity tasks.

The results of Pollock et al. were consistent. On tasks that emphasised procedures or concepts, isolating elements during an initial stage of learning was found to be effective. Both test scores and measures of cognitive load, particularly on high element interactivity tasks, supported this conclusion. However, this effect was only found with learners with low prior knowledge. Learners with greater prior knowledge did not need this progression from low to high intrinsic cognitive load as they were capable of learning just as well from the more complex materials without prior exposure to the simpler material. These results correspond with the expertise reversal effect (see Chapter 12).

To examine the staged progression strategy further, Ayres (2006b) used an isolated-elements approach in teaching basic algebraic concepts. Previous research by Ayres (2001, 2006a) found that bracket expansion tasks of the kind $4(3x - 6) - 5(7 - 2x)$ were high in element interactivity and found to be difficult for novice learners of algebra. To expand these brackets, only consecutive operations need to be performed; however, there is a high level of element interactivity caused by the way the numbers, signs, bracket operators and x variables are interrelated. Students need to decide what needs to be grouped together, when it needs to be grouped and how many calculations are to be completed overall. To create an isolated-elements environment, a set of worked examples was used that demonstrated only one calculation at a time. For example, using the problem above, students could study how to complete the fourth calculation $-5 \times (-2x)$ only. Then, using the paired worked-example strategy (see Chapter 8), learners practised using a similar calculation placed in the same position of a paired expansion task similar to $4(3x - 6) - 5(7 - 2x)$. In an identical fashion, students received worked-example pairs on the three other calculations.

This isolated-elements strategy was compared with an interacting-elements strategy where students were given full worked-example pairs showing all four calculations together, and a phased group, where students switched from an isolated-elements strategy to the full worked-examples strategy halfway through the acquisition stage. The prior mathematical knowledge of participating grade 8 students was measured. In this 2 (high vs low ability) × 3 (isolated vs interacting vs phased strategy) design, a significant interaction effect was found (an expertise reversal effect, see Chapter 12). Students with the least mathematical ability benefited from the isolated-elements approach, whereas students with the higher levels of mathematical ability benefited from the fully interacting worked-examples approach. The phased strategy did not provide a significant advantage for either level of ability. Notably, a difficulty rating scale as a measure of cognitive load collected post acquisition found that the isolated-elements approach was less difficult than the other two approaches, hence supporting the assumption of an overall reduction in cognitive load.

In a third study, Blayney, Kalyuga, and Sweller (2010) investigated the effectiveness of an isolated-elements approach with first-year undergraduate students learning how to construct spreadsheet formulae for basic accountancy concepts. In this study, a two-phase strategy was used similar to that of Pollock et al. (2002). In the first phase, two groups of students learning how to determine a budget received either isolated-elements or interacting-elements instructions. This initial phase was followed by a second instructional phase where both groups received instruction in a fully interacting elements format. Both phases used worked-examples to keep extraneous cognitive load to a minimum.

For the interacting-elements presentation, the whole formula consisting of several sub-calculations was combined together within one spreadsheet cell. In this format, the formula consisted of the maximum number of interacting elements that needed to be considered at once. In contrast, the isolated-elements group received one or more intermediary steps corresponding to the required sub-calculation in separate spreadsheet cells before these were combined in a separate cell to give the final answer. In this isolated-elements format, each formula had fewer interacting elements. This group had more steps to complete but each step had relatively few interacting elements.

For students with low prior knowledge, the initial use of the isolated-elements strategy was found to be more effective than the initial use of the fully interacting elements approach. In contrast, for students with high levels of prior knowledge, no difference was found between the two approaches.

Overall, these three studies (Ayres, 2006b; Blayney et al., 2010; Pollock et al., 2002) produced very similar results. Evidence emerged in each study that for low prior knowledge learners, use of an isolated-elements strategy is advantageous. That advantage disappeared or even reversed for higher prior knowledge learners. Reducing intrinsic load at an early stage for novices helps develop partial schemas held in long-term memory (information store principle), which due to the environmental organising and linking principle can overcome working memory limitations (narrow limits of change principle) as learning continues. In contrast, learners with higher levels of prior knowledge can use the environmental organising and linking principle as exemplified by sufficiently developed schemas or partial schemas to allow them to deal with high levels of element interactivity. It is notable that these three studies used different learning tasks with very diverse groups of learners (grade 8 students, undergraduate accountancy students and trade apprentices). The fact that similar results have been obtained with different learners and different tasks suggests that the results may be reasonably robust.

4C/ID Model for Complex Learning

The strategies described above all reduce intrinsic cognitive load using a part-task methodology. This strategy reduces intrinsic cognitive load because a part task contains fewer interacting elements than a full, whole task. In the 4C/ID model developed by van Merriënboer and colleagues (see van Merriënboer, Clark, & de Croock, 2002; van Merriënboer, Kester, & Paas, 2006; van Merriënboer & Kirschner, 2007; van Merriënboer, Kirschner, & Kester, 2003), part tasks are an integral component of an overall instructional model designed to organise learning tasks effectively and efficiently. The 4C/ID model consists of the following four components: learning tasks, supportive information, procedural information and part-task practice. Van Merriënboer et al. (2006) summarise *learning tasks* as the background of the training programme and are preferably taken from real-life scenarios: *supportive information* provides information that helps learners to problem-solve and reason in the domain, *procedural information* is provided to help learn routine procedures that need to be carried out under specific conditions and *part-task practice* is for routine tasks that need to become highly automated.

Even though this model is more focused on educational programmes than the design of instructional materials (van Merriënboer & Sluijsmans, 2009), it offers directions in reducing extraneous as well as intrinsic, cognitive load. By providing support and guidance when needed (just-in-time support) extraneous load is lowered. As expertise is increased, these scaffolding techniques are reduced according to a fading-guidance strategy (Renkl & Atkinson, 2003; van Merriënboer et al., 2003; see Chapter 13). Intrinsic load is lowered by using part tasks. However, such tasks are not necessarily a subset of original whole tasks, but can be basic skills that need to be mastered such as the multiplication tables. The initial presentation of part tasks helps consolidate procedures or rules, which can be applied to whole tasks at a later stage (van Merriënboer et al., 2002).

Nevertheless, in contradiction to the above approach emphasising a part-whole sequence, van Merriënboer et al. (2003) also suggested that under some circumstances, part-task practice should occur after whole tasks have been introduced, thus grounding the practice on part tasks in the context of a bigger picture. A key feature of the 4C/ID model is that initial tasks should be whole and meaningful, exposing the learner to a holistic view immediately (van Merriënboer et al., 2006). From this perspective, the model adopts a whole-part approach. Van Merriënboer et al. (2003) point out that a part-task approach may not be effective for complex learning environments that require the integration of a number of skills, knowledge and attitudes (see van Merriënboer & Kester, 2008, for a summary of the evidence). For complex motor tasks and many professional real-life tasks, it is essential that the learner understand and learn the relevant interactions and coordinations between the various subtasks. By learning the subtasks in isolation, these interactions may be missed. To ensure that all such interactions are identified, the 4C/ID model proposes that whole tasks should be presented initially, although in a more simplified (reduced intrinsic load) format before progressing to full complexity.

The Variability Effect

The above studies were all designed to decrease intrinsic cognitive load. Nevertheless, unlike extraneous cognitive load that should always be decreased where possible, intrinsic cognitive load should be optimised rather than decreased. If intrinsic cognitive load exceeds working memory capacity, learning and problem solving will be disrupted. Equally, if intrinsic cognitive load requires fewer cognitive resources than are available in working memory and the number of interacting elements relevant to the task can be increased, then learning will be enhanced by increasing intrinsic cognitive load.

When discussing the worked-example effect (see Chapter 8), many of the reviewed studies included transfer tasks. Cognitive load theory, in common with many other frameworks, has recognised the importance of testing for transfer. Showing that learned knowledge and skills can be applied to problems belonging to a different category to those previously studied may indicate that more sophisticated and flexible schemas have been constructed. Although early research indicated that worked examples could successfully foster transfer skills, researchers have investigated methods of structuring examples to specifically promote transfer. One such method is called variability, or *varied context examples* (Clark, Nguyen, & Sweller, 2006) which leads to the *variability effect*.

The variability effect occurs when example-based instruction (borrowing and organising principle) that includes highly variable examples results in enhanced transfer performance compared to less variable, more similar examples. Exposure to increased variability can be hypothesised to result in students learning how to differentiate relevant and irrelevant features of worked examples (van Merriënboer & Sweller, 2005). Through high variability, learners may be able to abstract schemas to transfer to long-term memory that incorporate knowledge of principles and learn when to apply those principles (Clark et al., 2006) via the environmental organising and linking principle, thus enhancing transfer.

Paas and van Merriënboer (1994) conducted the first investigation of variability from a cognitive load perspective. In this study, secondary technical school students were required to apply computer-controlled machinery programming to learn several geometrical principles such as Pythagoras' theorem. Low variability was achieved by using problems that only differed by changing the values of the problems, whereas for high variability, both values and problem formats were changed. For example, consider the problems in Fig. 16.1. The worked example shown in Fig. 16.1a gives an example of the calculation of the distance between two points. Figure 16.1b demonstrates a low variability example because only the numbers

a If P is (1, 1) and Q is (4, 5), find the length of PQ.

Answer: $\quad PQ = \sqrt{(4-1)^2 + (5-1)^2}$

$$= \sqrt{3^2 + 4^2}$$

$$= \sqrt{25}$$

$$= 5$$

b If P is (2, 3) and Q is (8, 11), find the length of PQ.

Answer: $\quad PQ = \sqrt{(8-2)^2 + (11-3)^2}$

$$= \sqrt{6^2 + 8^2}$$

$$= \sqrt{100}$$

$$= 10$$

c If P is (1, 1) and Q is (x, 13), and the length of PQ is 13, find x.

Answer: $\quad PQ = \sqrt{(x-1)^2 + (13-1)^2} = 13$

$$(x-1)^2 + 12^2 = 13^2$$

$$(x-1)^2 = 13^2 - 12^2$$

$$(x-1)^2 = 25$$

$$x - 1 = 5$$

$$\therefore x = 6$$

Fig. 16.1 (**a**) Worked example using distance formula. (**b**) Problem using distance formula with low variability. (**c**) Problem using distance formula with high variability

have changed, and the formula is applied in exactly the same way. In contrast, Fig. 16.1c shows a high variability example because the formula has to be applied and then manipulated to find the unknown 'x', as the solution demonstrates. There is considerable more thinking needed to solve this problem, including applications of algebra.

In Paas and van Merriënboer's study, using a 2×2 group design (worked example–high variability, worked example–low variability, problem solving–high variability, problem solving–low variability), it was found that worked examples led to better transfer with less mental effort than conventional problem solving. There was also an interaction indicating that variability was effective in the worked examples format but not effective in the conventional, problem-solving format. The high variation–worked examples combination had superior transfer outcomes than the other groups.

Quilici and Mayer (1996) also found that variability could accelerate the transfer of knowledge. In this study, which investigated the learning of statistics, two main strategies were compared. One strategy varied surface features but did not vary structural features, the second did not vary surface stories but did vary underlying structures. It was found that the strategy that varied structure led to superior sorting performance based on structure, and learners presented examples with increased structural variability were better able to select and categorise the correct statistical test to be used. It was concluded that categorising success could be improved by presenting examples where students can focus on differences in structural features instead of surface features.

A different form of variability is called *contextual interference* and involves the sequencing of problems. If problems are positioned next to each other in time and require the same set of skills for solution, then contextual interference is low. In contrast, if problems are positioned next to each other and require a different set of skills then contextual interference is high. Van Merriënboer et al. (2002, p. 14) used the following example to demonstrate the difference. Low contextual interference can be produced by blocked practice where the skills required for one problem are practised before moving on to a different problem (e.g. B-B-B, A-A-A, C-C-C). High contextual interference can be created by randomly linking together practise on the different skills (e.g. C-A-B, B-C-A, B-A-C).

De Croock, van Merriënboer, and Paas (1998) compared a high and low contextual approach in a study where learners were required to troubleshoot system failures. They found that learners who practised troubleshooting in a high contextual interference environment showed superior transfer skills than those who practised under lower interference. The advantage came at a cost. Students who practised under high interference conditions had delayed acquisition of the skill. De Croock et al. predicted that high contextual interference would generate more cognitive load. Although performance results concurred with this prediction, mental effort ratings during acquisition did not show any differences. In analysing this finding, van Merriënboer et al. (2002) argued that no mental effort differences were found because of the low complexity of the troubleshooting tasks.

In a later study, van Merriënboer et al. (2002) used a more complex learning environment in which engineering students learned various programming skills.

In Experiment 2, a high contextual interference group needed more time and invested more mental effort than a low contextual interference group during acquisition, thus providing evidence for increased cognitive load. Despite the increase in cognitive load, the high contextual interference group had fewer errors on a transfer test. Accordingly that increase in cognitive load was advantageous and so not due to extraneous cognitive load. There are theoretical reasons to suppose that the increase in cognitive load with increased variability is due to increases in intrinsic cognitive load leading to increases in germane load.

Variability and Increased Intrinsic Cognitive Load

The initial explanation for the advantages of increased variability was solely in terms of germane cognitive load (Paas & van Merriënboer, 1994; Sweller, van Merriënboer, & Paas, 1998). Van Merriënboer and Sweller (2005) further commented that through variability, learners have the opportunity to engage in deeper processing, building more flexible and well-connected schemas. That explanation is valid using the definition of germane resources used in this book (see Chapter 5). Recall that germane cognitive load is defined in terms of the working memory resources devoted to intrinsic cognitive load. We suggest that increases in variability increase intrinsic cognitive load and so on this formulation, additional working memory resources must be devoted to intrinsic cognitive load.

When variability is altered, so is the nature of the task, resulting in changes in intrinsic cognitive load. When problem variability is low, learners only need to learn how to solve problems with a particular structure. They can ignore the elements associated with variations in deep structure because deep structure is relatively constant. As variability increases, learners must take into account more and more elements associated with the various structures reflected in the problems and learn how to deal with those elements. Element interactivity and intrinsic cognitive load is increased with increased variability. That increase requires additional working memory resources devoted to dealing with this increased intrinsic load (germane resources). In effect, whenever variability is changed, the nature of the task facing learners changes with a concomitant change in element interactivity and intrinsic cognitive load. Learning how to deal with a greater range of problems increases knowledge that can, in turn, increase transfer performance to new tasks because the probability that the new task is similar to one already faced increases with variability. That result was obtained by Paas and van Merriënboer (1994).

Of course, increasing the number of interacting elements associated with intrinsic cognitive load only is a viable instructional strategy provided there is sufficient working memory capacity available to process the additional elements. If there is insufficient working memory capacity to handle the increased number of elements, increased variability will have negative rather than positive effects. Intrinsic cognitive load must be optimised rather than simply increased or decreased and the optimum level of intrinsic cognitive load will depend on the judgement of an instructor concerning the knowledge levels of learners. Higher knowledge levels may free sufficient capacity to enable an increase in intrinsic cognitive load without overwhelming working memory.

In conclusion, increasing the variability of worked examples increases intrinsic cognitive load because learners must process the additional interacting elements associated with increased variability. In turn, the additional knowledge acquired due to increased variability should facilitate transfer, explaining the empirical findings.

Conditions of Applicability

Intrinsic cognitive load is dependent upon the knowledge of the learner. Low prior knowledge learners are restricted in their ability to chunk information together into schemas and for complex material, learners are forced to simultaneously process a large number of interacting elements in working memory. Thus, for these learners it can be very difficult to learn complex materials. Consequently, for learners with low prior knowledge, there are considerable advantages to providing a part-task approach, where intrinsic load is considerably reduced by providing first a task with a lower level of element interactivity followed by a more complete task with higher levels of element interactivity. Having reduced intrinsic load, learners are more able to understand and learn the materials, and to develop partial schemas, enabling them to eventually progress to whole tasks. In contrast, learners with greater prior knowledge are able to process more interacting elements simultaneously without a heavy working memory load, and do not need the same scaffolding strategies provided by a part-task approach. In general, a part-whole sequence is an effective learning strategy.

On the other side of this particular ledger, if element interactivity is low, learning might be facilitated, by increasing intrinsic cognitive load through an increase in variability. As is the case for part-whole sequencing, changing element interactivity levels to an optimum level should only be done if knowledge levels are appropriate. Increasing variability when learners are having difficulty processing low variable information can be expected to decrease rather than increase learning.

Instructional Implications

The instructional implications are very clear. Learners with low prior knowledge may have difficulty learning complex materials unless element interactivity is lowered. Complexity can be lowered by a number of strategies such as using isolated elements. Learning of complex materials can be achieved by reducing element interactivity initially and then carefully progressing to full element interactivity in a simple-to-complex sequence. Similarly, optimal levels of element interactivity may be achieved by increasing variability of examples. The increased knowledge acquired as a consequence can be beneficial when solving transfer tasks.

In Chapter 5, we distinguished between understanding and learning by rote in terms of element interactivity. While learning with understanding is reserved for high element interactivity information, learning by rote can be applied to either low or high element interactivity information. When dealing with low element interactivity information, we assume that learning by rote is unavoidable because no other form of learning is available. In the studies reported in this chapter dealing with part-whole learning, element interactivity was reduced to the point that some aspects of the task could be easily rote-learned, with little understanding. However, having gained a degree of automation of such tasks, be they subgoals, vital procedures or subtasks, the partial knowledge acquired, even if rote-learned, acts as a crucial link in developing full understanding when learners are then exposed to complete tasks with all required interacting elements.

It can be beneficial to use a worked-examples approach in tandem with reducing intrinsic load. As previously discussed in Chapter 8, worked examples reduce extraneous cognitive load, and therefore a combination of both worked examples and reduced element interactivity can provide an ideal learning environment with a reduced cognitive load.

Conclusions

The studies reported in this chapter, conducted in different domains with a variety of learners, all have one thing in common: they optimised intrinsic cognitive load by either decreasing or increasing it. Decreasing intrinsic cognitive load was commonly accomplished through a sequence of simple to complex processing. Although the researchers have used different designations to describe the methods used such as pre-training, focusing on subgoals, separating procedural and conceptual processes, the net result in all cases is reduced element interactivity. Increasing intrinsic cognitive was accomplished by increasing the variability of examples.

The effectiveness of reducing element interactivity depends on levels of learner prior knowledge, leading to the expertise reversal effect. Novice learners tend to benefit more from a strategy of reducing the extent to which elements interact than more knowledgeable learners in the domain. Domain-specific knowledge enables students to process more interacting elements at a time, thus making strategies that reduce intrinsic load redundant for such learners (see Chapter 10 on the redundancy effect and Chapter 12 on the expertise reversal effect). A similar expertise reversal effect has not as yet been demonstrated for the variability effect but on theoretical grounds, we might expect the effect to be obtainable. For learners with sufficient knowledge, high variability could be beneficial. For learners with low levels of prior knowledge, increases in variability could overwhelm working memory and so decrease rather than increase learning.

In Chapter 5, we indicated that intrinsic cognitive load cannot be altered because it is intrinsic to a particular task. Indeed, if the learning task and the knowledge levels of learners remain constant, intrinsic cognitive load also remains constant.

Therefore, intrinsic cognitive load only can be altered by changing the nature of the task and the nature of what we expect students to learn (learning goals). Exactly, such a change occurred in all of the experiments described in this chapter. This change in what needs to be learned at a certain point in instruction can be contrasted to the consequences of altering extraneous cognitive load discussed in previous chapters. When varying extraneous cognitive load, what needs to be learned does not vary. Only the effectiveness and efficiency of learning the subject content vary when extraneous cognitive load is manipulated.

Similarly, by increasing the variability of examples, element interactivity and intrinsic cognitive load can be optimised by using the capacity of working memory to its full extent. An increase in learning eventuates.

Chapter 17
Emerging Themes in Cognitive Load Theory: The Transient Information and the Collective Working Memory Effects

The cognitive load effects previously described in this book are well established with significant supporting evidence collected across a number of studies and research groups. To complete our description of the various effects, we include two new effects in this chapter. Although their supporting research bases are in their infancy, there is mounting evidence that they are real, important cognitive load effects. In the next two sections, we describe the *Transient Information Effect* and the *Collective Working Memory Effect*.

The Transient Information Effect

Throughout this book we have argued that instructional designs that create an extraneous cognitive load are detrimental to learning. Central to this argument is the processing demands required of working memory. If working memory is engaged for example in conducting inefficient searches via the randomness as genesis principle, holding information while trying to process other information or integrating redundant information, its limited resources are consumed by processes that fail to foster schema acquisition. We have seen how asking learners to problem solve with a fixed goal or deal with materials in a split-attention format creates an extraneous cognitive load. In contrast, the presentation of goal-free problems or worked examples not only reduces extraneous cognitive load by reducing unnecessary interacting elements associated with extraneous cognitive load but also facilitates germane working memory resources directed to dealing with intrinsic cognitive load. These strategies are effective because they allow sufficient working memory resources (narrow limits of change principle) to be devoted to schema-building activities (information store principle). Schemas in turn can be used to drive action via the environmental organising and linking principle. We have documented a number of instructional design flaws (e.g. split-attention and redundancy) and suggested methods to avoid these procedures. In this section, we argue that there is a fundamental generator of extraneous cognitive load inherent in some modern, technologically driven instructional procedures. That excessive cognitive load can be caused by transient information.

Whenever a teacher orally explains something to a class or a pupil, whenever pupils talk to each other or hear speech, the information presented is transient. By its very nature, all speech is transient. Unless it is recorded, any spoken information disappears. If it is important information for the learner, then the learner must try to remember it. Remembering verbal information often can be more easily achieved if it is written down. Writing was invented primarily to turn transient oral information into a permanent form. In the absence of a permanent written record, the learner may need to use a mental rehearsal strategy to keep information alive in working memory before it dissipates. The more information there is to learn, the more difficult it becomes to remember, unless it is written down, or students have additional access to a permanent record. Furthermore, if spoken information requires complex processing, then the demands made on working memory become even more intrusive. For example, if a teacher explains a point using several spoken sentences, each containing information that must be integrated in order to understand the general gist, the demands made on working memory may be excessive. Information from one sentence may need to be held in working memory while information from another sentence is integrated with it. From this perspective, such information will create a heavy cognitive load. Accordingly, all spoken information has the potential to interfere with learning unless it is broken down into manageable proportions or supported by external offloads such as written notes.

We define the *Transient Information Effect* as a loss of learning due to information disappearing before the learner has time to adequately process it or link it with new information. While the major characteristic of information that leads to the transient information effect is, of course, that the information is transient, there is another equally important characteristic. Not only must the information be transient, it also must be high in information content. Element interactivity must be high. Transient information that can be readily held and processed in working memory will not result in a transient information effect.

There are two procedures that, with the advent of modern technology, frequently are used to transform permanent into transient information. First, written information can readily be transformed into spoken information and as indicated above, that transformation also transforms permanent into transient information. The modality effect (see Chapter 10) transforms written information into spoken information and so we might expect the modality effect to interact with the transient information effect. Second, static graphical information can be transformed into animated information. Static graphics are permanent while animation is transient. We will discuss both orally presented and animated information within a transient information context.

The Modality Effect and Transient Information

Combining auditory and visual information can have a positive effect on learning, as has been discussed in the chapter on the modality effect (see Chapter 10), provided the two sources of information refer to each other and are unintelligible in isolation. The advantage of using audio-visual rather than visual only information results in the modality effect. As previously indicated, the use of both auditory and visual channels reduces the load on the visual channel that occurs when all information is presented in visual form.

There are many independent demonstrations of the modality effect (see the Ginns, 2005b meta-analysis of 43 studies) but there also have been some puzzling exceptions. Some studies such as, for example, Tabbers, Martens, and van Merriënboer (2004) found visual only instructions to be superior to audio-visual instructions, thus obtaining a reverse modality effect. They used self-paced rather than system-paced conditions and suggested that the modality effect was more likely under system-paced conditions. Self-paced conditions provide time to trans-fer information from working to long-term memory and so effects due to a working memory overload may be eliminated. Nevertheless, the transient information effect may provide an alternative explanation for the reverse modality effect. Tabbers et al. used relatively lengthy textual material. Such material, when presented in spoken form may overload working memory. When presented in written form, it may be possible to skim simple sections and concentrate on more complex sections. The resultant advantage for written information may generate the reverse modality effect due to the transience of auditory information.

Wouters, Paas, and van Merriënboer (2009) also failed to obtain a modality effect when using self-paced conditions. This experiment, similar to the Tabbers et al. study, used relatively long spoken or written text that may have imposed a heavier working memory load under transitory, spoken conditions than permanent, written conditions.

Schmidt-Weigand, Kohnert, and Glowalla (2010) obtained only limited evidence for a modality effect but no evidence for the self-paced hypothesis. Neither speed of presentation nor system-controlled or self-paced conditions affected the modality effect. While generally no advantage was found for spoken over written instruc-tions, the spoken text condition was superior on a memory test of pictorial but not verbal information. The complexity of the textual/spoken instructions was provided as an explanation of the failure to obtain a modality effect, an explanation in accord with the suggestion that complex transient information may overload working memory more than permanent information.

Leahy and Sweller (in press) directly tested the transient information hypothesis and its relation to the modality effect in two experiments. In the first experiment, primary school children were taught how to read temperature–time graphs that indi-cated temperature changes during the day. Much of the verbal information was presented in lengthy chunks. The results indicated a strong, reverse modality effect with the written information superior to the spoken information. The second experi-ment used exactly the same material except that it was divided into much smaller chunks. In this experiment, a conventional modality effect was obtained with audio-visual information proving superior to visual only information. Furthermore, the time per word in the second experiment was longer than in the first and so it was unlikely that the modality effect was due to learners having insufficient time to pro-cess the information. Rather, the shorter verbal information reduced the influence of transience when presented with spoken text. Learners could remember the spoken text when processing the diagrams resulting in a conventional modality effect. With the longer text of the first experiment, learners could not hold the spoken information in working memory while processing the diagrams because there were too many interacting elements. It was easier to process the text in written than spoken form and so a reverse modality effect was obtained.

Transience when dealing with long, complex spoken information can overload working memory due to high element interactivity. That load can be reduced by presenting the information in written form resulting in the transient information effect. In written form, individual elements can be processed without the risk of totally missing other critical elements because of transience. Written information is permanent and so elements can be ignored at any given time and returned to later. Written information reduces effective element interactivity because it allows elements to be ignored until current elements have been processed.

It needs to be emphasised that the effect found by Leahy and Sweller only should apply to high element interactivity, biologically secondary information, as is the case for all cognitive load effects. We have no difficulty, for example, processing very lengthy spoken information during conversations, listening to speeches or watching films. Such information does not impose a heavy, intrinsic cognitive load and so cognitive load theory and findings are inapplicable.

Instructional Animations and Transient Information

Instructional animations or dynamic visual representations also use technology to transform information from permanent to transient form. An animation, in its many forms, from cartoon character depictions to video recordings of real-life events, can run for a few seconds to several hours. From an instructional perspective, it may take considerable time to provide enough information in a suitable form for learners to understand a particular concept. Animations, by their very nature, are dynamic and consist of a series of frames. Whether viewed on a computer or a television screen, as frames roll from one to another, visual information disappears from sight and the spoken word is no longer heard. Regardless of how well information is integrated, if information from previous frames is needed to understand later frames, then a transient information effect will occur. As we will argue later, the transience of animated information may be a key factor in explaining why instructional animations have not produced the consistently positive effects that have been anticipated. As Hegarty (2004) comments: 'we have learned that improving education is not a simple matter of adopting a new technology' (p. 344). Our understanding of how students learn from animations is far behind the technology advances themselves (Chandler, 2004). However, cognitive load theory may provide a better understanding of how students can learn effectively from animations, but first we will discuss some key aspects of animation research.

Animation Versus Static Presentations

A considerable amount of research has been conducted on the effectiveness of instructional animations. Much of this research has compared animations with static graphics (statics). The results have not been encouraging with many studies and reviews finding little advantage for animated instructional procedures (see Hegarty, Kriz, & Cate, 2003; Schnotz, Böckheler, & Grzondziel, 1999). A review by Tversky, Morrison, and Bétrancourt (2002) found little evidence that animations were consistently superior to static graphics. Instead, they found that many studies did not adequately create design formats with equivalent information. Consequently, advantages found for animated groups in some studies may have been simply due to more information presented in the animated than the static presentations. Tversky et al. (2002) concluded that for animations to be beneficial two principles must be followed. Firstly, according to the *correspondence principle*, there should be a very strong match between the structure and content of the animation, and that of the concept being represented. Secondly, according to the *apprehension principle*, the animation should be easily perceived and understood. However, they also noted that consistency with these two principles did not guarantee that an animation would be superior to its static equivalents. For example, statics have been found to be at least equal to, and sometimes superior to, animations in learning about mechanical systems (see Mayer, DeLeeuw, & Ayres, 2007; Mayer, Hegarty, Campbell, & Mayer, 2005) .

To explain why animated instructional designs have not led to the anticipated advantages, a number of possible reasons have been proposed. For example, Lowe (1999, 2003) argued that there often exists a conflict between perceptual salience and thematic relevance. Learners may need direct help in extracting domain-relevant information from an animation (Lowe, 2003). Koroghlanian and Klein (2004) found that animation required more learners' time than a static approach with no discernable learning differences. Furthermore they found that learners with high spatial abilities learned better in a static mode than in a dynamic one, with no differences found for learners with low spatial abilities. To explain this result, Koroghlanian and Klein proposed that while high spatial ability students had more cognitive resources available, they failed to make the necessary effort to integrate the various forms of information, which was consistent with the view of Schnotz et al. (1999). Hegarty et al. (2003) also argued that static diagrams could lead to more active learning. In a sequence of static diagrams, learners are required to *mentally integrate* the static diagrams to form a representation of the dynamic processes represented. It was suggested that this mental integration results in more active learning and deeper processing. Some researchers, consistent with the argument provided in this chapter, have also noted the transient nature of information. For example, Ainsworth and van Labeke (2004) observed that transience is a particular characteristic of dynamic representations that has ramifications for working memory load. Ainsworth and van Labeke used a previous analysis of animations by Stenning (1998), to point out that relevant previous states need to be held in working memory to integrate them with current states. Consequently, animations without user-control cannot be revisited, unlike static diagrams that usually are constantly accessible unless presented in a serial form with each static diagram replacing its predecessor.

Ainsworth and van Labeke's argument is based on considerations of cognitive load. From time to time other researchers have also noted that animations might create a high cognitive load (see, e.g. Ploetzner & Lowe, 2004); however, this suggestion has been one of several possible theoretical approaches considered and it has not been consistently applied. However, Ayres, Kalyuga, Marcus, and Sweller (2005), and Ayres and Paas (2007a, 2007b), have developed the cognitive load explanation further and constructed a more comprehensive theory, based on the transient information effect. By identifying information transience as a major problem in learning from animations, a number of conditions under which animations are effective can be predicted.

Some Conditions Under Which Animations Can Be Effective

Cognitive load theory has identified different sources of extraneous load that interfere with learning from static pictures and words. Violations of the basic principles of cognitive load theory result in the same learning decrements when dealing with animations. Most animations involve some combination of pictures and text, either spoken or written. Consequently, animated designs can be improved by using the previously described techniques for reducing extraneous cognitive load. For example, the split-attention, modality and redundancy effects need to be considered. Furthermore, animations also can be improved by cueing or signalling information because learners may have difficulty extracting the relevant information from an animation (Lowe, 2003). Many studies have shown the effectiveness of strategies that use cueing or signalling techniques (Boucheix & Guignard, 2005; De Koning, Tabbers, Rikers, & Paas, 2007; Mautone & Mayer, 2001; Moreno, 2007).

Nevertheless, in spite of these general improvements to the design of animations, extraneous load may also be created by transient information that may not be alleviated by other cognitive load effects. The following sections examine some strategies that have been used to improve the effectiveness of animations.

Learner Control. If transience of information creates problems in learning from an animation, then potentially a simple solution is to stop or slow down the animation. Providing an appropriate speed of animation can be achieved by giving an appropriate level of control to the learner. Slowing or stopping the flow of information that has to be simultaneously processed lessens the load on working memory. Evidence in support of this strategy has been found in several studies. Mayer and Chandler (2001) found that learners performed better with than without control over the animation. Control in this case allowed learners to stop and restart the instructional sequence. In a more dynamic use of interactivity, Schwan and Riempp (2004) compared a continuous video recording of knot tying with an interactive version.

Learners in the interactive group were able to stop the animation at any time, change its speed, and even play it backwards. Results indicated that the interactive group developed a better understanding of the processes observed and were able to tie the knots with less practice.

Hasler, Kersten, and Sweller (2007) found that learner control , either as a pause and continue facility or as the restart of a predefined segment facility, led to superior learning than a continuous animation with high element interactivity materials. Learners who had access to these facilities rarely actually stopped the animation. So there was little difference from the continuous animation condition. The availability of a stop–start facility alone was sufficient to activate different cognitive processes even if the facility was not used. Bétrancourt (2005) argued that complete control of an animation should benefit more advanced learners only, as they have the necessary monitoring skills to know when to stop the animation. In the Hasler et al. study, the participants were novices in the domain, and therefore the findings support Bétrancourt's prediction that the learners would not use the stop–start function. Nevertheless, even though the learners did not use the facility, they still benefited from it.

Segmenting. The importance of complexity when considering the transient information effect applies equally to animations as to speech. As indicated when discussing the transient properties of speech, transience only is likely to be a problem when dealing with lengthy, complex information incorporating high element interactivity. Short, simple, low element interactivity information is less likely to cause a working memory overload even if it is transient. It can be held and processed in working memory either during or even after its presentation. As occurred in the case of Leahy and Sweller's (in press) experiments on the modality and reverse modality effects discussed above, we should not expect transience caused by animation to constitute a problem when dealing with very short sequences. Indeed, we suggest that at least some of the variability in the effectiveness of animations compared to static graphics is due to the length and complexity of the material presented. Short animations may be superior to the equivalent static graphics while long animations may be worse than static graphics. This hypothesised effect only should apply to high element interactivity material.

We can vary the length of animations by the use of segmentation. Just as stopping an animation under user-control can reduce the effect of transient information, so can segmenting it into smaller pieces. The less information that has to be held in working memory and integrated with future information, the more likely it is that learning can occur. Consequently, segmenting an animation into smaller sections is one method to reduce such load. For example, Mayer, Moreno, Boire, and Vagge (1999) demonstrated that the temporal split-attention effect would disappear if animations and narratives were divided into smaller segments (see Chapter 9). Florax and Ploetzner (2010) also found evidence that split-attention was moderated by the amount of information presented. Mayer and Chandler (2001) showed that an animation subdivided into segments generated superior learning outcomes than the same animation that was run continuously without segmentation. As described in the previous section, Mayer and Chandler used a pause and restart procedure that linked user-control to segmenting. Considerable evidence that segmenting helps learners to deal with the working memory overload generated by animations has been found (see Boucheix & Guinard, 2005; Hasler et al., 2007; Moreno, 2007; Spanjers, van Gog, & van Merriënboer, 2010).

Prior Knowledge. Prior knowledge allowing use of the environmental organising and linking principle has a similar effect on instructional effectiveness of animations to that of reducing the length and complexity of information and so might be expected to have a similar effect to segmenting information. Both prior knowledge and segmenting can reduce the complexity of information by reducing the number of interacting elements with which learners must deal. Ayres et al. (2005) argued that learners with higher levels of prior knowledge may be able to deal with the transient information generated by animations better than learners with lower levels of prior knowledge. It was anticipated that prior knowledge would allow learners to more readily chunk information that has to be stored temporarily in working memory, leaving more spare capacity available for learning. Kalyuga (2008a) found evidence in support of this hypothesis. In a 2 (static vs animation) × 2 (experts vs novices) design, learners who were more knowledgeable in mathematics learned more with an animated format than an equivalent static format, while novice students learned better using the static than the animated format. The Kalyuga findings are in accord with an expertise reversal effect (see Chapter 12). This effect has also been found in studies that have investigated segmentation of animations. Both Boucheix and Guinard (2005) and Spanjers et al. (2010) found that the advantages of segmenting disappeared for learners with high levels of prior knowledge, suggesting that the strategy was redundant for such learners. Low knowledge learners need segmenting to reduce a high working memory load in order to overcome the effects of transience while higher knowledge learners do not need a reduction in working memory load because their knowledge itself reduces the load.

As was the case with the presentation of spoken information, reducing the element interactivity associated with transient animations should reduce cognitive load and facilitate learning. Learner control, segmentation and prior knowledge all have the effect of reducing the number of interacting elements with which learners must deal. That reduction can ameliorate the negative effects of transience when using animated instructional presentations. Of course, as is the case for speech, if an animation does not impose a heavy cognitive load due to transient, interacting elements, the need to reduce that load may be eliminated. In the next section, we suggest one set of circumstances where many interacting elements can be readily handled by the human cognitive system.

Learning Human Movement or Motor Skills: A Special Case

Despite some early pessimism about the impact of instructional animation, a meta-analysis by Höffler and Leutner (2007) did find a number of studies where animations had produced better learning outcomes than static equivalents. In particular, they found that if animations were highly realistic or involved learning about perceptual-motor knowledge, then they could be more effective than static diagrams. In fact, the condition with the largest effect size was on perceptual-motor tasks such as disassembling a machine gun (Spangenberg, 1973). Two studies, based on a cognitive load theoretical framework and featuring hand manipulation tasks, have provided additional evidence that human movement could be a special case in overcoming the negative effects of transient information.

In the first study, Wong et al. (2009) compared an animated and static approach in learning to make origami shapes. In the animated format learners simply observed a sheet of paper being folded into the target shape in a continuous presentation. In contrast, the static group for the same amount of time studied a series of key frames taken from the animation. On a test to physically make the origami shape, the animated group made more successful completions than the static group in both experiments. In the second study Ayres, Marcus, Chan, and Qian (2009) compared the effectiveness of the two formats in tying knots and solving puzzle-rings. Again, the animated groups performed better than the static groups in physically completing the tasks. In a second experiment, subjective cognitive load measures were collected, showing that the animated group found the task easier than the static group, suggesting that the animation strategy created less cognitive load.

Arguel and Jamet (2009) used first-aid materials to find additional support for human movement as a special case. A characteristic of many first-aid strategies is that they involve manipulating the human body, for example manoeuvring the patient's body into different positions according to the specific illness or accident. In teaching learners about first-aid techniques, Arguel and Jamet found that an animated format was superior to a static format.

The results of comparisons between animations and static graphics when dealing with human movement seem to favour animations. This result contrasts with the results of tasks depicting the movement of mechanical or abstract entities that do not include human movement. The evidence strongly suggests that the transience associated with animation depicting human movement can be much more easily overcome than the transience depicting mechanical movement that does not involve human movement. There are theoretical reasons for these results based on human cognitive architecture.

The Role of Biologically Primary Knowledge

The findings reported above in learning domains associated with motor movement, as well as the meta-analysis of Höffler and Leutner (2007) suggest that information transience caused by animation has a different effect to information transience caused by mechanical, non-human movement. Specifically, we appear to be able to process much larger amounts of information without strains on working memory when human movement is involved. From a theoretical perspective, transience only should be a problem when we must deal with large amounts of information that may exceed working memory capacity. Why should the amount of information with which working memory can deal be larger for tasks involving human movement?

To provide a plausible explanation, van Gog, Paas, Marcus, Ayres, and Sweller (2009) used an interdisciplinary approach combining evolutionary biological theory and neuroscience within a CLT framework (Ayres & Paas, 2009). As previously argued in Chapter 1, biologically primary knowledge can be acquired quite effortlessly (Geary, 2007, 2008). We suggest that imitating human movement is a biologically primary task. Humans have evolved to observe and copy various forms of human movement and motor skills. It is feasible that such skills might be essential in our survival and development. If imitating human movement is a biologically primary task, then learning based on imitating human movement can occur with less impact on working memory resources, helping to overcome the transient information associated with animations. We may have evolved to readily process the interacting elements associated with human movement. In contrast, learning about mechanical systems, which are not related to human movement, may have a much larger secondary knowledge component requiring more effortful learning with a greater working memory load. We have not evolved to handle the interacting elements associated with the movement of machines, for example.

The Role of Mirror Neurons. There are physiological grounds for suggesting that human movement might have a unique status. Van Gog et al. (2009) proposed mirror neurons as an explanatory mechanism for the superiority of animations over static graphics when learning human movement. Evidence has been collected indicating that mirror neurons enable humans to engage in imitative learning (see Blandin, Lhuisset, & Proteau, 1999). A number of relevant neuroscience effects have been observed. For example, brain-imaging techniques have shown that the human motor system has a mirroring capacity (see Rizzolatti & Craighero, 2004). The same cortical circuits that are activated in completing an action also are activated when observing someone else engaging in the same action. In other words, similar brain activities occur when doing or observing motor actions. These actions are not just imitated, but also incorporate understanding of the action (Rizzolatti, 2005; Rizzolatti & Craighero, 2004). Furthermore, evidence has been collected that learning even takes place from observing de facto human behaviour (e.g. a robot arm), provided the goal of the action is clear (Gazzola, Rizzolatti, Wicker, & Keysers, 2007) or listening to someone describe human movement activities (Tettamanti et al., 2005).

These findings suggest that we may have evolved to imitate human movement with the mirror neuron system providing the physiological mechanism. If so, animation incorporating human movement may make heavy use of the biologically primary system thus reducing the role of working memory limitations. It may be recalled that working memory limitations apply primarily to the biologically secondary system. The negative effects of transience associated with animations may be reduced or eliminated when dealing with the human motor system with its close ties to biologically primary knowledge.

Conditions of Applicability

Whether or not transient information interferes with learning is entirely dependent on the cognitive load imposed by that information. Transient information that imposes a low cognitive load may be entirely beneficial if the positive effects of speech or animation outweigh the negative effects of transience. However, if the information is complex and lengthy, the effects of transience can be catastrophic and it should be avoided. Alternatively, information may be simplified by appropriately segmenting it or ensuring that levels of expertise allow the information to be held and processed in working memory. If the information deals with human movement, transience may not be a problem due to the heavy role of biologically primary knowledge in human movement.

Instructional Implications

The transient information effect indicates that under some conditions, transient information can have negative effects on learning. The effect will occur when information that is needed to understand future information has disappeared from the learner's view or hearing. In this case the learner is required to hold that initial information temporarily in working memory in order to integrate it with future information at a later time. The result can be an increased cognitive load and reduced learning.

We should be wary of accidentally introducing transience as part of educational technology. The simple existence of a specific technological tool never is a sufficient reason for its introduction in instruction. Transience introduced as speech or animation can substantially reduce learning compared to permanent forms of communication such as written information or static graphics.

There can be considerable advantages to speech and animation because both are closely aligned with the biologically primary tasks we have evolved to handle. Nevertheless, for the biologically secondary knowledge that is central to most instructional curricula, cognitive load considerations should be remembered when introducing transient information.

Conclusions

Areas associated with transient information have produced mixed, difficult to interpret results. Consistently positive results for both the use of speech and the use of animations have not been obtained. Both speech and animations produce transient information. By considering transience from a cognitive load perspective, it appears possible to interpret and understand the findings. Cognitive load theory can explain why transient information is harmful and predict the types of instructional conditions that will lead to positive and negative learning outcomes. It can explain why instructional animations have led to variable results and why learning about human movement might be a special case. While work on the transience effect is in its infancy, considerable data has been produced and those data strongly suggest that a cognitive load theory interpretation may be promising.

The Collective Working Memory Effect

Research into learning by collaboration has a long history. It is usually approached from a motivational perspective (students are motivated by being grouped together) or from a social constructivist point of view (knowledge is best constructed by discourse between students). However, Kirschner, Paas, and Kirschner (2009a) have conceptualised collaborative learning from a cognitive load theory perspective. By considering collaboration between learners from a cognitive load theory viewpoint, a more fundamental explanation of when and how group work can be effective may be developed. The *Collective Working Memory Effect* is a new cognitive load theory effect that occurs when individuals obtain higher learning outcomes through collaborative work than when learning alone.

Collaborative learning shifts cognitive load theory's emphasis on the borrowing and reorganising principle from instructors or other knowledgeable experts to other learners. Rather than obtaining all or most information from instructors, the use of collaborative learning allows students to obtain much of their information from other students.

In a review of the literature on collaborative learning environments, Kirschner, Paas, and Kirschner (2009a) concluded that the findings on the value of collaborative learning are inconclusive. For example, they pointed out that some studies have shown that students become more actively engaged in the learning process and meta-cognitive skills are fostered. Other research has found collaborative learning to be inefficient considering the resources invested. Collaborative learning can also lead to social loafing in which some learners rely on others with little personal involvement in the collaboration. Kirschner et al. (2009a) identified four possible reasons why the results seem to be mixed. Firstly, group processes are often tested instead of direct measurement of learning outcomes. Secondly, carefully randomised controlled experiments are rarely carried out. Thirdly, goals are often poorly defined, and fourthly, individual outcomes of group members are often not measured. To obtain more conclusive results, Kirschner et al. suggest that 'research should base its claims on direct measurements of learning in a test phase, should study one important or fundamental aspect of the learning environment at a time, and should focus on performance of the group members rather than on the group as a whole' (p. 35). Furthermore, they proposed that more consideration needs to be given to human cognitive architecture in order to fully understand the cognitive processes during collaborative learning.

F. Kirschner et al. applied a cognitive load approach to collaborative learning by considering groups as information processing systems. In particular, they argued that a group of learners potentially have an expanded processing capacity because the intrinsic cognitive load caused by a task can be effectively subdivided across a number of cooperating working memories. For complex tasks that make substantial demands on working memory, sharing the load is predicted to provide a significant advantage. Kirschner, Paas, and Kirschner (2009b) also considered the role played by the *transaction costs* associated with collaboration. An important aspect of collaborative learning is sharing and coordinating information, which Kirschner et al. (2009b) refer to as transaction costs. Completing such transactions requires working memory resources, which have the potential to nullify the advantage of sharing working memory resources if they are too high. In other words, collaboration may come at an extra cost. Hence, transaction costs were considered an important factor in developing their theoretical model.

From the perspective of element interactivity, sharing the cognitive load means dividing the interacting elements between several working memories. Of course, such sharing will not be beneficial if the transaction costs exceed the advantages gained by off-loading some of the elements to other people. For complex tasks, there should be advantages to dividing the elements amongst several people because the transaction costs should be less than the cost of processing a large number of elements. For simpler, low element interactivity tasks, the transaction costs may exceed any reduction in element interactivity obtained by sharing.

Kirschner et al. (2009b) investigated a cognitive load approach in an experiment where learners in collaborative groups were provided only part of the essential information relevant to learning about biological heredity. Each member of a group of three had one third of the amount of information required to solve heredity problems during a learning phase. Consequently, information had to be shared between group members in order for problems to be solved. In contrast, individual learners were provided with all the elements of information necessary to solve the tasks. On a test phase, all learners were tested individually regardless of whether they initially learned in groups or individually. Results indicated that on tests of retention, individuals were more efficient learners, but on tests of transfer, group members learned more efficiently, where efficiency was calculated by combining performance with mental effort measures (see Chapter 6). Using these cognitive load measures, Kirschner et al. (2009b) concluded that transaction costs were low and enabled group members to more deeply process the information elements, leading to better transfer results. Individual learners were only able to process the elements at more superficial levels, leading to better retention of surface information.

Kirschner et al. (in press) investigated the impact of problem complexity on the effectiveness of collaborative learning. They argued that research into collaboration suggests that group learning is superior on complex problem-solving tasks (Laughlin, Bonner, & Miner, 2002; Laughlin, Hatch, Silver, & Boh, 2006), but individual learning is superior on less complex tasks (Andersson & Rönnberg, 1995; Meudell, Hitch, & Kirby, 1992), a pattern also previously identified by Kirschner et al. (2009b). To explain these effects, Kirschner et al. (in press) hypothesised that for simple tasks, individuals have enough working memory capacity to complete them, whereas group members have to deal with additional transaction costs. Thus, the collaborative approach may increase cognitive load on simple tasks, rendering group learning worse than individual learning. For more complex tasks, individuals may lack sufficient working memory capacity to complete the tasks, whereas group members can share the working memory load. If complexity of a task is sufficiently high, transaction costs may be minor in comparison to the reduction in cognitive load achieved by sharing the task. Even when transaction costs are added, group work members may experience a lower cognitive load than individual learners.

To test their hypothesis, Kirschner et al. (in press) used a similar design to Kirschner et al. (2009b) using a biology topic but, rather than partitioning information amongst group members, they provided all group members with all the necessary information. Using levels of element interactivity (Sweller & Chandler, 1994) to measure problem complexity, a set of low-complexity and high-complexity learning tasks was designed. Test results from a 2 (individual vs group learning) × 2 (high- vs low-complexity tasks) design indicated an interaction for mental effort scores. Mental effort was lower for students who learned individually rather than in groups on low-complexity tasks, but higher for students who learned individually rather than in groups on high-complexity tasks. The same interaction was also found on efficiency scores and solution times, but not raw performance scores. Kirschner et al. (in press) concluded that individual learning from low-complexity tasks was more efficient because these learners invested less mental effort than group learners. However, for more complex learning tasks, individual learning was less efficient than group learning because individual learners had to invest more mental effort.

The results from the two studies by Kirschner et al. (2009b, in press) are consistent. Both sets of findings suggest that individual and group-based learning environments generate different levels of cognitive load, leading to different learning efficiencies. These results are also consistent with other research findings indicating that collaboration is best suited to more complex learning tasks.

Two other recent studies have also taken a cognitive load approach to collaborative learning. Retnowati, Ayres, and Sweller (2010) found that groups could benefit more from learning from worked examples rather than from problem solving (see Chapter 8). Zhang, Ayres, and Chan (2011) compared collaborative learning groups with an individualised learning approach on complex tasks to design webpages. Test results indicated that a collaborative approach was significantly better than an individual approach provided students were allowed some choice in the content of the webpage. Furthermore, cognitive load measures indicated that students working collaboratively experienced less mental effort than those working individually, consistent with the studies of Kirschner et al.

Conditions of Applicability

The collective working memory effect indicates that collaboration is more likely to be effective in learning tasks with high levels of element interactivity. For tasks low in element interactivity, individualised learning is more likely to lead to higher learning outcomes. The transaction costs are important in explaining the effectiveness of collaborative learning. If the reduction in cognitive load associated with collaboration exceeds the transaction costs, collaborative learning is more effective than individual learning. If the transaction costs exceed the reduction in cognitive load due to collaboration, individual learning is superior to collaborative learning.

Instructional Implications

The studies reported in this section suggest that considerations of cognitive load may be important for understanding how collaborative learning works. The collective working memory effect indicates that collaboration can be used to share the working memory load on complex learning tasks. Under appropriate conditions, collaboration can enhance learning. Nevertheless, we need to recognise that under other conditions, individual learning may be superior to collaborative learning. Cognitive load theory can be used to predict and explain those conditions.

Conclusions

The collective working memory effect is a potentially new cognitive load effect with little data available at the time of writing. Nevertheless, it is an interesting effect that goes a long way towards making sense of an area that hitherto has made little sense with seemingly random experimental results. Cognitive load theory throws new light on collaborative learning and may have the potential to place it on a sounder footing with the collection of additional data.

Part V
Conclusions

Chapter 18
Cognitive Load Theory in Perspective

Cognitive load theory differs from many instructional theories in several respects. First, the theory places a heavy reliance on the cognitive implications of biological evolution. As indicated in Part I, it divides knowledge into biologically primary and biologically secondary knowledge. Biologically secondary knowledge is a new, culturally important knowledge that we have not specifically evolved to acquire. Cognitive load theory is largely concerned with that biologically secondary knowledge that is taught in schools and other educational and training institutions. The theory is concerned with biologically primary knowledge only to the extent that primary knowledge is needed for and influences the acquisition of secondary knowledge.

The second way in which cognitive load theory differs from many other instructional theories is its emphasis on human cognitive architecture, which is also treated from an evolutionary perspective as discussed in Part II. We suggest that both human cognition and evolution by natural selection are closely analogous, natural information processing systems. The theory considers our knowledge of human cognitive architecture to be critical to instructional design. Human cognitive architecture, based on the distinction between working and long-term memory, is not merely relevant to cognitive load theory, it is integral.

Our understanding of the role of working and long-term memory in human cognitive architecture allows us to categorise sources of cognitive load as discussed in Part III. That categorisation provides the third way in which cognitive load theory differs from most other theories. Working memory and long-term memory are central to human cognitive architecture when dealing with the biologically secondary information that is the subject of instruction. Working memory load is determined by element interactivity while element interactivity in turn is determined by an interaction between the contents of long-term memory and instructional material. A large number of interacting elements will impose a heavy working memory load unless they are incorporated in schemas held in long-term memory. Those interacting elements can constitute either an intrinsic or extraneous cognitive load depending on the purpose and nature of the instruction. If they are essential to learning, they are classed as imposing an intrinsic cognitive load. If they are unnecessary to learning and are merely a function of a particular instructional procedure, they are

J. Sweller et al., *Cognitive Load Theory*, Explorations in the Learning Sciences, Instructional Systems and Performance Technologies 1, DOI 10.1007/978-1-4419-8126-4_18, © Springer Science+Business Media, LLC 2011

classed as imposing an extraneous cognitive load. In either case, they will be processed in an identical fashion by the cognitive system. Germane cognitive load also is dependent on element interactivity. To the extent that working memory is dealing largely with elements intrinsic to the task at hand, germane cognitive load is high. To the extent that working memory is dealing with elements extraneous to the task at hand, germane cognitive load is low.

The cognitive load effects of Part IV of this book flow from these relations and provide the ultimate purpose and justification for the preceding sections. Cognitive load theory was devised in order to allow us to generate the instructional effects discussed in Part IV and those effects provide the most important component of cognitive load theory. The cognitive load theory effects also indicate the fourth and fifth way in which cognitive load theory differs from many other theories.

The fourth manner in which cognitive load theory differs from most instructional theories is associated with its assumptions concerning the nature of teachable/learnable knowledge. Modern instructional theories tend to place a heavy emphasis on what can best be described as general cognitive strategies, including meta-cognitive and general problem-solving strategies. Such strategies are independent of curriculum areas and so can be expected to function without close relations to the content being taught. Cognitive load theory assumes such strategies exist but most, even if not all, are biologically primary and so acquired easily, automatically and unconsciously at a young age. They usually cannot be readily taught, not because they are difficult to learn but rather, because they are easy to learn and so readily acquired by normal humans who have evolved to acquire such strategies without explicit instruction or assistance.

In contrast, cognitive load theory assumes that when learners are faced with new, complex curriculum areas, the difficulty those learners have functioning in the new environment is due largely to the complexity of the new material rather than to the absence of learned, general cognitive strategies. Evidence that most general strategies already have been acquired by learners and do not need to be taught comes from the fact that there seem to be few general cognitive strategies that people fail to use automatically when working in a familiar environment. If general strategies are used in familiar contexts but not unfamiliar complex areas, it follows that the major difficulty faced by learners is likely to be in assimilating novel, complex information rather than learning general cognitive strategies. For this reason, cognitive load theory places its primary emphasis on assisting learners to acquire domain-specific knowledge in complex areas rather than acquiring very general, cognitive strategies. Our cognitive architecture with its large long-term memory, limited working memory and a particular ability to obtain information from other people has evolved for this process. The cognitive load effects generated from this architecture and discussed in Part IV indicate relevant techniques.

The fifth way in which cognitive load theory differs from many instructional theories concerns the methodology used to test the hypotheses that resulted in the cognitive load effects of Part IV. The major point is that cognitive load theory *does* test hypotheses. Many instructional theories do not. All of the instructional effects discussed in Part IV have been tested using randomised controlled experiments in which commonly used instructional procedures act as a control condition with novel techniques generated by cognitive load theory acting as an experimental condition. Without exception, the instructional effects discussed in Part IV have been validated using randomised controlled experiments, usually replicated under a variety of conditions.

Critically, those experiments have conformed with the standard requirement of any scientific experiment in that only one variable was altered at a time, a requirement frequently flouted in educational research. For example, comparing 'traditional' classrooms with 'inquiry-based' classrooms is a pointless exercise. We know before such an experiment is carried out that a well-run, interesting lesson based on explicit instruction is almost invariably going to result in better learner outcomes than a chaotic, poorly designed inquiry-based lesson in which learners have little idea why they are in the class or what they are supposed to be doing. Equally, poorly organised, excruciatingly boring, explicitly presented instruction is highly likely to be worse than carefully organised, inquiry-based instruction with intelligently designed questions for learners to investigate, along with lots of assistance when needed. Such comparisons can yield all possible results and are scientifically worthless. In contrast, comparing for example, problem solving with worked examples will provide one procedure for validly testing the importance of guidance during learning. The two conditions are identical apart from learners having to solve problems in one condition while they study the equivalent worked examples in the other condition. Any differences between the two conditions can be properly attributed to the difference between problems and worked examples rather than to a very large number of possible alternative factors. We believe there are always procedures available to run properly structured randomised controlled experiments in areas associated with cognitive processes and instructional design. There is never a justification for running experiments that cannot possibly isolate causal factors because multiple variables have been altered simultaneously.

Advocacy that is not based on data from validly run randomised controlled experiments can be badly misplaced. We need to know whether learners provided with new instructional procedures have superior outcomes than when using older, more conventional procedures. Randomised controlled experiments altering one variable at a time can provide that assurance. The cognitive load theory effects discussed in Part IV all are based on such experiments.

None of these five characteristics – the division of knowledge into biologically primary and biologically secondary knowledge, an emphasis on human cognitive architecture, the division of cognitive load into categories, the assumption of the primacy of domain-specific rather than domain-general cognitive strategies, and an emphasis on collecting data through the use of randomised controlled experiments – is necessarily unique to cognitive load theory. Individually, they can be found in other theories. Together, they may be unique to cognitive load theory. The assumptions of the theory have led directly to the data from randomised controlled experiments that constitute the cognitive load theory effects discussed in Part IV of this book. Ultimately, the usefulness of those effects in providing instructional guidelines determines the usefulness of cognitive load theory.

The first cognitive load effect studied was the goal-free effect. The rationale of the effect depends on the assumption that the number of interacting elements that a problem solver must process when solving a conventional problem using means–ends analysis can overwhelm working memory. One of the simplest ways of reducing element interactivity associated with conventional problem solving is to change the nature of problem solving by using goal-free problems. By reducing the specificity of a problem goal, means–ends analysis becomes impossible and the large number of interacting elements associated with the strategy is reduced. Learners, faced with a goal-free problem only consider each problem state along with any moves that can be made from that state, rather than attempting to compare a current state with a goal state and find problem-solving operators that will reduce differences between them.

Studies of the worked example and problem completion effects similarly were motivated by the assumption that conventional problem solving imposed an excessive cognitive load because of the large number of interacting elements associated with a means–ends strategy. Rather than changing the problem-solving strategy to reduce the number of interacting elements, worked examples were used as a substitute for problem solving, with completion problems having a similar effect for a similar reason.

Of the cognitive load effects outlined in Part IV, the worked example effect has attracted the most attention. It has been studied extensively by many investigators over many years. The attention the worked example effect has attracted is understandable. On the one hand, it conflicts with constructivist and inquiry-oriented views of instruction and on the other hand it is arguably the major cognitive load theory effect. The worked example effect indicates the unity and centrality of the cognitive architecture used by cognitive load theory and the connection of that architecture to instructional design. Studying worked examples should assist in the acquisition of domain-specific knowledge structures in long-term memory in accord with the information store principle. Worked examples provide information from other people in accord with the borrowing and reorganising principle. In contrast, as specified by the randomness as genesis principle, problem solving includes a high element interactivity, random generation and test procedure intended to provide a problem solution rather than to build organised knowledge structures in long-term memory. As suggested by the narrow limits of change principle, working memory is necessarily limited when dealing with novel information that requires random generation and test resulting in a heavy extraneous working memory load imposed by problem solving. That extraneous working memory load is due to the large number of interacting elements that must be manipulated by a conventional problem-solving procedure. Lastly, based on the environmental organising and linking principle, once information from a worked example is successfully stored in long-term memory, the characteristics of working memory change and that information can be readily used in further problem solving and learning, explaining the advantage of worked examples over problem solving. As can be seen, the principles that underpin human cognitive architecture are closely tied to the worked example effect.

Other cognitive load theory effects are equally tied to the cognitive architecture used by cognitive load theory. The problem completion effect can be explained by the cognitive architecture in exactly the same way as the worked example effect. The split-attention, modality and redundancy effects all assume that information needs to be obtained from others via explicit instruction. That instruction needs to be structured so that the high element interactivity associated with split-source or redundant information is reduced to ensure optimal functioning of working memory and the transfer of information to long-term memory. In the case of split-attention, element interactivity can be reduced by integrating multiple sources of information into a single source. As an alternative to integrating multiple sources of visual information, dual-modality presentation increases the functionality of working memory under dual-modality conditions. In the case of redundancy, multiple sources of information can be reduced by eliminating redundant information.

The expertise reversal effect derives from all of these effects while the guidance-fading effect derives from the worked example effect. Both effects rely heavily on the environmental organising and linking principle. Once relevant information is stored in long-term memory it guides activity and so renders instructional guidance redundant. Instructional guidance in the presence of the same information held in long-term memory merely increases the number of extraneous, interacting elements with which learners must deal, resulting in working memory inefficiency. When sufficient information is stored in long-term memory, it may be better to practice imagining that information rather than attempting to process it during instructional presentations, leading to the imagination effect. Similarly, we may speculate that self-explanations are more likely to be effective once sufficient knowledge has been acquired to permit learners to engage in self-explanations without overloading working memory.

Element interactivity is readily associated with intrinsic cognitive load, and indeed element interactivity was first described within an intrinsic cognitive load framework. Without high element interactivity associated with a high intrinsic cognitive load, any element interactivity associated with an extraneous cognitive load may not exceed working memory limits. If working memory limits are not exceeded, cognitive load effects cannot be obtained. The element interactivity effect occurs when a low intrinsic cognitive load results in a failure to obtain effects usually associated with an extraneous cognitive load.

There can be other consequences if element interactivity associated with intrinsic cognitive load is too low. If intrinsic cognitive load is low, the task can be changed by *increasing*, rather than decreasing, what students must learn. Increasing what students learn is accomplished by increasing the number of intrinsic, interacting elements. Increasing the variability of worked examples will change what students must learn. Instead of just learning to solve a particular class of problems, students must learn to solve several classes of problems and learn to distinguish between them. In this way element interactivity associated with intrinsic cognitive load is increased by increasing what students learn. Of course, this procedure only can be effective if spare processing capacity is available.

At the other extreme, if element interactivity is associated with a very high intrinsic cognitive load that itself exceeds working memory limits, reducing element interactivity associated with an extraneous cognitive load may not be able to help. Intrinsic cognitive load itself may need to be reduced by changing what learners are expected to learn in the early stages of learning, leading to the isolated elements effect. This effect relies on presenting learners with high element interactivity information but treating it as though it is low. The procedure results in students learning material but not fully understanding it until further learning occurs.

These effects, based on both extraneous and intrinsic cognitive load, are well established. The cognitive architecture used by cognitive load theory is continuing to generate novel instructional effects that, at the time of writing, are less well established. The transient information effect suggests that if information is presented in a transient form as occurs when speech or animation is used, and if the information presented is high in element interactivity due to intrinsic cognitive load, any advantages due to the modality effect or due to animation effects may be neutralised or reversed due to the exceeding of working memory limits. Preliminary analyses of previous data along with new data provide support for the transient information effect.

The collective working memory effect provides another new cognitive load effect. If the element interactivity associated with the intrinsic cognitive load of a task exceeds working memory limits, sharing the task with others may render the task more tractable provided the transaction costs of sharing do not exceed the benefits of off-loading information to others.

Cognitive load theory, with its emphasis on human cognitive architecture, domain-specific knowledge and instructional effects based on randomised controlled experiments has generated a considerable range of instructional procedures. The integration of these facets into a unified whole has been productive. Cognitive load theory is that unified theory. We believe the theory has the potential to alter our understanding of instructional procedures.

References

Ainsworth, S., & Van Labeke, N. (2004). Multiple forms of dynamic representation. *Learning and Instruction, 14*, 241–255.

Amadieu, F., Tricot, A., & Mariné, C. (2009). Prior knowledge in learning from a non-linear electronic document: Disorientation and coherence of the reading sequences. *Computers in Human Behavior, 25*, 381–388.

Amadieu, F., van Gog, T., Paas, F., Tricot, A., & Mariné, C. (2009). Effects of prior knowledge and concept-map structure on disorientation, cognitive load, and learning. *Learning and Instruction, 19*, 376–386.

Anderson, J. R. (1996). ACT: A simple theory of complex cognition. *The American Psychologist, 51*, 355–365.

Anderson, J. R., Corbett, A. T., Koedinger, K. R., & Pelletier, R. (1995). Cognitive tutors: Lessons learned. *Journal of the Learning Sciences, 4*, 167–207.

Andersson, J., & Rönnberg, J. (1995). Recall suffers from collaboration: Joint recall effects of friendship and task complexity. *Applied Cognitive Psychology, 9*, 199–211.

Antonenko, P. D., & Niederhauser, D. S. (2010). The influence of leads on cognitive load and learning in a hypertext environment. *Computers in Human Behavior, 26*, 140–150.

Antonenko, P., Paas, F., Grabner, R., & van Gog, T. (2010). Using electroencephalography to measure cognitive load. *Educational Psychology Review, 22*, 425–438.

Arguel, A., & Jamet, E. (2009). Using video and static pictures to improve learning of procedural contents. *Computers in Human Behavior, 25*, 354–359.

Atkinson, R. K. (2002). Optimizing learning from examples using animated pedagogical agents. *Journal of Educational Psychology, 94*, 416–427.

Atkinson, R. K., Derry, S. J., Renkl, A., & Wortham, D. (2000). Learning from examples: Instructional principles from the worked examples research. *Review of Educational Research, 70*, 181–214.

Atkinson, R. K., Mayer, R. E., & Merrill, M. M. (2005). Fostering social agency in multimedia learning: Examining the impact of an animated agent's voice. *Contemporary Educational Psychology, 30*, 117–139.

Atkinson, R. K., Renkl, A., & Merrill, M. M. (2003). Transitioning from studying examples to solving problems: Effects of self-explanation prompts and fading worked-out steps. *Journal of Educational Psychology, 95*, 774–783.

Atkinson, R. K., & Renkl, A. (2007). Interactive example-based learning environments: Using interactive elements to encourage effective processing of worked examples. *Educational Psychology Review, 19*, 375–386.

Atkinson, R. C., & Shiffrin, R. M. (1968). Human memory: A proposed system and its control processes. In J. T. Spence & K. W. Spence (Eds.), *The psychology of learning and motivation* (Vol. 2, pp. 89–195). Oxford/England: Academic.

Austin, K. A. (2009). Multimedia learning: Cognitive individual differences and display design techniques predict transfer learning with multimedia learning modules. *Computers and Education, 53,* 1339–1354.

Ayres, P. L. (1993). Why goal-free problems can facilitate learning. *Contemporary Educational Psychology, 18,* 376–381.

Ayres, P. (1998). The effectiveness of a no-goal approach in solving Pythagorean problems. In C. Kanes, M. Goos, & E. Warren (Eds.), *Published Proceedings of the Mathematical Education Research Group of Australasia (MERGA 21)* (pp. 68–73). Gold Coast, Australia.

Ayres, P. L. (2001). Systematic mathematical errors and cognitive load. *Contemporary Educational Psychology, 26,* 227–248.

Ayres, P. (2006a). Impact of reducing intrinsic cognitive load on learning in a mathematical domain. *Applied Cognitive Psychology, 20,* 287–298.

Ayres, P. (2006b). Using subjective measures to detect variations of intrinsic cognitive load within problems. *Learning and Instruction, 16,* 389–400.

Ayres, P., Kalyuga, S., Marcus, N., & Sweller, J. (2005, August). *The conditions under which instructional animation may be effective.* Unpublished paper presented at the International workshop Extending Cognitive Load Theory and Instructional Design to the Development of Expert Performance, Open University of the Netherlands, Heerlen, The Netherlands.

Ayres, P., Marcus, N., Chan, C., & Qian, N. (2009). Learning hand manipulative tasks: When instructional animations are superior to equivalent static representations. *Computers in Human Behavior, 25,* 348–353.

Ayres, P., & Paas, F. (2007a). Can the cognitive load approach make instructional animations more effective? *Applied Cognitive Psychology, 21,* 811–820.

Ayres, P., & Paas, F. (2007b). Making instructional animations more effective: A cognitive load approach. *Applied Cognitive Psychology, 21,* 695–700.

Ayres, P., & Paas, F. (2009). Interdisciplinary perspectives inspiring a new generation of cognitive load research. *Educational Psychology Review, 21,* 1–9.

Ayres, P., & Sweller, J. (1990). Locus of difficulty in multistage mathematics problems. *The American Journal of Psychology, 103,* 167–193.

Ayres, P., & Sweller, J. (2005). The split-attention principle in multimedia learning. In R. E. Mayer (Ed.), *The Cambridge handbook of multimedia learning* (pp. 135–146). New York: Cambridge University Press.

Ayres, P., & Youssef, A. (2008). Investigating the influence of transitory information and motivation during instructional animations. In P. A. Kirschner, F. Prins, V. Jonker, & G. Kanselaar (Eds.), *Published Proceedings of the Eighth International Conference for the Learning Sciences* (Vol. 1, pp. 68–75). Utrecht, The Netherlands.

Baddeley, A. (1986). *Working memory.* New York: Oxford University Press.

Baddeley, A. (1992). Working memory. *Science, 255,* 556–559.

Baggett, P. (1984). Role of temporal overlap of visual and auditory material in forming dual media associations. *Journal of Educational Psychology, 76,* 408–417.

Bandura, A. (1986). *Social foundations of thought and action: A social cognitive theory.* Englewood Cliffs: Prentice-Hall.

Bartlett, F. C. (1932). *Remembering: A study in experimental and social psychology.* Oxford/ England: Macmillan.

Berthold, K., Eysink, T. H. S., & Renkl, A. (2009). Assisting self-explanation prompts are more effective than open prompts when learning with multiple representations. *Instructional Science, 37,* 345–363.

Berry, D. C., & Broadbent, D. E. (1984). On the relationship between task performance and associated verbalizable knowledge. *The Quarterly Journal of Experimental Psychology: Human Experimental Psychology, 36A,* 209–231.

Bétrancourt, M. (2005). The animation and interactivity principles in multimedia learning. In R. E. Mayer (Ed.), *The Cambridge handbook of multimedia learning* (pp. 287–296). New York: Cambridge University Press.

Bétrancourt, M., & Bisseret, A. (1998). Integrating textual and pictorial information via pop-up windows: An experimental study. *Behaviour and Information Technology, 17*, 263–273.

Bielaczyk, K., Pirolli, P. L., & Brown, A. L. (1995). Training in self-explanation and self-regulation strategies: Investigating the effects of knowledge acquisition activities on problem solving. *Cognition and Instruction, 13*, 221–252.

Blandin, Y., Lhuisset, L., & Proteau, L. (1999). Cognitive processes underlying observational learning of motor skills. *The Quarterly Journal of Experimental Psychology: Human Experimental Psychology, 52A*, 957–979.

Blayney, P., Kalyuga, S., & Sweller, J. (2010). Interactions between the isolated–interactive elements effect and levels of learner expertise: Experimental evidence from an accountancy class. *Instructional Science, 38*, 277–287.

Bobis, J., Sweller, J., & Cooper, M. (1993). Cognitive load effects in a primary-school geometry task. *Learning and Instruction, 3*, 1–21.

Bobis, J., Sweller, J., & Cooper, M. (1994). Demands imposed on primary-school students by geometric models. *Contemporary Educational Psychology, 19*, 108–117.

Bodemer, D., Ploetzner, R., Feuerlein, I., & Spada, H. (2004). The active integration of information during learning with dynamic and interactive visualisations. *Learning and Instruction, 14*, 325–341.

Borrás, I., & Lafayette, R. C. (1994). Effects of multimedia courseware subtitling on the speaking performance of college students of French. *Modern Language Journal, 78*, 61–75.

Boucheix, J.-M., & Guignard, H. (2005). What animated illustrations conditions can improve technical document comprehension in young students? Format, signaling and control of the presentation. *European Journal of Psychology of Education, 20*, 369–388.

Bratfisch, O., Borg, G., & Dornic, S. (1972). *Perceived item-difficulty in three tests of intellectual performance capacity (Tech. Rep. No. 29)*. Stockholm: Institute of Applied Psychology.

Britton, B. K., & Tesser, A. (1982). Effects of prior knowledge on use of cognitive capacity in three complex cognitive tasks. *Journal of Verbal Learning and Verbal Behavior, 21*, 421–436.

Bruner, J. (1961). The art of discovery. *Harvard Educational Review, 31*, 21–32.

Brünken, R., Plass, J. L., & Leutner, D. (2004). Assessment of cognitive load in multimedia learning with dual-task methodology: Auditory load and modality effects. *Instructional Science, 32*, 115–132.

Brünken, R., Steinbacher, S., Plass, J. L., & Leutner, D. (2002). Assessment of cognitive load in multimedia learning using dual-task methodology. *Experimental Psychology, 49*, 109–119.

Brunstein, A., Betts, S., & Anderson, J. R. (2009). Practice enables successful learning under minimal guidance. *Journal of Educational Psychology, 101*, 790–802.

Burns, B. D., & Vollmeyer, R. (2002). Goal specificity effects on hypothesis testing in problem solving. *The Quarterly Journal of Experimental Psychology: Human Experimental Psychology, 55A*, 241–261.

Camp, G., Paas, F., Rikers, R., & van Merriënboer, J. (2001). Dynamic problem selection in air traffic control training: A comparison between performance, mental effort and mental efficacy. *Computers in Human Behavior, 17*, 575–595.

Carlson, R., Chandler, P., & Sweller, J. (2003). Learning and understanding science instructional material. *Journal of Educational Psychology, 95*, 629–640.

Carroll, W. M. (1994). Using worked examples as an instructional support in the algebra classroom. *Journal of Educational Psychology, 86*, 360–367.

Catrambone, R. (1998). The subgoal learning model: Creating better examples so that students can solve novel problems. *Journal of Experimental Psychology: General, 127*, 355–376.

Cerpa, N., Chandler, P., & Sweller, J. (1996). Some conditions under which integrated computer-based training software can facilitate learning. *Journal of Educational Computing Research, 15*, 345–367.

Chandler, P. (2004). The crucial role of cognitive processes in the design of dynamic visualizations. *Learning and Instruction, 14*, 353–357.

Chandler, P., & Sweller, J. (1991). Cognitive load theory and the format of instruction. *Cognition and Instruction, 8*, 293–332.

Chandler, P., & Sweller, J. (1992). The split-attention effect as a factor in the design of instruction. *The British Journal of Educational Psychology, 62*, 233–246.

Chandler, P., & Sweller, J. (1996). Cognitive load while learning to use a computer program. *Applied Cognitive Psychology, 10*, 151–170.

Chase, W. G., & Simon, H. A. (1973). Perception in chess. *Cognitive Psychology, 4*, 55–81.

Chi, M. T. H. (2000). Self-explaining expository texts: The dual process of generating inferences and repairing mental models. In R. Glaser (Ed.), *Advances in instructional psychology: Educational design and cognitive science* (pp. 161–238). Mahwah, NJ: Erlbaum.

Chi, M. T., Bassok, M., Lewis, M. W., Reimann, P., & Glaser, R. (1989). Self-explanations: How students study and use examples in learning to solve problems. *Cognitive Science, 13*, 145–182.

Chi, M. T. H., de Leeuw, N., Chiu, M.-H., & LaVancher, C. (1994). Eliciting self-explanations improves understanding. *Cognitive Science, 18*, 439–477.

Chi, M., Glaser, R., & Rees, E. (1982). Expertise in problem solving. In R. Sternberg (Ed.), *Advances in the psychology of human intelligence* (pp. 7–75). Hillsdale: Lawrence Erlbaum.

Chiesi, H. L., Spilich, G. J., & Voss, J. F. (1979). Acquisition of domain-related information in relation to high and low domain knowledge. *Journal of Verbal Learning and Verbal Behavior, 18*, 257–273.

Chung, K. K. H. (2007). Presentation factors in the learning of Chinese characters: The order and position of Hanyu pinyin and English translations. *Educational Psychology, 27*, 1–20.

Chung, J., & Reigeluth, C. M. (1992). Instructional prescriptions for learner control. *Educational Technology Research and Development, 32*, 14–20.

Cierniak, G., Scheiter, K., & Gerjets, P. (2009a). Expertise reversal in multimedia learning: Subjective load ratings and viewing behavior as cognitive process indicators. In N. A. Taatgen & H. van Rijn (Eds.), *Proceedings of the 31st Annual Conference of the Cognitive Science Society* (pp. 1906–1911). Austin: Cognitive Science Society.

Cierniak, G., Scheiter, K., & Gerjets, P. (2009b). Explaining the split-attention effect: Is the reduction of extraneous cognitive load accompanied by an increase in germane cognitive load? *Computers in Human Behavior, 25*, 315–324.

Clark, L. V. (1960). Effect of mental practice on the development of a certain motor skill. *Research Quarterly of the American Association for Health, Physical Education, and Recreation, 31*, 560–569.

Clark, R. C., & Mayer, R. E. (2003). *E-learning and the science of instruction*. San Francisco: Jossey-Bass/Pfeiffer.

Clark, R., Nguyen, F., & Sweller, J. (2006). *Efficiency in learning: Evidence-based guidelines to manage cognitive load*. San Francisco: Pfeiffer.

Clarke, T., Ayres, P., & Sweller, J. (2005). The impact of sequencing and prior knowledge on learning mathematics through spreadsheet applications. *Educational Technology Research and Development, 53*, 15–24.

Cohen, J. (1988). *Statistical power analysis for the behavioural sciences*. New York: Academic.

Cooper, G., & Sweller, J. (1987). Effects of schema acquisition and rule automation on mathematical problem-solving transfer. *Journal of Educational Psychology, 79*, 347–362.

Cooper, G., Tindall-Ford, S., Chandler, P., & Sweller, J. (2001). Learning by imagining. *Journal of Experimental Psychology: Applied, 7*, 68–82.

Corbalan, G., Kester, L., & van Merriënboer, J. J. G. (2008). Selecting learning tasks: Effects of adaptation and shared control on learning efficiency and task involvement. *Contemporary Educational Psychology, 33*, 733–756.

Corbin, C. B. (1967). The effects of covert rehearsal on the development of a complex motor skill. *The Journal of General Psychology, 76*, 143–150.

Cowan, N. (2001). The magical number 4 in short-term memory: A reconsideration of mental storage capacity. *The Behavioral and Brain Sciences, 24*, 87–185.

Craig, S. D., Gholson, B., & Driscoll, D. M. (2002). Animated pedagogical agents in multimedia educational environments: Effects of agent properties, picture features and redundancy. *Journal of Educational Psychology, 94*, 428–434.

Cronbach, L. (1967). How can instruction be adapted to individual differences. In R. Gagne (Ed.), *Learning and individual differences* (pp. 23–39). Columbus: Merrill.

Cronbach, L. J., & Snow, R. E. (1977). *Aptitudes and instructional methods: A handbook for research on interactions.* New York: Irvington.

Crooks, S., White, D., Srinivasan, S., & Wang, Q. (2008). Temporal, but not spatial, contiguity effects while studying an interactive geographic map. *Journal of Educational Multimedia and Hypermedia, 17*, 145–169.

Cuevas, H. M., Fiore, S. M., & Oser, R. L. (2002). Scaffolding cognitive and metacognitive processes in low verbal ability learners: Use of diagrams in computer-based training environments. *Instructional Science, 30*, 433–464.

De Croock, M. B. M., van Merriënboer, J. J. G., & Paas, F. G. W. C. (1998). High versus low contextual interference in simulation-based training of troubleshooting skills: Effects on transfer performance and invested mental effort. *Computers in Human Behavior, 14*, 249–267.

De Groot, A. (1965). *Thought and choice in chess.* The Hague: Mouton. Original work published 1946.

De Groot, A., & Gobet, F. (1996). *Perception and memory in chess: Studies in the heuristics of the professional eye.* Assen, The Netherlands: Van Gorcum.

De Koning, B. B., Tabbers, H. K., Rikers, R. M. J. P., & Paas, F. (2007). Attention cueing as a means to enhance learning from an animation. *Applied Cognitive Psychology, 21*, 731–746.

De Westelinck, K., Valcke, M., De Craene, B., & Kirschner, P. (2005). Multimedia learning in social sciences: Limitations of external graphical representations. *Computers in Human Behavior, 21*, 555–573.

DeLeeuw, K. E., & Mayer, R. E. (2008). A comparison of three measures of cognitive load: Evidence for separable measures of intrinsic, extraneous, and germane load. *Journal of Educational Psychology, 100*, 223–234.

Diao, Y., Chandler, P., & Sweller, J. (2007). The effect of written text on comprehension of spoken English as a foreign language. *The American Journal of Psychology, 120*, 237–261.

Diao, Y., & Sweller, J. (2007). Redundancy in foreign language reading comprehension instruction: Concurrent written and spoken presentations. *Learning and Instruction, 17*, 78–88.

Dillon, A., & Jobst, J. (2005). Multimedia learning with hypermedia. In R. E. Mayer (Ed.), *The Cambridge handbook of multimedia learning* (pp. 569–588). New York: Cambridge University Press.

Driskell, J. E., Copper, C., & Moran, A. (1994). Does mental practice enhance performance? *The Journal of Applied Psychology, 79*, 481–492.

Dunbar, R. I. M. (2000). Causal reasoning, mental rehearsal, and the evolution of primate cognition. In C. Heyes & L. Luber (Eds.), *The evolution of cognition: Vienna series in theoretical biology* (pp. 205–219). Cambridge, MA: MIT Press.

Dunsworth, Q., & Atkinson, R. K. (2007). Fostering multimedia learning of science: Exploring the role of an animated agent's image. *Computers and Education, 49*, 677–690.

Dutke, S., & Rinck, M. (2006). Multimedia learning: Working memory and the learning of word and picture diagrams. *Learning and Instruction, 16*, 526–537.

Egan, D. E., & Schwartz, B. J. (1979). Chunking in recall of symbolic drawings. *Memory and Cognition, 7*, 149–158.

Egstrom, G. H. (1964). Effects of an emphasis on conceptualizing techniques during early learning of a gross motor skill. *Research Quarterly, 35*, 472–481.

Erhel, S., & Jamet, E. (2006). Using pop-up windows to improve multimedia learning. *Journal of Computer Assisted Learning, 22*, 137–147.

Ericsson, K. A., & Charness, N. (1994). Expert performance: Its structure and acquisition. *The American Psychologist, 49*, 725–747.

Ericsson, K. A., & Kintsch, W. (1995). Long-term working memory. *Psychological Review, 102*, 211–245.

Ericsson, K. A., Krampe, R. T., & Tesch-Römer, C. (1993). The role of deliberate practice in the acquisition of expert performance. *Psychological Review, 100*, 363–406.

Etnier, J. L., & Landers, D. M. (1996). The influence of procedural variables on the efficacy of mental practice. *The Sport Psychologist, 10*, 48–57.

Federico, P.-A. (1980). Adaptive instruction: Trends and issues. In R. Snow, P.-A. Federico, & W. Montague (Eds.), *Aptitude, learning, and instruction* (Cognitive process analyses of aptitude, Vol. 1, pp. 1–26). Hillsdale: Lawrence Erlbaum.

Federico, P.-A. (1999). Hypermedia environments and adaptive instruction. *Computers in Human Behavior, 15*, 653–692.

Florax, M., & Ploetzner, R. (2010). What contributes to the split-attention effect? The role of text segmentation, picture labelling, and spatial proximity. *Learning and Instruction, 20*, 216–224.

Garza, T. J. (1991). Evaluating the use of captioned video materials in advanced foreign language learning. *Foreign Language Annals, 24*, 239–258.

Gazzola, V., Rizzolatti, G., Wicker, B., & Keysers, C. (2007). The anthropomorphic brain: The mirror neuron system responds to human and robotic actions. *Neuroimage, 35*, 1674–1684.

Geary, D. C. (2007). Educating the evolved mind: Conceptual foundations for an evolutionary educational psychology. In J. S. Carlson & J. R. Levin (Eds.), *Psychological perspectives on contemporary educational issues* (pp. 1–99). Greenwich: Information Age Publishing.

Geary, D. C. (2008). An evolutionarily informed education science. *Educational Psychologist, 43*, 179–195.

Geddes, B. W., & Stevenson, R. J. (1997). Explicit learning of a dynamic system with a non-salient pattern. *The Quarterly Journal of Experimental Psychology: Human Experimental Psychology, 50A*, 742–765.

Gerjets, P., Scheiter, K., & Catrambone, R. (2004). Designing instructional examples to reduce intrinsic cognitive load: Molar versus modular presentation of solution procedures. *Instructional Science, 32*, 33–58.

Gerjets, P., Scheiter, K., & Catrambone, R. (2006). Can learning from molar and modular worked examples be enhanced by providing instructional explanations and prompting self-explanations? *Learning and Instruction, 16*, 104–121.

Gerjets, P., Scheiter, K., Opfermann, M., Hesse, F. W., & Eysink, T. H. S. (2009). Learning with hypermedia: The influence of representational formats and different levels of learner control on performance and learning behavior. *Computers in Human Behavior, 25*, 360–370.

Gerjets, P., Scheiter, K., & Schuh, J. (2008). Information comparisons in example-based hypermedia environments: Supporting learners with processing prompts and an interactive comparison tool. *Educational Technology Research and Development, 56*, 73–92.

Ginns, P. (2005a). Imagining instructions: Mental practice in highly cognitive domains. *Australian Journal of Education, 49*, 128–140.

Ginns, P. (2005b). Meta-analysis of the modality effect. *Learning and Instruction, 15*, 313–331.

Ginns, P. (2006). Integrating information: A meta-analysis of the spatial contiguity and temporal contiguity effects. *Learning and Instruction, 16*, 511–525.

Ginns, P., Chandler, P., & Sweller, J. (2003). When imagining information is effective. *Contemporary Educational Psychology, 28*, 229–251.

Goldsmith, T. E., Johnson, P. J., & Acton, W. H. (1991). Assessing structural knowledge. *Journal of Educational Psychology, 83*, 88–96.

Goolkasian, P. (2000). Pictures, words, and sounds: From which format are we best able to reason? *The Journal of General Psychology, 127*, 439–459.

Grafton, S., Arbib, M., Fadiga, L., & Rizzolatti, G. (1996). Localization of grasp representations in humans by positron emission tomography: 2. Observation compared with imagination. *Experimental Brain Research, 112*, 103–111.

Greeno, J. G. (1976). Indefinite goals in well-structured problems. *Psychological Review, 83*, 479–491.

Greeno, J. G. (1978). Natures of problem-solving abilities. In W. K. Estes (Ed.), *Handbook of learning and cognitive processes* (Vol. 5, pp. 239–270). Oxford/England: Lawrence Erlbaum.

Grouios, G. (1992). The effect of mental practice on diving performance. *International Journal of Sport Psychology, 23*, 60–69.

Halford, G. S., Maybery, M. T., & Bain, J. D. (1986). Capacity limitations in children's reasoning: A dual-task approach. *Child Development, 57*, 616–627.

Harskamp, E. G., Mayer, R. E., & Suhre, C. (2007). Does the modality principle for multimedia learning apply to science classrooms? *Learning and Instruction, 17*, 465–477.

Hart, S. G. (2006). NASA-Task Load Index (NASA-TLX); 20 years later. *Proceedings of the Human Factors and Ergonomics Society 50th Annual Meeting* (pp. 904–908). Santa Monica: Human Factors and Ergonomics Society.

Hart, S. G., & Staveland, L. E. (1988). Development of NASA-TLX (Task Load Index): Results of empirical and theoretical research. In P. A. Hancock & N. Meshkati (Eds.), *Human mental workload* (Advances in psychology, Vol. 52, pp. 139–183). Amsterdam: North-Holland.

Hasler, B. S., Kersten, B., & Sweller, J. (2007). Learner control, cognitive load and instructional animation. *Applied Cognitive Psychology, 21*, 713–729.

Hazler, R. J., & Hipple, T. E. (1981). The effects of mental practice on counselling behaviours. *Counselor Education and Supervision, 20*, 211–218.

Hegarty, M. (2004). Dynamic visualizations and learning: Getting to the difficult questions. *Learning and Instruction, 14*, 343–351.

Hegarty, M., Kriz, S., & Cate, C. (2003). The roles of mental animations and external animations in understanding mechanical systems. *Cognition and Instruction, 21*, 325–360.

Hilbert, T. S., & Renkl, A. (2009). Learning how to use a computer-based concept-mapping tool: Self-explaining examples helps. *Computers in Human Behavior, 25*, 267–274.

Hilbert, T. S., Renkl, A., Kessler, S., & Reiss, K. (2008). Learning to prove in geometry: Learning from heuristic examples and how it can be supported. *Learning and Instruction, 18*, 54–65.

Hirai, A. (1999). The relationship between listening and reading rates of Japanese EFL learners. *Modern Language Journal, 83*, 367–384.

Höffler, T. N., & Leutner, D. (2007). Instructional animation versus static pictures: A meta-analysis. *Learning and Instruction, 17*, 722–738.

Hoffman, B., & Schraw, G. (2010). Conceptions of efficiency: Applications in learning and problem solving. *Educational Psychologist, 45*, 1–14.

Holliday, W. G. (1976). Teaching verbal chains using flow diagrams and texts. *AV Communication Review, 24*, 63–78.

Homer, B. D., & Plass, J. L. (2010). Expertise reversal for iconic representations in science visu-alizations. *Instructional Science, 38*, 259–276.

Homer, B. D., Plass, J. L., & Blake, L. (2008). The effects of video on cognitive load and social presence in multimedia-learning. *Computers in Human Behavior, 24*, 786–797.

Hummel, H. G. K., Paas, F., & Koper, E. J. R. (2004). Cueing for transfer in multimedia pro-grammes: Process worksheets vs. worked-out examples. *Journal of Computer Assisted Learning, 20*, 387–397.

Iacoboni, M., Woods, R. P., Brass, M., Bekkering, H., Mazziotta, J. C., & Rizzolatti, G. (1999). Cortical mechanisms of human imitation. *Science, 286*, 2526–2528.

Jablonka, E., & Lamb, M. J. (1995). *Epigenetic inheritance and evolution.* New York: Oxford University Press.

Jablonka, E., & Lamb, M. J. (2005). *Evolution in four dimensions: Genetic, epigenetic, behavioral, and symbolic variation in the history of life.* Cambridge, MA: MIT Press.

Jamet, E., & Le Bohec, O. (2007). The effect of redundant text in multimedia instruction. *Contemporary Educational Psychology, 32*, 588–598.

Jeffries, R., Turner, A., Polson, P., & Atwood, M. (1981). Processes involved in designing soft-ware. In J. R. Anderson (Ed.), *Cognitive skills and their acquisition* (pp. 255–283). Hillsdale: Lawrence Erlbaum.

Jeung, H.-J., Chandler, P., & Sweller, J. (1997). The role of visual indicators in dual sensory mode instruction. *Educational Psychology, 17*, 329–343.

Kahneman, D., & Beatty, J. (1966). Pupil diameter and load on memory. *Science, 154*, 1583–1585.

Kalyuga, S. (2006a). Assessment of learners' organised knowledge structures in adaptive learning environments. *Applied Cognitive Psychology, 20*, 333–342.

Kalyuga, S. (2006b). Rapid assessment of learners' proficiency: A cognitive load approach. *Educational Psychology, 26*, 735–749.

Kalyuga, S. (2006c). Rapid cognitive assessment of learners' knowledge structures. *Learning and Instruction, 16*, 1–11.

Kalyuga, S. (2007). Expertise reversal effect and its implications for learner-tailored instruction. *Educational Psychology Review, 19*, 509–539.

Kalyuga, S. (2008a). Relative effectiveness of animated and static diagrams: An effect of learner prior knowledge. *Computers in Human Behavior, 24*, 852–861.

Kalyuga, S. (2008b). When less is more in cognitive diagnosis: A rapid online method for diagnosing learner task-specific expertise. *Journal of Educational Psychology, 100*, 603–612.

Kalyuga, S., Ayres, P., Chandler, P., & Sweller, J. (2003). The expertise reversal effect. *Educational Psychologist, 38*, 23–31.

Kalyuga, S., Chandler, P., & Sweller, J. (1998). Levels of expertise and instructional design. *Human Factors, 40*, 1–17.

Kalyuga, S., Chandler, P., & Sweller, J. (1999). Managing split-attention and redundancy in multimedia instruction. *Applied Cognitive Psychology, 13*, 351–371.

Kalyuga, S., Chandler, P., & Sweller, J. (2000). Incorporating learner experience into the design of multimedia instruction. *Journal of Educational Psychology, 92*, 126–136.

Kalyuga, S., Chandler, P., & Sweller, J. (2001). Learner experience and efficiency of instructional guidance. *Educational Psychology, 21*, 5–23.

Kalyuga, S., Chandler, P., & Sweller, J. (2004). When redundant on-screen text in multimedia technical instruction can interfere with learning. *Human Factors, 46*, 567–581.

Kalyuga, S., Chandler, P., Tuovinen, J., & Sweller, J. (2001). When problem solving is superior to studying worked examples. *Journal of Educational Psychology, 93*, 579–588.

Kalyuga, S., & Renkl, A. (2010). Expertise reversal effect and its instructional implications: Introduction to the special issue. *Instructional Science, 38*, 209–215.

Kalyuga, S., & Sweller, J. (2004). Measuring knowledge to optimize cognitive load factors during instruction. *Journal of Educational Psychology, 96*, 558–568.

Kalyuga, S., & Sweller, J. (2005). Rapid dynamic assessment of expertise to improve the efficiency of adaptive e-learning. *Educational Technology Research and Development, 53*, 83–93.

Kelsey, I. B. (1961). Effects of mental practice and physical practice upon muscular endurance. *Research Quarterly of the American Association for Health, Physical Education, and Recreation, 32*, 47–54.

Kerr, B. (1973). Processing demands during mental operations. *Memory and Cognition, 1*, 401–412.

Kester, L., & Kirschner, P. A. (2009). Effects of fading support on hypertext navigation and performance in student-centered e-learning environments. *Interactive Learning Environments, 17*, 165–179.

Kester, L., Kirschner, P. A., & van Merriënboer, J. J. G. (2005). The management of cognitive load during complex cognitive skill acquisition by means of computer-simulated problem solving. *The British Journal of Educational Psychology, 75*, 71–85.

Kester, L., Kirschner, P. A., & van Merriënboer, J. J. G. (2006). Just-in-time information presentation: Improving learning a troubleshooting skill. *Contemporary Educational Psychology, 31*, 167–185.

Kester, L., Kirschner, P. A., van Merriënboer, J. J. G., & Baumer, A. (2001). Just-in-time information presentation and the acquisition of complex cognitive skills. *Computers in Human Behavior, 17*, 373–391.

Khawaja, M. A., Chen, F., & Marcus, N. (2010). Using language complexity to measure cognitive load for adaptive interaction design. *Proceedings of the 14th International Conference on Intelligent User Interfaces (IUI10)* (pp. 333–336). *Hong Kong, China.*

Kirschner, P., Ayres, P., & Chandler, P. (2011). Contemporary cognitive load theory: the good, bad and the ugly. *Computers in Human Behavior, 27*, 99–105.

Kirschner, F., Paas, F., & Kirschner, P. (in press). Task complexity as a driver for collaborative learning efficiency: The collective working-memory effect. *Applied Cognitive Psychology.*

Kirschner, F., Paas, F., & Kirschner, P. A. (2009a). A cognitive load approach to collaborative learning: United brains for complex tasks. *Educational Psychology Review, 21*, 31–42.

Kirschner, F., Paas, F., & Kirschner, P. A. (2009b). Individual and group-based learning from complex cognitive tasks: Effects on retention and transfer efficiency. *Computers in Human Behavior, 25*, 306–314.

Kirschner, P. A., Sweller, J., & Clark, R. E. (2006). Why minimal guidance during instruction does not work: An analysis of the failure of constructivist, discovery, problem-based, experiential, and inquiry-based teaching. *Educational Psychologist, 41*, 75–86.

Klahr, D., & Nigam, M. (2004). The equivalence of learning paths in early science instruction: Effects of direct instruction and discovery learning. *Psychological Science, 15*, 661–667.

Koedinger, K. R., & Aleven, V. (2007). Exploring the assistance dilemma in experiments with cognitive tutors. *Educational Psychology Review, 19,* 239–264.

Koroghlanian, C., & Klein, J. D. (2004). The effect of audio and animation in multimedia instruction. *Journal of Educational Multimedia and Hypermedia, 13,* 23–46.

Kotovsky, K., Hayes, J. R., & Simon, H. A. (1985). Why are some problems hard? Evidence from Tower of Hanoi. *Cognitive Psychology, 17,* 248–294.

Kyun, S. A., Kalyuga, S., & Sweller, J. (in preparation). The effect of worked examples when learning English literature.

Larkin, J., McDermott, J., Simon, D. P., & Simon, H. A. (1980a). Expert and novice performance in solving physics problems. *Science, 208,* 1335–1342.

Larkin, J. H., McDermott, J., Simon, D. P., & Simon, H. A. (1980b). Models of competence in solving physics problems. *Cognitive Science, 4,* 317–345.

Laughlin, P. R., Bonner, B. L., & Miner, A. G. (2002). Groups perform better than the best individuals on letters-to-numbers problems. *Organizational Behavior and Human Decision Processes, 88,* 605–620.

Laughlin, P. R., Hatch, E. C., Silver, J. S., & Boh, L. (2006). Groups perform better than the best individuals on letters-to-numbers problems: Effects of group size. *Journal of Personality and Social Psychology, 90,* 644–651.

Leahy, W. & Sweller, J. (in press). Cognitive Load Theory, Modality of Presentation and the Transient Information Effect. *Applied Cognitive Psychology.*

Leahy, W., & Sweller, J. (2004). Cognitive load and the imagination effect. *Applied Cognitive Psychology, 18,* 857–875.

Leahy, W., & Sweller, J. (2005). Interactions among the imagination, expertise reversal, and element interactivity effects. *Journal of Experimental Psychology: Applied, 11,* 266–276.

Leahy, W., & Sweller, J. (2008). The imagination effect increases with an increased intrinsic cognitive load. *Applied Cognitive Psychology, 22,* 273–283.

Lee, C. H., & Kalyuga, S. (in press). Effectiveness of different pinyin presentation formats in learning Chinese characters: A cognitive load perspective. *Language Learning.*

Lee, C. H., & Kalyuga, S. (2011). Effectiveness of on-screen pinyin in learning Chinese: An expertise reversal for multimedia redundancy effect. *Computers in Human Behavior, 27,* 11–15.

Lee, H., Plass, J. L., & Homer, B. D. (2006). Optimizing cognitive load for learning from computer-based science simulations. *Journal of Educational Psychology, 98,* 902–913.

Lesh, R., Behr, M., & Post, T. (1987). Rational number relations and proportions. In C. Janvier (Ed.), *Problems of representation in the teaching and learning of mathematics.* Hillsdale: Lawrence Erlbaum.

Leutner, D., Leopold, C., & Sumfleth, E. (2009). Cognitive load and science text comprehension: Effects of drawing and mentally imagining text content. *Computers in Human Behavior, 25,* 284–289.

Lohman, D. F. (1986). Predicting mathemathanic effects in the teaching of higher-order thinking skills. *Educational Psychologist, 21,* 191–208.

Lowe, R. K. (1999). Extracting information from an animation during complex visual learning. *European Journal of Psychology of Education, 14,* 225–244.

Lowe, R. K. (2003). Animation and learning: Selective processing of information in dynamic graphics. *Learning and Instruction, 13,* 157–176.

Luchins, A. S. (1942). Mechanization in problem solving – The effect of Einstellung. *Psychological Monographs, 54,* 95.

Marcus, N., Cooper, M., & Sweller, J. (1996). Understanding instructions. *Journal of Educational Psychology, 88,* 49–63.

Markham, P. L. (1999). Captioned videotape and second-language listening word recognition. *Foreign Language Annals, 32,* 321–328.

Mautone, P. D., & Mayer, R. E. (2001). Signaling as a cognitive guide in multimedia learning. *Journal of Educational Psychology, 93,* 377–389.

Mawer, R. F., & Sweller, J. (1982). Effects of subgoal density and location on learning during problem solving. *Journal of Experimental Psychology. Learning, Memory, and Cognition, 8,* 252–259.

Mayer, R. E. (1989). Systematic thinking fostered by illustrations in scientific text. *Journal of Educational Psychology, 81*, 240–246.

Mayer, R. E. (1997). Multimedia learning: Are we asking the right questions? *Educational Psychologist, 32*, 1–19.

Mayer, R. E. (2004). Should there be a three-strikes rule against pure discovery learning? The case for guided methods of instruction. *The American Psychologist, 59*, 14–19.

Mayer, R. E. (Ed.). (2005). *Cambridge handbook of multimedia learning*. New York: Cambridge University Press.

Mayer, R. E. (2009). *Multimedia learning* (2nd ed.). New York: Cambridge University Press.

Mayer, R. E., & Anderson, R. B. (1991). Animations need narrations: An experimental test of a dual-coding hypothesis. *Journal of Educational Psychology, 83*, 484–490.

Mayer, R. E., & Anderson, R. B. (1992). The instructive animation: Helping students build connections between words and pictures in multimedia learning. *Journal of Educational Psychology, 84*, 444–452.

Mayer, R. E., & Chandler, P. (2001). When learning is just a click away: Does simple user interaction foster deeper understanding of multimedia messages? *Journal of Educational Psychology, 93*, 390–397.

Mayer, R. E., DeLeeuw, K. E., & Ayres, P. (2007). Creating retroactive and proactive interference in multimedia learning. *Applied Cognitive Psychology, 21*, 795–809.

Mayer, R. E., Dow, G. T., & Mayer, S. (2003). Multimedia learning in an interactive self-explaining environment: What works in the design of agent-based microworlds? *Journal of Educational Psychology, 95*, 806–812.

Mayer, R. E., & Gallini, J. K. (1990). When is an illustration worth ten thousand words? *Journal of Educational Psychology, 82*, 715–726.

Mayer, R. E., Hegarty, M., Mayer, S., & Campbell, J. (2005). When static media promote active learning: Annotated illustrations versus narrated animations in multimedia instruction. *Journal of Experimental Psychology: Applied, 11*, 256–265.

Mayer, R. E., Heiser, J., & Lonn, S. (2001). Cognitive constraints on multimedia learning: When presenting more material results in less understanding. *Journal of Educational Psychology, 93*, 187–198.

Mayer, R. E., & Johnson, C. I. (2008). Revising the redundancy principle in multimedia learning. *Journal of Educational Psychology, 100*, 380–386.

Mayer, R. E., Mathias, A., & Wetzell, K. (2002). Fostering understanding of multimedia messages through pre-training: Evidence for a two-stage theory of mental model construction. *Journal of Experimental Psychology: Applied, 8*, 147–154.

Mayer, R. E., Mautone, P., & Prothero, W. (2002). Pictorial aids for learning by doing in a multimedia geology simulation game. *Journal of Educational Psychology, 94*, 171–185.

Mayer, R. E., & Moreno, R. (1998). A split-attention effect in multimedia learning: Evidence for dual processing systems in working memory. *Journal of Educational Psychology, 90*, 312–320.

Mayer, R. E., & Moreno, R. (2002). Aids to computer-based multimedia learning. *Learning and Instruction, 12*, 107–119.

Mayer, R. E., & Moreno, R. (2003). Nine ways to reduce cognitive load in multimedia learning. *Educational Psychologist, 38*, 43–52.

Mayer, R. E., Moreno, R., Boire, M., & Vagge, S. (1999). Maximizing constructivist learning from multimedia communications by minimizing cognitive load. *Journal of Educational Psychology, 91*, 638–643.

Mayer, R. E., & Sims, V. K. (1994). For whom is a picture worth a thousand words? Extensions of a dual-coding theory of multimedia learning. *Journal of Educational Psychology, 86*, 389–401.

Mayer, R. E., Sobko, K., & Mautone, P. D. (2003). Social cues in multimedia learning: Role of speaker's voice. *Journal of Educational Psychology, 95*, 419–425.

Mayer, R. E., Steinhoff, K., Bower, G., & Mars, R. (1995). A generative theory of textbook design: Using annotated illustrations to foster meaningful learning of science text. *Educational Technology Research and Development, 43*, 31–43.

Mayer, R. E., Stiehl, C. C., & Greeno, J. G. (1975). Acquisition of understanding and skill in relation to subjects' preparation and meaningfulness of instruction. *Journal of Educational Psychology, 67*, 331–350.

McNamara, D. S., Kintsch, E., Songer, N. B., & Kintsch, W. (1996). Are good texts always better? Interactions of text coherence, background knowledge, and levels of understanding in learning from text. *Cognition and Instruction, 14*, 1–43.

Meadow, A., Parnes, S. J., & Reese, H. (1959). Influence of brainstorming instructions and problem sequence on a creative problem solving test. *The Journal of Applied Psychology, 43*, 413–416.

Mendoza, D., & Wichman, H. (1978). 'Inner' darts: Effects of mental practice on performance of dart throwing. *Perceptual and Motor Skills, 47*, 1195–1199.

Merrill, M. D. (1975). Learner control: Beyond aptitude-treatment interactions. *AV Communication Review, 23*, 217–226.

Meudell, P. R., Hitch, G. J., & Kirby, P. (1992). Are two heads better than one? Experimental investigations of the social facilitation of memory. *Applied Cognitive Psychology, 6*, 525–543.

Miller, W. (1937). The picture crutch in reading. *Elementary English Review, 14*, 263–264.

Miller, G. A. (1956). The magical number seven, plus or minus two: Some limits on our capacity for processing information. *Psychological Review, 63*, 81–97.

Miller, C. S., Lehman, J. F., & Koedinger, K. R. (1999). Goals and learning in microworlds. *Cognitive Science, 23*, 305–336.

Moreno, R. (2004). Decreasing cognitive load for novice students: Effects of explanatory versus corrective feedback in discovery-based multimedia. *Instructional Science, 32*, 99–113.

Moreno, R. (2007). Optimising learning from animations by minimising cognitive load: Cognitive and affective consequences of signalling and segmentation methods. *Applied Cognitive Psychology, 21*, 765–781.

Moreno, R., & Durán, R. (2004). Do multiple representations need explanations? The role of verbal guidance and individual differences in multimedia mathematics learning. *Journal of Educational Psychology, 96*, 492–503.

Moreno, R., & Mayer, R. E. (1999). Cognitive principles of multimedia learning: The role of modality and contiguity. *Journal of Educational Psychology, 91*, 358–368.

Moreno, R., & Mayer, R. E. (2002). Verbal redundancy in multimedia learning: When reading helps listening. *Journal of Educational Psychology, 94*, 156–163.

Moreno, R., Mayer, R. E., Spires, H. A., & Lester, J. C. (2001). The case for social agency in computer-based teaching: Do students learn more deeply when they interact with animated pedagogical agents? *Cognition and Instruction, 19*, 177–213.

Mousavi, S. Y., Low, R., & Sweller, J. (1995). Reducing cognitive load by mixing auditory and visual presentation modes. *Journal of Educational Psychology, 87*, 319–334.

Moussa, J., Ayres, P., & Sweller, J. (2007). *Cognitive load and the impact of spoken English on learning English as a foreign language.* Paper presented at the International Conference on Cognitive Load Theory, Sydney, UNSW.

Mwangi, W., & Sweller, J. (1998). Learning to solve compare word problems: The effect of example format and generating self-explanations. *Cognition and Instruction, 16*, 173–199.

Nadolski, R. J., Kirschner, P. A., & van Merriënboer, J. J. G. (2005). Optimizing the number of steps in learning tasks for complex skills. *The British Journal of Educational Psychology, 75*, 223–237.

Newell, A., & Simon, H. A. (1972). *Human problem solving.* Englewood Cliffs: Prentice Hall.

Niemiec, R. P., Sikorski, C., & Walberg, H. J. (1996). Learner-control effects: A review of reviews and a meta-analysis. *Journal of Educational Computing Research, 15*, 157–174.

Nückles, M., Hübner, S., Dümer, S., & Renkl, A. (2010). Expertise reversal effects in writing-to-learn. *Instructional Science, 38*, 237–258.

O'Neil, H. F., & Chuang, S. S. (2007). *An audio/text after-action review in a computer-based collaborative problem solving task.* Los Angeles: National Center for Research on Evaluation, Standards, and Student Testing (CRESST). University of California.

Oksa, A., Kalyuga, S., & Chandler, P. (2010). Expertise reversal effect in using explanatory notes for readers of Shakespearean text. *Instructional Science, 38*, 217–236.

Osborn, A. F. (1953). *Applied imagination.* New York: Scribners.

Osman, M. (2008). Observation can be as effective as action in problem solving. *Cognitive Science, 32*, 162–183.

Owen, E., & Sweller, J. (1985). What do students learn while solving mathematics problems? *Journal of Educational Psychology, 77*, 272–284.

Owens, P., & Sweller, J. (2008). Cognitive load theory and music instruction. *Educational Psychology, 28*, 29–45.

Paas, F. G. (1992). Training strategies for attaining transfer of problem-solving skill in statistics: A cognitive-load approach. *Journal of Educational Psychology, 84*, 429–434.

Paas, F., Ayres, P., & Pachman, M. (2008). Assessment of cognitive load in multimedia learning: Theory, methods and applications. In D. H. Robinson & G. Schraw (Eds.), *Recent innovations in educational technology that facilitate student learning* (pp. 11–35). Charlotte: Information Age Publishing.

Paas, F., Camp, G., & Rikers, R. (2001). Instructional compensation for age-related cognitive declines: Effects of goal specificity in maze learning. *Journal of Educational Psychology, 93*, 181–186.

Paas, F., Renkl, A., & Sweller, J. (2003). Cognitive load theory and instructional design: Recent developments. *Educational Psychologist, 38*, 1–4.

Paas, F., Renkl, A., & Sweller, J. (2004). Cognitive load theory: Instructional implications of the inter-action between information structures and cognitive architecture. *Instructional Science, 32*, 1–8.

Paas, F., Tuovinen, J. E., Tabbers, H., & van Gerven, P. W. M. (2003). Cognitive load measurement as a means to advance cognitive load theory. *Educational Psychologist, 38*, 63–71.

Paas, F. G. W. C., & van Merriënboer, J. J. G. (1993). The efficiency of instructional conditions: An approach to combine mental effort and performance measures. *Human Factors, 35*, 737–743.

Paas, F. G. W. C., & van Merriënboer, J. J. G. (1994). Variability of worked examples and transfer of geometrical problem-solving skills: A cognitive-load approach. *Journal of Educational Psychology, 86*, 122–133.

Paas, F. G. W. C., van Merriënboer, J. J. G., & Adam, J. J. (1994). Measurement of cognitive load in instructional research. *Perceptual and Motor Skills, 79*, 419–430.

Pashler, H., Bain, P. M., Bottqe, B. A., Graesser, A., Koedinger, K., McDaniel, M., et al. (2007). *Organizing instruction and study to improve student learning. IES practice guide. NCER 2007–2004.*

Pawley, D., Ayres, P., Cooper, M., & Sweller, J. (2005). Translating words into equations: A cognitive load theory approach. *Educational Psychology, 25*, 75–97.

Penney, C. G. (1989). Modality effects and the structure of short-term verbal memory. *Memory and Cognition, 17*, 398–422.

Perry, H. M. (1939). The relative efficiency of actual and 'imaginary' practice in five selected tasks. *Archives of Psychology, 243*, 76.

Peterson, L., & Peterson, M. J. (1959). Short-term retention of individual verbal items. *Journal of Experimental Psychology, 58*, 193–198.

Phipps, S. J., & Morehouse, C. A. (1969). Effects of mental practice on the acquisition of motor skills of varied difficulty. *Research Quarterly, 40*, 773–778.

Piaget, J. (1928). *Judgement and reasoning in the child.* New York: Harcourt.

Pillay, H. K. (1994). Cognitive load and mental rotation: Structuring orthographic projection for learning and problem solving. *Instructional Science, 22*, 91–113.

Plass, J. L., Chun, D. M., Mayer, R. E., & Leutner, D. (2003). Cognitive load in reading a foreign language text with multimedia aids and the influence of verbal and spatial abilities. *Computers in Human Behavior, 19*, 221–243.

Ploetzner, R., & Lowe, R. (2004). Dynamic visualisations and learning. *Learning and Instruction, 14*, 235–240.

Pociask, F. D., & Morrison, G. R. (2008). Controlling split attention and redundancy in physical therapy instruction. *Educational Technology Research and Development, 56*, 379–399.

Pollock, E., Chandler, P., & Sweller, J. (2002). Assimilating complex information. *Learning and Instruction, 12*, 61–86.

Polya, G. (1957). *How to solve it: A new aspect of mathematical method.* Garden City: Doubleday.

Portin, P. (2002). Historical development of the concept of the gene. *The Journal of Medicine and Philosophy, 27*, 257–286.

Purnell, K. N., Solman, R. T., & Sweller, J. (1991). The effects of technical illustrations on cognitive load. *Instructional Science, 20*, 443–462.

Quilici, J. L., & Mayer, R. E. (1996). Role of examples in how students learn to categorize statistics word problems. *Journal of Educational Psychology, 88*, 144–161.

Rakestraw, P. G., Irby, D. M., & Vontver, L. A. (1983). The use of mental practice in pelvic examination instruction. *Journal of Medical Education, 58*, 335–340.

Rawlings, E. I., & Rawlings, I. L. (1974). Rotary pursuit tracking following mental rehearsal as a function of voluntary control of visual imagery. *Perceptual and Motor Skills, 38*, 302.

Reder, L. M., & Anderson, J. R. (1980). A comparison of texts and their summaries: Memorial consequences. *Journal of Verbal Learning and Verbal Behavior, 19*, 121–134.

Reder, L. M., & Anderson, J. R. (1982). Effects of spacing and embellishment on memory for the main points of a text. *Memory and Cognition, 10*(2), 97–102.

Reigeluth, C. M. (2007). Order, first step to mastery: An introduction to sequencing in instructional design. In order to learn: How the sequence of topics influences learning. In F. E. Ritter, J. Nerb, E. Lehtinen, & T. M. O'Shea (Eds.), *In order to learn: How the sequence of topics influences learning* (Oxford series on cognitive models and architectures, pp. 19–40). New York: Oxford University Press.

Reisslein, J. (2005). *Learner achievement and attitudes under varying paces of transitioning to independent problem solving.* Unpublished dissertation presented in partial fulfillment of the requirements for the degree Doctor of Philosophy, Arizona State University, Tempe, Arizona.

Reisslein, J., Atkinson, R. K., Seeling, P., & Reisslein, M. (2006). Encountering the expertise reversal effect with a computer-based environment on electrical circuit analysis. *Learning and Instruction, 16*, 92–103.

Renkl, A. (1997). Learning from worked-out examples: A study on individual differences. *Cognitive Science, 21*, 1–29.

Renkl, A. (1999). Learning mathematics from worked-out examples: Analyzing and fostering self-explanations. *European Journal of Psychology of Education, 14*, 477–488.

Renkl, A. (2005). The worked-out examples principle in multimedia learning. In R. E. Mayer (Ed.), *The Cambridge handbook of multimedia learning* (pp. 229–245). New York: Cambridge University Press.

Renkl, A., & Atkinson, R. K. (2001, August). *The effects of gradually increasing problem-solving demands in cognitive skill acquisition.* Paper presented at the 9th European Conference for Research on Learning and Instruction, Fribourg, Switzerland.

Renkl, A., & Atkinson, R. K. (2003). Structuring the transition from example study to problem solving in cognitive skill acquisition: A cognitive load perspective. *Educational Psychologist, 38*, 15–22.

Renkl, A., Atkinson, R. K., & Große, C. S. (2004). How fading worked solution steps works – A cognitive load perspective. *Instructional Science, 32*, 59–82.

Renkl, A., Atkinson, R. K., & Maier, U. H. (2000). From studying examples to solving problems: Fading worked-out solution steps helps learning. In L. Gleitman & A. K. Joshi (Eds.), *Proceedings of the 22nd Annual conference of the Cognitive Science Society* (pp. 393–398). Mahwa: Lawrence Erlbaum.

Renkl, A., Atkinson, R. K., Maier, U. H., & Staley, R. (2002). From example study to problem solving: Smooth transitions help learning. *Journal of Experimental Education, 70*, 293–315.

Renkl, A., Schwonke, R., Wittwer, J., Krieg, C., Aleven, V., & Salden, R. (2007, March). *Worked-out examples in an intelligent tutoring system: Do they further improve learning?* Paper presented at the International Cognitive Load Theory Conference, Sydney, Australia.

Renkl, A., Stark, R., Gruber, H., & Mandl, H. (1998). Learning from worked-out examples: The effects of example variability and elicited self-explanations. *Contemporary Educational Psychology, 23*, 90–108.

Retnowati, E., Ayres, P., & Sweller, J. (2010). Worked example effects in individual and group work settings. *Educational Psychology, 30*, 349–367.

Ritter, F. E., Nerb, J., Lehtinen, E., & O'Shea, T. M. (Eds.). (2007). *In order to learn: How the sequence of topics influences learning* (Oxford series on cognitive models and architectures). New York: Oxford University Press.

Rizzolatti, G. (2005). The mirror neuron system and imitation. In S. Hurley & N. Chater (Eds.), *Perspectives on imitation: From neuroscience to social science* (Mechanisms of imitation and imitation in animals, Vol. 1, pp. 55–76). Cambridge, MA: MIT Press.

Rizzolatti, G., & Craighero, L. (2004). The mirror-neuron system. *Annual Review of Neuroscience, 27*, 169–192.

Romero, K., & Silvestri, L. (1990). The role of mental practice in the acquisition and performance of motor skills. *Journal of Instructional Psychology, 17*, 218–221.

Rose, J. M. (2002). The effects of cognitive load on decision aid users. *Advances in Accounting Behavioral Research, 5*, 115–140.

Rose, J. M., & Wolfe, C. J. (2000). The effects of system design alternatives on the acquisition of tax knowledge from a computerized tax decision aid. *Accounting, Organizations and Society, 25*, 285–306.

Rourke, A., & Sweller, J. (2009). The worked-example effect using ill-defined problems: Learning to recognise designers' styles. *Learning and Instruction, 19*, 185–199.

Roy, M., & Chi, M. T. H. (2005). The self-explanation principle in multimedia learning. In R. E. Mayer (Ed.), *The Cambridge handbook of multimedia learning* (pp. 271–286). New York, NY: Cambridge University Press.

Sackett, R. S. (1934). The influence of symbolic rehearsal upon the retention of a maze habit. *The Journal of General Psychology, 10*, 376–398.

Sackett, R. S. (1935). The relationship between amount of symbolic rehearsal and retention of a maze habit. *The Journal of General Psychology, 13*, 113–130.

Salden, R. J. C. M., Aleven, V., Schwonke, R., & Renkl, A. (2010). The expertise reversal effect and worked examples in tutored problem solving. *Instructional Science, 38*, 289–307.

Salden, R. J. C. M., Paas, F., Broers, N. J., & van Merriënboer, J. J. G. (2004). Mental effort and performance as determinants for the dynamic selection of learning tasks in air traffic control training. *Instructional Science, 32*, 153–172.

Salden, R. J. C. M., Paas, F., & van Merriënboer, J. J. G. (2006a). A comparison of approaches to learning task selection in the training of complex cognitive skills. *Computers in Human Behavior, 22*, 321–333.

Salden, R. J. C. M., Paas, F., & van Merriënboer, J. J. G. (2006b). Personalised adaptive task selection in air traffic control: Effects on training efficiency and transfer. *Learning and Instruction, 16*, 350–362.

Saunders, R. J., & Solman, R. T. (1984). The effect of pictures on the acquisition of a small vocabulary of similar sight-words. *The British Journal of Educational Psychology, 54*, 265–275.

Scheiter, M., & Gerjets, P. (2007). Making your own order: Order effects in system- and user-controlled settings for learning and problem solving. In F. Ritter, J. Nerb, E. Lehtinen, & T. O'Shea (Eds.), *In order to learn: How the sequence of topics influences learning* (pp. 195–212). New York: Oxford University Press.

Schirmer, B. R. (2003). Using verbal protocols to identify the reading strategies of students who are deaf. *Journal of Deaf Studies and Deaf Education, 8*, 157–170.

Schmidt-Weigand, F., Kohnert, A., & Glowalla, U. (2010). A closer look at split visual attention in system- and self-paced instruction in multimedia learning. *Learning and Instruction, 20*, 100–110.

Schneider, W., & Detweiler, M. (1987). A connectionist/control architecture for working memory. In G. H. Bower (Ed.), *The psychology of learning and motivation: Advances in research and theory* (Vol. 21, pp. 53–119). New York: Academic.

Schneider, W., & Shiffrin, R. M. (1977). Controlled and automatic human information processing: I. Detection, search, and attention. *Psychological Review, 84*, 1–66.

Schnotz, W. (2005). An integrated model of text and picture comprehension. In R. E. Mayer (Ed.), *The Cambridge handbook of multimedia learning* (pp. 49–69). Cambridge, UK: Cambridge University Press.

Schnotz, W., & Bannert, M. (2003). Construction and interference in learning from multiple representation. *Learning and Instruction, 13*, 141–156.

Schnotz, W., Böckheler, J., & Grzondziel, H. (1999). Individual and co-operative learning with interactive animated pictures. *European Journal of Psychology of Education, 14*, 245–265.

Schnotz, W., & Rasch, T. (2005). Enabling, facilitating, and inhibiting effects of animations in multimedia learning: Why reduction of cognitive load can have negative results on learning. *Educational Technology Research and Development, 53*, 47–58.

Schooler, J. W., & Engstler-Schooler, T. Y. (1990). Verbal overshadowing of visual memories: Some things are better left unsaid. *Cognitive Psychology, 22*, 36–71.

Schwan, S., & Riempp, R. (2004). The cognitive benefits of interactive videos: Learning to tie nautical knots. *Learning and Instruction, 14*, 293–305.

Schwonke, R., Renkl, A., Krieg, C., Wittwer, J., Aleven, V., & Salden, R. (2009). The worked-example effect: Not an artefact of lousy control conditions. *Computers in Human Behavior, 25*, 258–266.

Schworm, S., & Renkl, A. (2006). Computer-supported example-based learning: When instructional explanations reduce self-explanations. *Computers & Education, 46*, 426–445.

Schworm, S., & Renkl, A. (2007). Learning argumentation skills through the use of prompts for self-explaining examples. *Journal of Educational Psychology, 99*, 285–296.

Seufert, T. (2003). Supporting coherence formation in learning from multiple representations. *Learning and Instruction, 13*, 227–237.

Seufert, T., Schütze, M., & Brünken, R. (2009). Memory characteristics and modality in multimedia learning: An aptitude-treatment-interaction study. *Learning and Instruction, 19*, 28–42.

Shapiro, A. M. (1999). The relationship between prior knowledge and interactive overviews during hypermedia-aided learning. *Journal of Educational Computing Research, 20*, 143–167.

Shick, M. (1970). Effects of mental practice on selected volleyball skills for college women. *Research Quarterly, 41*, 88–94.

Shiffrin, R. M., & Schneider, W. (1977). Controlled and automatic human information processing: II. Perceptual learning, automatic attending and a general theory. *Psychological Review, 84*, 127–190.

Shin, E. C., Schallert, D. L., & Savenye, W. C. (1994). Effects of learner control, advisement, and prior knowledge on young students' learning in a hypertext environment. *Educational Technology Research and Development, 42*, 33–46.

Shute, V. J., & Gluck, K. A. (1996). Individual differences in patterns of spontaneous online tool use. *Journal of the Learning Sciences, 5*, 329–355.

Simon, H. A., & Gilmartin, K. (1973). A simulation of memory for chess positions. *Cognitive Psychology, 5*, 29–46.

Simon, H. A., & Lea, G. (1974). Problem solving and rule induction: A unified view. Knowledge and cognition. In L. W. Gregg (Ed.), *Knowledge and cognition.* Oxford/England: Lawrence Erlbaum.

Simon, D. P., & Simon, H. A. (1978). Individual differences in solving physics problems. In R. S. Siegler (Ed.), *Children's thinking: What develops?* (pp. 325–348). Hillsdale: Lawrence Erlbaum.

Snow, R. E. (1989). Aptitude-treatment interaction as a framework for research on individual differences in learning. In P. L. Ackerman, R. J. Sternberg, & R. Glaser (Eds.), *Learning and individual differences: Advances in theory and research* (pp. 13–59). New York: W. H. Freeman.

Snow, R. E. (1994). Abilities in academic tasks. In R. J. Sternberg & R. K. Wagner (Eds.), *Mind in context: Interactionist perspectives on human intelligence* (pp. 3–37). Cambridge, MA: Cambridge University Press.

Snow, R. E., & Lohman, D. F. (1984). Toward a theory of cognitive aptitude for learning from instruction. *Journal of Educational Psychology, 76*, 347–376.

Spangenberg, R. W. (1973). The motion variable in procedural learning. *AV Communication Review, 21*, 419–436.

Spanjers, I. A. E., Van Gog, T., & van Merriënboer, J. J. G. (2010). A theoretical analysis of how segmentation of dynamic visualizations optimizes students' learning. *Educational Psychology Review, 22*, 411–423.

Spiro, R. J., & DeSchryver, M. (2009). Constructivism: When it's the wrong idea and when it's the only idea. In S. Tobias & M. Thomas (Eds.), *Constructivist instruction: Success or failure?* (pp. 106–123). New York: Routledge/Taylor & Francis.

Steinberg, E. R. (1977). Review of student control in computer-assisted instruction. *Journal of Computer-Based Instruction, 3*, 84–90.

Steinberg, E. R. (1989). Cognition and learner control: A literature review, 1977–1988. *Journal of Computer-Based Instruction, 16*, 117–121.

Stenning, K. (1998). Distinguishing semantic from processing explanations of usability of representations: Applying expressiveness analysis to animation. In J. Lee (Ed.), *Intelligence and multimodality in multimedia interfaces: Research and applications.* Cambridge, MA: AAAI Press.

Stotz, K., & Griffiths, P. (2004). Genes: Philosophical analyses put to the test. *History and Philosophy of the Life Sciences, 26*, 5–28.

Surburg, P. R. (1968). Audio, visual and audio-visual instruction with mental practice in developing the forehand tennis drive. *Research Quarterly, 39*, 728–734.

Sweller, J. (1980). Transfer effects in a problem solving context. *The Quarterly Journal of Experimental Psychology, 32*, 233–239.

Sweller, J. (1983). Control mechanisms in problem solving. *Memory and Cognition, 11*, 32–40.

Sweller, J. (1988). Cognitive load during problem solving: Effects on learning. *Cognitive Science, 12*, 257–285.

Sweller, J. (1994). Cognitive load theory, learning difficulty, and instructional design. *Learning and Instruction, 4*, 295–312.

Sweller, J. (1999). *Instructional design in technical areas.* Camberwell: ACER Press.

Sweller, J. (2003). Evolution of human cognitive architecture. In B. Ross (Ed.), *The psychology of learning and motivation* (Vol. 43, pp. 215–266). San Diego: Academic.

Sweller, J. (2004). Instructional design consequences of an analogy between evolution by natural selection and human cognitive architecture. *Instructional Science, 32*, 9–31.

Sweller, J. (2008). Instructional implications of David C. Geary's evolutionary educational psychology. *Educational Psychologist, 43*, 214–216.

Sweller, J. (2009a). *What human cognitive architecture tells us about constructivism Constructivist instruction: Success or failure?* (pp. 127–143). New York: Routledge.

Sweller, J. (2009b). Cognitive bases of human creativity. *Educational Psychology Review, 21*, 11–19.

Sweller, J. (2010). Element interactivity and intrinsic, extraneous, and germane cognitive load. *Educational Psychology Review, 22*, 123–138.

Sweller, J., & Chandler, P. (1994). Why some material is difficult to learn. *Cognition and Instruction, 12*, 185–233.

Sweller, J., Chandler, P., Tierney, P., & Cooper, M. (1990). Cognitive load as a factor in the structuring of technical material. *Journal of Experimental Psychology: General, 119*, 176–192.

Sweller, J., & Cooper, G. A. (1985). The use of worked examples as a substitute for problem solving in learning algebra. *Cognition and Instruction, 1*, 59–89.

Sweller, J., & Gee, W. (1978). Einstellung, the sequence effect, and hypothesis theory. *Journal of Experimental Psychology: Human Learning and Memory, 4*, 513–526.

Sweller, J., & Levine, M. (1982). Effects of goal specificity on means–ends analysis and learning. *Journal of Experimental Psychology. Learning, Memory, and Cognition, 8*, 463–474.

Sweller, J., Mawer, R. F., & Howe, W. (1982). Consequences of history-cued and means–end strategies in problem solving. *The American Journal of Psychology, 95*, 455–483.

Sweller, J., Mawer, R. F., & Ward, M. R. (1983). Development of expertise in mathematical problem solving. *Journal of Experimental Psychology: General, 112*, 639–661.

Sweller, J., & Sweller, S. (2006). Natural information processing systems. *Evolutionary Psychology, 4*, 434–458.

Sweller, J., van Merriënboer, J. J. G., & Paas, F. G. W. C. (1998). Cognitive architecture and instructional design. *Educational Psychology Review, 10*, 251–296.

Tabbers, H. K., Martens, R. L., & van Merriënboer, J. J. G. (2000). *Multimedia instructions and cognitive load theory: Split-attention and modality effects.* Unpublished paper presented at the Onderwijs Research Dagen, at Leiden, The Netherlands.

Tabbers, H. K., Martens, R. L., & van Merriënboer, J. J. G. (2004). Multimedia instructions and cognitive load theory: Effects of modality and cueing. *The British Journal of Educational Psychology, 74*, 71–81.

Tarmizi, R. A., & Sweller, J. (1988). Guidance during mathematical problem solving. *Journal of Educational Psychology, 80*, 424–436.

Tennyson, R. D. (1975). Adaptive instructional models for concept acquisition. *Educational Technology, 15*, 7–15.

Tettamanti, M., Buccino, G., Saccuman, M. C., Gallese, V., Danna, M., Scifo, P., et al. (2005). Listening to action-related sentences activates fronto-parietal motor circuits. *Journal of Cognitive Neuroscience, 17*, 273–281.

Tindall-Ford, S., Chandler, P., & Sweller, J. (1997). When two sensory modes are better than one. *Journal of Experimental Psychology: Applied, 3*, 257–287.

Tindall-Ford, S., & Sweller, J. (2006). Altering the modality of instructions to facilitate imagination: Interactions between the modality and imagination effects. *Instructional Science, 34*, 343–365.

Tobias, S. (1976). Achievement treatment interactions. *Review of Educational Research, 46*, 61–74.

Tobias, S. (1987). Mandatory text review and interaction with student characteristics. *Journal of Educational Psychology, 79*, 154–161.

Tobias, S. (1988). Teaching strategic text review by computer and interaction with student characteristics. *Computers in Human Behavior, 4*, 299–310.

Tobias, S. (1989). Another look at research on the adaptation of instruction to student characteristics. *Educational Psychologist, 24*, 213–227.

Torcasio, S., & Sweller, J. (2010). The use of illustrations when learning to read: A cognitive load theory approach. *Applied Cognitive Psychology, 24*, 659–672.

Trafton, J. G., & Reiser, R. J. (1993). The contribution of studying examples and solving problems to skill acquisition. In M. Polson (Ed.), *Proceedings of the 15th Annual Conference of the Cognitive Science Society* (pp. 1017–1022). Hillsdale: Lawrence Erlbaum.

Trumpower, D. L., Goldsmith, T. E., & Guynn, M. J. (2004). Goal specificity and knowledge acquisition in statistics problem solving: Evidence for attentional focus. *Memory and Cognition, 32*, 1379–1388.

Tuovinen, J. E., & Sweller, J. (1999). A comparison of cognitive load associated with discovery learning and worked examples. *Journal of Educational Psychology, 91*, 334–341.

Tversky, B., Morrison, J. B., & Betrancourt, M. (2002). Animation: Can it facilitate? *International Journal of Human Computer Studies, 57*, 247–262.

Underwood, G., Jebbett, L., & Roberts, K. (2004). Inspecting pictures for information to verify a sentence: Eye movements in general encoding and in focused search. *The Quarterly Journal of Experimental Psychology: Human Experimental Psychology, 57A*, 165–182.

Ungerleider, S., & Golding, J. M. (1991). Mental practice among Olympic athletes. *Perceptual and Motor Skills, 72*, 1007–1017.

VanLehn, K., Jones, R., & Chi, M. (1992). A model of the self-explanation effect. *Journal of the Learning Sciences, 2*, 1–60.

Van Gerven, P. W. M., Paas, F., van Merriënboer, J. J. G., Hendriks, M., & Schmidt, H. G. (2003). The efficiency of multimedia learning into old age. *The British Journal of Educational Psychology, 73*, 489–505.

Van Gerven, P. W. M., Paas, F., van Merriënboer, J. J. G., & Schmidt, H. G. (2004). Memory load and the cognitive pupillary response in aging. *Psychophysiology, 41*, 167–174.

Van Gerven, P. W. M., Paas, F., van Merriënboer, J. J. G., & Schmidt, H. G. (2006). Modality and variability as factors in training the elderly. *Applied Cognitive Psychology, 20*, 311–320.

Van Gog, T., & Paas, F. (2008). Instructional efficiency: Revisiting the original construct in educational research. *Educational Psychologist, 43*, 16–26.

Van Gog, T., Paas, F., Marcus, N., Ayres, P., & Sweller, J. (2009). The mirror neuron system and observational learning: Implications for the effectiveness of dynamic visualizations. *Educational Psychology Review, 21*, 21–30.

Van Gog, T., Paas, F., & van Merriënboer, J. J. G. (2004). Process-oriented worked examples: Improving transfer performance through enhanced understanding. *Instructional Science, 32*, 83–98.

Van Gog, T., Paas, F., & van Merriënboer, J. J. G. (2008). Effects of studying sequences of process-oriented and product-oriented worked examples on troubleshooting transfer efficiency. *Learning and Instruction, 18*, 211–222.

Van Gog, T., Rikers, R. M. J. P., & Ayres, P. (2008). Data collection and analysis: Assessment of complex performance. In J. M. Spector, M. D. Merrill, J. J. G. van Merriënboer, & M. P. Driscoll (Eds.), *Handbook of research on educational communications and technology* (3 revth ed., pp. 783–789). London/England: Routledge.

Van Gog, T., & Scheiter, K. (2010). Eye tracking as a tool to study and enhance multimedia learning. *Learning and Instruction, 20*, 95–99.

Van Meer, J. P., & Theunissen, N. C. M. (2009). Prospective educational applications of mental simulation: A meta-review. *Educational Psychology Review, 21*, 93–112.

Van Merriënboer, J. J. G. (1990). Strategies for programming instruction in high school: Program completion vs. program generation. *Journal of Educational Computing Research, 6*, 65–285.

Van Merriënboer, J. J. G. (1997). *Training complex cognitive skills: A four-component instructional design model for technical training.* Englewood Cliffs: Educational Technology Publications.

Van Merriënboer, J. J. G., Clark, R. E., & de Croock, M. B. M. (2002). Blueprints for complex learning: The 4C/ID-Model. *Educational Technology Research and Development, 50*, 39–64.

Van Merriënboer, J. J. G., & de Croock, M. B. (1992). Strategies for computer-based programming instruction: Program completion vs. program generation. *Journal of Educational Computing Research, 8*, 365–394.

Van Merriënboer, J. J. G., & Kester, L. (2008). Whole-task models in education. In J. M. Spector, M. D. Merrill, J. J. G. van Merriënboer, & M. P. Driscoll (Eds.), *Handbook of research on educational communications and technology* (3rd ed., pp. 441–456). New York: Lawrence Erlbaum.

Van Merriënboer, J. J. G., Kester, L., & Paas, F. (2006). Teaching complex rather than simple tasks: Balancing intrinsic and germane load to enhance transfer of learning. *Applied Cognitive Psychology, 20*, 343–352.

Van Merriënboer, J. J. G., & Kirschner, P. A. (2007). *Ten steps to complex learning: A systematic approach to four-component instructional design:.* Mahwah: Lawrence Erlbaum.

Van Merriënboer, J. J. G., Kirschner, P. A., & Kester, L. (2003). Taking the load off a learner's mind: Instructional design for complex learning. *Educational Psychologist, 38*, 5–13.

Van Merriënboer, J. J. G., & Krammer, H. P. (1987). Instructional strategies and tactics for the design of introductory computer programming courses in high school. *Instructional Science, 16*, 251–285.

Van Merriënboer, J. J. G., & Paas, F. G. W. C. (1990). Automation and schema acquisition in learning elementary computer programming: Implications for the design of practice. *Computers in Human Behavior, 6*, 273–289.

Van Merriënboer, J. J. G., Schuurman, J. G., de Croock, M. B. M., & Paas, F. G. W. C. (2002). Redirecting learners' attention during training: Effects on cognitive load, transfer test performance and training efficiency. *Learning and Instruction, 12*, 11–37.

Van Merriënboer, J. J. G., & Sluijsmans, D. M. A. (2009). Toward a synthesis of cognitive load theory, four-component instructional design, and self-directed learning. *Educational Psychology Review, 21*, 55–66.

Van Merriënboer, J. J. G., & Sweller, J. (2005). Cognitive load theory and complex learning: Recent developments and future directions. *Educational Psychology Review, 17*, 147–177.

Vollmeyer, R., & Burns, B. D. (2002). Goal specificity and learning with a hypermedia program. *Experimental Psychology, 49*, 98–108.

Vollmeyer, R., Burns, B. D., & Holyoak, K. J. (1996). The impact of goal specificity on strategy use and the acquisition of problem structure. *Cognitive Science, 20*, 75–100.

Ward, M., & Sweller, J. (1990). Structuring effective worked examples. *Cognition and Instruction, 7*, 1–39.

West-Eberhard, M. (2003). *Developmental plasticity and evolution.* New York: Oxford University Press.

Whelan, R. R. (2007). Neuroimaging of cognitive load in instructional multimedia. *Educational Research Review, 2*(1), 1–12.

Wirth, J., Künsting, J., & Leutner, D. (2009). The impact of goal specificity and goal type on learning outcome and cognitive load. *Computers in Human Behavior, 25*, 299–305.

Wong, A., Marcus, N., Ayres, P., Smith, L., Cooper, G. A., Paas, F., et al. (2009). Instructional animations can be superior to statics when learning human motor skills. *Computers in Human Behavior, 25*, 339–347.

Wouters, P., Paas, F., & van Merriënboer, J. J. G. (2009). Observational learning from animated models: Effects of modality and reflection on transfer. *Contemporary Educational Psychology, 34*, 1–8.

Xie, B., & Salvendy, G. (2000). Prediction of mental workload in single and multiple tasks environments. *International Journal of Cognitive Ergonomics, 4*, 213–242.

Yeung, A. S., Jin, P., & Sweller, J. (1998). Cognitive load and learner expertise: Split-attention and redundancy effects in reading with explanatory notes. *Contemporary Educational Psychology, 23*, 1–21.

Zhang, L., Ayres, P., & Chan, K. (2011). Examining different types of collaborative learning in a complex computer-based environment: A cognitive load approach. *Computers in Human Behavior, 27*, 94–98.

Zhu, X., & Simon, H. A. (1987). Learning mathematics from examples and by doing. *Cognition and Instruction, 4*, 137–166.

Index

CPSIA information can be obtained
at www.ICGtesting.com
Printed in the USA
LVHW082120251218
601613LV00011B/385/P